Corporate FINANCE

Guan Jun Wang
Savannah State University

Kendall Hunt
publishing company

Cover image © Shutterstock, Inc.

Kendall Hunt
publishing company

www.kendallhunt.com
Send all inquiries to:
4050 Westmark Drive
Dubuque, IA 52004-1840

Copyright © 2015 by Kendall Hunt Publishing Company

ISBN 978-1-4652-7979-8

All rights reserved. No part of this publication may be reproduced, stored in a retrieval system, or transmitted, in any form or by any means, electronic, mechanical, photocopying, recording, or otherwise, without the prior written permission of the copyright owner.

Printed in the United States of America

Contents

Preface v

Chapter 1 Introduction and Overview 1

Chapter 2 Financial Statement Analysis 19

Chapter 3 Overview of the Financial Markets 55

Chapter 4 Time Value of Money: The Basic Concepts 87

Chapter 5 Time Value of Money: Advanced Topics 111

Chapter 6 Financial Securities 153

Chapter 7 Valuation of Bonds and Stocks and the Cost of Capital 167

Chapter 8 Risk and Return and the Capital Asset Pricing Model 201

Chapter 9 Basics of Capital Budgeting 223

Chapter 10 Advanced Topics in Capital Budgeting 257

Appendix A 291
Appendix B 295
Appendix C 299
Appendix D 303

Preface

It has been my desire to have a Corporate (Business) Finance textbook that is affordable, easy and fun to read while without sacrificing rigor, accuracy, or clarity. This book serves such purposes.

Though this book (chapters 1, 2, 4, 5, 6, 7, 9 & 10) was mainly built upon Kale and Fendler's "Lectures in corporate finance" and Chapters 3 and 8 Woolridge and Gray's "Basic principles of finance", most chapters have undergone varying degrees of revision: rearranged the order of material, deleted unnecessary material and added new content to improve the depth and effectiveness of the presentation. Throughout the text, all financial market and business information for which more current data are available have been updated. Not only have the exhibits been updated, but firm information, financial values such as interest rates, and foreign currency exchange rates have been updated throughout the discussion in text, examples and end-of-chapter problems. Time value of money tables were added to provide students an alternative way to solve TVM problems.

I hope that you enjoy the book.

Guan Jun Wang, Ph.D.

Chapter 1

Introduction and Overview

1.1 **The Exciting and Relevant World of Finance**
1.2 **The Mysterious World of Finance**
1.3 **Finance as a Field of Study**
1.4 **Forms of Business Organization**
1.5 **The Goal of Corporate Financial Management**
1.6 **The Relationship between Accounting and Finance**
1.7 **Value and the Importance of Cash**
1.8 **Careers in Finance**
1.9 **Purpose and Organization of Text**
    Questions

After studying Chapter 1, you should be able to:

- Understand why sound financial management is vital to the survival of a business.
- Identify the three main subject areas in the field of finance.
- Describe different forms of business organization.
- Explain why the goal of a financial manager should be to maximize the wealth of the firm's shareholders and why this particular goal is preferred over other goals.

From *Lectures in Corporate Finance*, 6th Edition by Jayant R. Kale and Richard J. Fendler. Copyright © 2013 by Kendall Hunt Publishing Company. Reprinted by permission.

- Describe the basic difference between financial management and accounting.
- Understand the importance of cash and the basic relationship between cash flow and value.

1.1 The Exciting and Relevant World of Finance

As professors, we are often asked by students why we chose to study finance in school, why we are active in financial research and consulting, and why we are so passionate about teaching finance. The answers to these questions are the same and quite simple. We chose finance as a career and we choose to teach finance for three reasons:

1. Finance is exciting because it is all around us. You see finance in action every time you watch the nightly news or read the paper. Many decisions made by individuals, companies, and government agencies involve a financial component. We strongly hope that as you read this book, you will learn to see finance in action and that will stir you to make understanding more about finance and financial decision making a lifetime learning goal.

2. Finance is about money and nearly everyone likes to talk, or has some opinion, about money:
   - "Money is better than poverty, if only for financial reasons." (Woody Allen)
   - "Early to bed and early to rise—till you get enough money to do otherwise." (Peter's Almanac)
   - "The only thing I like about rich people is their money." (Lady Nancy Astor)
   - "Money frees you from doing things you dislike. Since I dislike doing nearly everything, money is handy." (Grocho Marx)
   - "The trick is to stop thinking of it as 'your' money." (IRS auditor)
   - "For the love of money is the root of all evil." (The Bible)
   - "The lack of money is the root of all evil." (Mark Twain)
   - "Money is the root of all evil, and yet it is such a useful root that we cannot get on without it any more than we can without potatoes." (Louisa May Alcott)
   - "Too many people spend money they haven't earned, to buy things they don't want, to impress people they don't like." (Will Smith)
   - "Money isn't the most important thing in life, but it's reasonably close to oxygen on the 'gotta have it' scale." (Zig Ziglar)
   - "You already know, you light I'm heavy roll, heavy dough. Mic macheted your flow, your paper falls slow like confetti, mines a steady grow." (Jay-Z)

At the most basic level, finance is the study of the creation and management of wealth. More specifically, finance is the study of how investors, financial institutions, and company executives manage money in order to make more money. Because nearly every decision made within a company involves some financial component, finance impacts every area of a business. Understanding the basics of finance will help you be a better and more valuable employee to whatever organization you work for during your career.

3. Financial management is essential to the success of any organization, from a major corporation to a small business to a government agency to an individual household. Even though this is a book about corporate finance, you will learn principles as you read this book that apply to the management of your own future income and savings. You have undoubtedly heard of individuals, often athletes and entertainers, who make millions of dollars per year and yet go bankrupt and retire in poverty. There are also countless, less well-publicized stories, of wise and frugal individuals who earned relatively minimal amounts of money during their working years, yet retired with several million dollars in their retirement account. Knowledge of finance does not guarantee successful management of your finances, but it will help you to understand and make wiser money related decisions during your life.

1.2 The Mysterious World of Finance

Most successful business enterprises have the following in common: a product (or service) that people want or need, an efficient method of production and/or delivery, effective marketing, quality managers, a trained work force, and a vision and strategy for future growth. The managers of successful firms also usually possess a thorough understanding of the principles of financial management. In fact, the managers of most of the best corporations in the United States devote at least as much time to the finances of their firms as they do to operations and sales. This is probably why so many current top managers and CEOs majored in finance in college or graduate school and/or were promoted out of their (or some other) company's finance department. They know that whereas even the most excellent financial management cannot save a firm with a bad product, poor financial management can cause a firm that efficiently produces, markets, and delivers a high-demand product to fail. The following story illustrates the importance of financial management to a firm.

When at 7 years of age, Bennie Feldhaus completely disassembled and then rebuilt his father's riding lawnmower, doubling the mower's top speed and power while reducing its gas consumption by 30%, his parents knew that Bennie was destined to be something special. By age 10, Bennie had rebuilt the engines in both the family automobiles, achieving similar results. By 14, Bennie had memorized the engine specifications of every car made in the United States over the past five years. By 16, he knew the specifications of all foreign made automobiles as well.

Bennie, however, disliked school. To him school was boring and a waste of time. He wanted to be working on automobiles. So, after he finally graduated from high school at age 20, Bennie started working in his uncle's auto garage. Bennie, who was personable and funny as well as talented, soon gained a reputation as a master auto mechanic. Mechanics from all over the city would call Bennie regularly for advice.

After 10 years of working for his uncle, Bennie decided that there had to be a better way to profit from his talent. Accordingly, at age 30, Bennie took all of the money that he had and started an auto parts store. His plan was simple. He would use his reputation and experience among the mechanics in the city to build a solid customer base, and he would use his personality and knowledge to provide better instruction and service than any other auto parts store around.

Bennie's Auto Parts and Service Center was an immediate success. Within a year Bennie was making more money than he ever thought possible. He worked 12 hours per day, seven days per week, and even at that rate, he could not keep up with the demand for his products and services.

Unfortunately, Bennie had one, what he considered to be minor, problem. He didn't understand the principles of corporate finance. Approximately 40% of Bennie's customers paid with checks. When he received a check from a customer, Bennie would stuff it into a drawer in the counter. Because he was so busy, often he would not deposit the checks for weeks. Another 30% of Bennie's customers paid with credit cards. Bennie never verified the credit cards, and in any given month approximately 10% of these purchases would be returned by the credit card company unpaid. The rest of Bennie's customers requested that Bennie bill them for their purchases. Again, because he was so busy, often Bennie did not accurately record the credit purchases. Accordingly, any time a customer complained about his bill, Bennie would adjust or wipe out the debt. If a customer did not pay after Bennie sent out a second notice, Bennie would stop sending bills. Collections took too much time and besides, he reasoned, his sales growth would easily make up for a few uncollected accounts.

Bennie did not have an inventory system. He ordered parts whenever it seemed like he needed them, and when they arrived he put them on whatever shelves were mostly empty. Often he would order a part for a customer only to find out later that the needed part was sitting on a shelf in another part of his storeroom. Cataloging inventory took too much time and besides, he reasoned, with the rate his sales were growing, having a few extra parts laying around couldn't be all that detrimental to his firm's health.

Finally, Bennie never paid much attention to the bills he received from his suppliers. He was too busy selling products and making money. He would send payments only after he began to receive threatening letters or phone calls. However, because he was so busy he never bothered to balance his checkbook, and consequently often the checks he sent bounced. In one particularly bad month, his bounced check fees to the bank exceeded $1,500.

Halfway into his second year of operations, Bennie's suppliers began to demand immediate payment for all outstanding bills and refused to ship new parts without first receiving payment in cash or cashiers check. As Bennie began to have trouble getting parts, he started to lose customers. Soon his cash flow dried up, and Bennie was forced to go to the bank to seek a loan to consolidate all of his outstanding debt.

Not surprisingly, the bank officer laughed at his request. Bennie had a long history of bounced checks, he did not have any type of financial statements to show to the banker, and he did not have any definite plan for how he was going to repay the loan. Without the loan, Bennie was forced to declare bankruptcy. To make matters worse, one year later he was indicted for tax fraud by the federal government. Because he was too busy to bother with minor details like financial records, Bennie never bothered to send any money to the IRS. Today, Bennie is in jail making license plates pondering, in his spare time, the mysterious world of finance.

A thorough reading of this book will not necessarily qualify you to be a successful financial manager nor will it reveal all of the mysteries of the financial world. It will, however, help you to understand the repercussions of Bennie's actions (or lack thereof) and perhaps allow you to keep from making the same mistakes that Bennie made if you decide to start a business of your own. Who knows—had Bennie read this book before starting Bennie's Auto Parts and Service Center, he might be spending his spare time playing golf instead of making license plates!

1.3 Finance as a Field of Study

Finance is a very broad-based subject matter. To organize its study, the (actually non-mysterious) field of finance is divided into three separate, although inter-related, topic areas: corporate financial management, investments, and financial markets and institutions.

Financial markets and institutions studies the determinants of interest rates, the regulation of financial institutions (banks, credit unions, insurance companies, pension funds, and so on), the structure and functioning of the various financial markets, such as the stock and bond markets, and the various financial assets (and the secondary markets for the assets) issued by governments, corporations and financial institutions (such as mortgages, auto loans, collateralized mortgage obligations, and certificates of deposit).

Investments focuses on how individuals and financial institutions make decisions concerning the allocation of securities within their investment portfolios. The major securities studied in Investments are stocks, bonds, options, and futures contracts. A central theme of this subject area is the determination and management of risk.

Corporate financial management, also often referred to as business or corporation finance, involves the actual financial management of a business enterprise. This is the broadest subject area of finance. It includes topics such as financial reporting and financial analysis, cash flow analysis, financial forecasting, the management of inventory and accounts receivable, current liability management, security valuation, the measurement and analysis of risk, capital budgeting, dividend policy, capital structure, bankruptcy, mergers and acquisitions, and international financial management. Also, because financial managers must deal with investors and financial institutions when they need to raise outside funds, any study of corporation finance must include at least a survey of the other two subject areas. To see why this is so, consider the following.

In the most basic sense, finance is concerned with the process through which funds are transferred from savers to borrowers. Savers, or surplus units, are those households, businesses, and governments whose income exceeds their consumption. Borrowers, or deficit units, are those households, businesses, and governments whose consumption exceeds their income. Although any household, business, or government may be either a surplus or a deficit unit, in the economy as a whole, most deficit units are businesses and most surplus units are households (in this context, surplus units are commonly referred to as investors).

The transfer of funds from surplus units (investors) to deficit units (businesses) takes place in a financial market or through a financial institution:

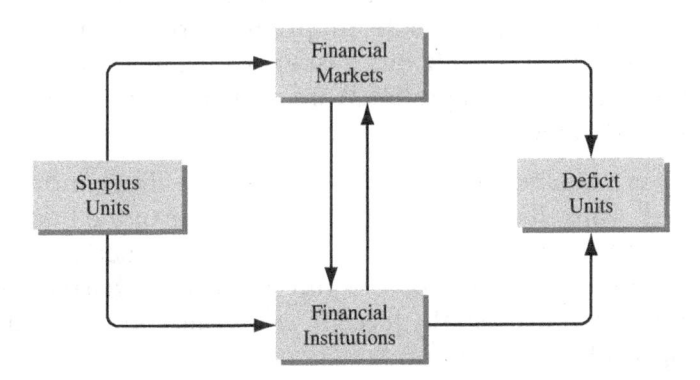

Businesses (deficit units) borrow money to purchase physical assets such as machinery, raw materials, real estate, plant, and equipment. This money is obtained either directly from investors (surplus units) through a financial market (such as the stock or bond market) or indirectly through a financial institution. In exchange for the funds they receive, these deficit units issue claims (called financial assets) against the cash flows that the physical assets that they purchase are expected to generate.

For example, a firm that borrows $1,000,000 to purchase a plant gives to the provider(s) of the $1,000,000 financial assets that promise the owner(s) of these financial assets a part of the actual annual cash flow that the plant produces.

Investors lend money, that is, purchase financial assets, to earn an expected return. This return is a function of the annual cash flow that the physical asset purchased with the investor's funds is expected to generate. As long as the actual cash flow equals or exceeds the expected cash flow, investors are content. If, however, the actual cash flow is less than the expected cash flow, the investor loses. In the extreme, the actual cash flow can even be negative, implying that investors can lose part or all of their initial investment.

The fact that actual cash flows can, and most often always do, deviate from expected cash flows is what causes financial assets to be risky. Identifying, managing, and valuing risky cash flows is the essence of finance. These are the central themes that integrate the three subject areas of finance. Financial markets and institutions, which encompasses the mechanisms that allow businesses to issue and investors to purchase financial assets, primarily concerns the risks that different trading systems add to, or subtract from, financial assets. Investments primarily concerns the manner in which investors evaluate financial asset risk and determine expected cash flows, and use this information to determine financial asset values. Finally, financial management primarily concerns the process whereby business managers apply the same risk measurement and valuation principals used by investors to determine and manage physical asset risk, and to raise the funds necessary to expand their businesses.

The primary purpose of this book is to present an overview of the Corporate Financial Management subject area. In it we outline the basic principles of corporate financial management. After reading and working through this book you should know and appreciate the role and duties of a financial manager. And, should you decide to take additional courses in finance, you will possess a solid foundation upon which you can build future knowledge.

1.4 Forms of Business Organization

All businesses must be organized in some legal manner. In the United States, there are three main forms of business organizations: sole proprietorships, partnerships, and corporations. Although other types of business organizations (specifically, limited partnerships, limited liability partnerships, and professional corporations) are growing in popularity, the three main types listed above dominate the business world.

A *sole proprietorship* is a business that is 100% owned by a single individual. In most sole proprietorships, this owner is also the operator or chief manager of the business. A sole proprietorship is simple and inexpensive to establish. In most states, one merely obtains a business license and begins operations. Sole proprietorships require no formal charter and are subject to fewer government regulations. They also usually face lower tax rates on earned income than other business organizations, especially corporations.

There are two drawbacks to the sole proprietorship business organization. First, it is very difficult for such companies to raise large amounts of capital. The main sources of capital for sole proprietorships are the owner, friends and family, and commercial banks. The first source is limited to the personal wealth of the owner, and even in the case of a wealthy owner, the owner might not wish to invest a significant amount of wealth in a single entity. The second source usually involves difficult personal relationships, and identifying an acceptable return to friends and family in the event of success is often tricky. Borrowing from a commercial bank usually requires much red tape, can involve potential intervention in the management of the business, and, most significant, is limited to the amount of money invested in the business by the first two sources. A bank generally will not contribute any more to a business than the owner of the business is willing to contribute.

A second drawback to the sole proprietorship business organization is that the owner of a sole proprietorship has unlimited personal liability to the debt of the business. If the business fails, the creditors of the business are entitled to not only all of the assets of the business, they can also take the personal assets of the owner (until the full value of all of their claims are satisfied). Due to this unlimited liability feature, the bankruptcy of a sole proprietorship will usually result in personal bankruptcy for the owner.

Another form of business organization is a *partnership*. A partnership is essentially the same as a sole proprietorship, except that the business is owned and operated by two or more individuals. These individuals must agree on who will provide the initial start-up capital, who does what work, and how the profits (or losses) of the business will be shared.

Partnerships have most of the same benefits and drawbacks as sole proprietorships, although some differences exist. Multiple partners might be able to contribute more capital to the business than a single owner. On the other hand, unlimited personal liability applies to all owners, regardless of the percent of ownership. Thus, if a business of two partners goes bankrupt and one of the partners with little personal wealth also goes bankrupt, the other owner who might have substantial wealth is responsible for all of the remaining debts of the business. Finally, the transfer of ownership of a partnership is often difficult. If one of the owners of the business dies or decides to leave the business, the other owner(s) must buy out the departed owner (or survivors). If the remaining owner does not have sufficient personal wealth to do this, the business usually folds.

In terms of numbers, more than 85% of all businesses in the United States are organized as sole proprietorships or partnerships. In terms of revenue, however, more than 80% of all business in the country is conducted by corporations. A *corporation* is a legal entity, separate and apart from its owners or managers. Although much more complex and costly to establish, the corporate form of business organization offers three distinct advantages over the other forms of organization:

1. *Limited Liability.* As a separate legal entity, a corporation bears the entire burden of all debt in the event of bankruptcy. That is, the owners (or shareholders) of a corporation cannot ever lose more than the amount they invested in the company. If a shareholder purchases 1,000 shares of stock in a corporation at $100 per share and that corporation later goes bankrupt, the shareholder will lose only the $100,000 that was originally invested. If in the bankruptcy the creditors are due $10,000,000 and the total value of all liquidated assets of the firm is only worth $6,000,000, then all assets will be liquidated and the creditors will only get $6,000,000. The owners (that is, shareholders) of the firm are not in any way liable for the additional $4,000,000 in claims.

2. *Ability to Raise Capital.* Due to the limited liability feature, corporations are able to attract more investors than unincorporated businesses. In fact, the stock of many corporations is public, meaning that the company's stock trades in an organized stock market, such as the New York Stock Exchange. Companies whose stock trades publicly have access to almost unlimited capital (of course, the company must provide an attractive potential return to obtain this capital). Also, corporations with large amounts of equity capital can attract large amounts of debt capital. As noted above, banks, and other creditors, view owner equity as a sign of faith in the future prospects of the company.

3. *Easy Transfer of Ownership.* The ownership of a corporation is represented by shares of stock. Owners of corporations who decide to liquidate their interest in the corporations need only sell their shares of stock. If the company is a public company (that is, its shares trade on an organized exchange), this merely involves a call to a broker or a click of the mouse.

The principles of financial management described in this book apply directly to a publicly traded corporation. Sole proprietorships and partnerships have specific management and operational issues that are unique to those organizations. Nonetheless, the basic goal of financial management and the importance and valuation of cash flow expressed throughout the book apply to all forms of business organization.

1.5 The Goal of Corporate Financial Management

The goal of any corporation must be to create value for its stockholders. Stockholders are the owners of the corporation, and their basic reason for investing in the company in the first place is to make money. The managers of any corporation are merely the employees of the owners of the firm, the shareholders. As such, managers are sometimes referred to as "agents." Agents are hired by owners to run the company to create as much value for the owners as possible. If the agents do not perform their duties to the satisfaction of the owners, they can be fired or replaced.

To a stockholder, value is represented by the price of the company's common stock. Note that at any given time, the price per share multiplied by the total number of shares outstanding is simply equal to the total value of the equity of the company. This total value is owned by all shareholders in the company according to their percentage ownership (that is, the number of shares they own divided by the total number of shares outstanding). If the price per share increases, the value of each stockholder's stake in the company (that is, his or her personal wealth) increases. Thus, all else constant, the goal of a financial manager must be to maximize the price per share of the company's stock.

Note that maximizing the price per share of the company's stock is not necessarily equivalent to maximizing the firm's profit. Profit maximization is not a well defined corporate objective because it leaves open the question of which year's profit, and higher profits does not necessarily mean a better rate of return, and lastly profits can be changed by using different accounting rules.

1.6 The Relationship between Accounting and Finance

Because much of finance involves the analysis and management of a firm's income statement and balance sheet, it is common to ask: "What is the difference between finance and accounting?" The most direct answer to this question is that whereas accounting is backward-looking (literally, to some of us), finance is forward-looking. Accounting statements present a historical account of the money earned, raised, and spent by a firm from its inception through the current period. It focuses on the book value of the firm's assets and how the purchase of those assets was financed. Conversely, finance is the study of all of the future cash that the firm's current and prospective collection of assets can potentially earn. It focuses on the market value of the firm. In essence, though related, the two subjects can be said to be diametrically opposed. The following story illustrates the relationship between book (accounting) value and market (finance) value.

Joe Vitale is a third-year business major at Urban University, a 32,000-student campus located in the downtown area of a large metropolitan city. "Urb-U" is not a traditional campus. Instead, it is actually a disjointed collection of university classroom buildings, labs, offices, dormitories, and other buildings that are interspersed throughout the downtown area.

As fate would have it, the two sets of buildings with the greatest distance between them (approximately three miles) are the dormitories and the general classroom buildings. To further complicate matters for students, whereas parking near the dormitories is adequate, parking near the classroom buildings is essentially nonexistent. The university refuses to provide a free shuttle service for monetary reasons and is not allowed to run a for-profit service for political reasons. Students are encouraged to walk, bike, or use the public transit system. Most consider the first method to require excessive time and unacceptable effort and the second to be hazardous to life and limb. The city transit system is expensive, slow, overcrowded, and seldom on schedule.

Joe, a budding entrepreneur, realizes that this situation has the potential to earn someone a sizeable amount of money. Following several conversations with his finance professor/consultant, Joe has decided to start a shuttle service between the dorms and the classroom buildings. He plans to use money that his grandfather gave him for MBA school to buy a transport van. The van costs $30,000, has a four-year life, and will be depreciated on a straight-line basis to a zero salvage value. Joe and his consultant estimate that the business is capable of producing the following cash flow series:

Table 1.1 Joe's Shuttle Company

Year	Estimated Cash Flow
1	$20,000
2	$15,000
3	$15,000
4	$10,000

These cash flows are the revenue that Joe expects to collect minus the payment of all expenses (gas, insurance, vehicle maintenance, advertising, wages to drivers, applicable taxes, consultant fees, and so on), and a salary to himself as the manager of the operation. These are *residual cash flows*—those left over after all expenses have been paid. They belong to the provider(s) of capital. In this example, the cash flow series above represents Joe's expected return for providing the $30,000 to buy the necessary asset(s) to start and run the business (that is, Joe's expected return as the owner of the business).

Assuming that Joe starts his business today and that his only asset is the transport van, what is the *book value* (i.e., accounting value) of his firm? The answer is, of course, $30,000. That is, the original purchase price of the van.

What will the book value of the firm be after one year? Note that annual depreciation of the van is:

(Purchase Price − Salvage Value)/Useful Life = ($30,000 − 0)/4 = $7,500 per year for 4 years.

Thus, the book value of the van (and therefore, of Joe's firm) after one year is:

Purchase Price − One year of depreciation = $30,000 − $7,500 = $22,500.

What will the book value of the firm be after (a) two years? (b) three years? (c) four years?

Answers: (a) $15,000   (b) $7,500   (c) $0.

Now for a more difficult question. Assuming that Joe starts his business today, what is the *market value* of his firm? The answer to this question has little to do with the cost or book value of the firm. Instead, the answer depends on the cash flows that Joe's firm is expected to generate in the future. Specifically, the firm's market value depends on what someone else would be willing to pay today in exchange for these expected future cash flows.

To illustrate this point, consider the following. Assume that Joe has a very rich uncle to whom Joe has explained the business opportunity and the expected future cash flow series shown in Table 1.1. Joe's uncle believes that Joe's assumptions and estimates are fair, reasonable, and accurate. In fact, the uncle is willing to give Joe $34,000 today if Joe will agree to sign over to him all of the net cash that the business actually generates for each of the next four years—that is, if Joe agrees to sell complete ownership of the business to his uncle. If the business generates less cash than expected, Joe's uncle loses. If, however, it generates more than expected, Joe's uncle gets the expected cash plus the extra cash.

Why would Joe's uncle propose such a deal? Is it solely because he is related to Joe? Actually, Joe's uncle is quite shrewd. He is merely investing his money in Joe's firm. He has many alternative investments from which to choose. Instead of investing in Joe's firm, he could deposit the $34,000 into a savings account, buy a CD (certificate of deposit), buy government or corporate bonds, buy publicly traded stock, or invest in some other type of asset. Joe's uncle chooses Joe's firm because he considers it to represent the best expected return available given the risks involved (specifically, the risk that the actual cash flow will be significantly less than the expected cash flow).

Do such transactions actually occur? In fact, they occur all the time. Other than risk, this transaction is not unlike a car loan. The bank gives me $34,000 to buy a car in exchange for my promise to pay $649.44 per month for the next 60 months. That is, an amount today in exchange for a future expected cash flow series. A similar comparison can be made with a house loan, credit card line of credit, stock purchase, and so on.

Obviously, my loan payments to the bank are probably more certain than Joe's cash payments to his uncle. That is why the expected return on the bank loan is substantially less than the expected return on the investment in Joe's firm. Whereas (as will be shown later in this book) the expected cash flow stream on the bank loan represents a 5.5% annual return, the expected cash flow from Joe's firm represents a 31.15% annual return!

Returning to our earlier question, what is the market value of Joe's firm? The answer is $34,000 because that is what an investor is willing to give Joe today in exchange for all of the future cash the firm is expected to generate.

Note the difference between market value and book value. Whereas the book value of Joe's firm is $30,000, the market value of his firm is $34,000. Whereas book value is what was actually paid for the asset(s), market value is what the asset(s) is (are) worth in terms of its ability to produce expected future cash flow within the context of a firm.

Recall that the goal of a financial manager is to create value for the firm's shareholders. The most direct way to achieve this goal is to find, purchase, or manage assets so that their market value exceeds their book value.

One final question concerning the relationship between finance and accounting: Given the fundamental difference between the two subjects, why does much of finance involve the analysis of a firm's income statement and balance sheet? Financial managers, outside analysts, creditors, and stockholders analyze accounting data to identify trends concerning, in particular, cash flow. Accounting statements, as shown in the next chapter, do not specifically list cash flow. However, taken together, income statements and balance sheets provide valuable information concerning the flow of cash during a given accounting period. And, although these are historical values, to the degree that historical trends and relationships will continue into the future, they can be important indicators of future potential cash flow—and thus useful in determining and managing market value. Thus, just as potential employers would use your school records (that is, grade point average, major, extracurricular activities) as indicators of the type of employee you might be for their firms, financial analysts use accounting data as indicators of the potential of a given business enterprise.

1.7 Value and the Importance of Cash

Count the number of times that the terms *cash* and *value* have been used to this point in the book. The answers are *cash* (47 times) and *value* (33 times). Obviously, there is an important connection between these two terms. Consider the following.

Suppose that the shares of ABC Co. trade on the New York Stock Exchange (NYSE). At nine o'clock in the morning, the price of ABC's stock is $30 per share. Soon after you observe this price, the management of ABC makes the following announcement: "The company's R&D division has discovered that with a slight modification in its manufacturing process, ABC will be able to generate significant reductions in manufacturing costs." Assume that the cost of modifying the manufacturing process is negligible and that it will take very little time to incorporate the modification into the manufacturing process. In other words, the cost savings will begin to be realized almost immediately. Also suppose that the announcement made by the firm is truthful and completely believable. What do you think will happen to the price of ABC's shares? Will the share price increase, decrease, or remain unchanged?

The answer to this question is obvious—the share price will rise. If your answer was that the share price would increase, you already know the most important concept in finance. Let us spend a few minutes on the obvious reason why the share price will rise. To do this, let us begin by answering the following seemingly simple question. (You must circle the one answer that you think is most correct).

Why does a typical investor buy stock in a firm such as ABC?

A. The CEO of ABC is the investor's favorite uncle.

B. The investor loves the company's name ABC.

C. ABC manufactures products that have great social value.

D. The investor believes that ABC's share price will increase substantially in the future.

Which answer did you choose? Our guess is that you circled D and, if so, your choice was the most correct. Note that answers A, B, and C are not wrong. It is possible that some investors buy shares for one or more of these reasons. However, we are interested in the reason for the *typical investor* and, clearly, the most probable reason why an investor buys shares is to make money. Therefore, answer D is the most correct answer. This is one of the most fundamental rules in finance and it is also a very simple rule. Buying shares is just one form of investment and, in fact, this rule applies to all investments.

People make investments to make money.

Let us now go to the next question. Again, you must circle the most correct answer.

What determines the current price (that is, the price today) of a firm's share of common stock?

A. The growth rate of the company's sales.

B. The quality of the firm's products.

C. How much money the shareholder will make from owning the firm's share.

Which answer did you circle? You will notice that, unlike the first question, the answer is not immediately obvious. All three choices appear to be important factors in determining the current share price. Which one, however, is the most important?

Let us consider the choices one by one. Suppose that the sales of a firm increase by leaps and bounds. Although high sales and high sales growth are generally favorable signs, the profits that these sales generate depend upon the firm's costs—high sales result in high profits only if costs are less than revenues. A firm might be better off by reducing sales of products whose production costs are greater than the price that they fetch. Therefore, the volume of sales and/or sales growth is not the most important determinant of the share price.

How about the quality of the firm's products? Again, it depends upon the cost of achieving quality. If the marginal (that is, additional) cost of producing a high-quality (as opposed to say an average quality) product exceeds the marginal revenue from the product, then the firm is better off making only average-quality products. Thus, product quality alone cannot be the most important determinant of the share price.

That leaves us with the third choice, what the share price will be in the future. Aside from the fact that it is the only alternative left, there is another reason why this is the best answer. Recall that the main reason an investor buys a share is to make money. The money that an investor will make depends upon what the future share price will be—if the price in the future is high, the investor will make more money. We have just argued that increases in sales or product quality do not necessarily translate into more money for the shareholder. Therefore, the most important determinant of the current price of a share is how much money the investor can make from owning that share. This leads us to the next rule.

The price of an investment depends upon how much money that investment will generate.

These two simple rules justify your answer to the original question that the price of ABC's shares will increase as a result of the cost-reducing modification to the manufacturing process. Because the modification reduces costs, the profits of the firm will be higher. These higher profits will ultimately result in more money for the shareholders (for example, in the form of higher dividends). Finally, because the price of the share depends upon how much money the shareholders will make, the fact that they expect to make more money will result in an increase in the price that they would be willing to pay for the share and, consequently, the share price will go up.

This brings us to the fundamental concept (mentioned earlier) in finance:

The <u>value</u> of an investment is determined by the <u>expected future cash flows</u> that the investment generates for the investor.

The concept above might, at first, appear to be a simple restatement of what we had been discussing before. However, some important words have been changed and added. These are italicized. First, the word *price* was replaced with value. Second, the fact that it is the cash flows in the *future* that are relevant was never made explicit before. Finally, the term *cash flows* was substituted for money. There are reasons for these changes.

The terms *price* and *value* are usually considered to be equivalent in finance. One way to see this equivalence is to consider an asset, say a share of ABC company's stock. Suppose that this share belongs to you, and that you believe (on the basis of how much money this share is going to generate for you) that this share is worth $30. In other words, you value this share at $30. If you received an offer from a buyer for this share of $35, would you sell the share? The answer is yes. If the offer price were $28? No. In other words, you, the seller, would be willing to sell your share at a price that is no less than $30, the value that you place on the share. Now suppose that the buyer is a person just like you and knows exactly what you know about ABC Co. and, consequently, also places a value of $30 on the share. Would this buyer buy this share at $28? The answer is yes. At $35? Certainly not! In other words, the buyer would be willing to buy this share at a price no greater than $30. Therefore, if a transaction involving this share of ABC did take place between you and the buyer, it could take place only at the price of $30, the value that both you and the buyer place on the share.

Next, let us consider the concept that only the money that the asset generates in the *future* determines its value. The rationale underlying this concept is quite straightforward. When you buy an asset, what the asset generated in the past went to its previous owner, not to you. The only money that you will get is what the asset will generate for you after you buy it, that is, in the future. Therefore, the value that you place on an asset will be determined solely by the money that the asset will generate in the future. This is not to say that the money that the asset generated in the past is not useful information. However, it is useful only to the extent that it might provide you with some idea as to what the asset will generate in the future.

Finally, let us turn to the use of the phrase "cash flows" instead of money. The reason for considering only *cash* flows is simple. The only thing that an investor can spend is cash. Therefore the only thing that the investor cares about is the stream of cash flows that the asset will generate in the future. This fact might seem somewhat trivial at this point, but its importance will become apparent later in the course.

1.8 Careers in Finance

As finance professors, we are often asked the following questions from our students:

1. How much money does a finance major make?
2. What kinds of jobs are available to finance majors?

These are relevant and important questions for anyone considering any major in college. However, as important as these questions are, the answers to these questions should not overly influence your career choices. Be careful to pick your major based on what you like to do as opposed to the job you might desire to have, or how much money you can make. It is much more important to be happy at what you do than to have a prestigious title or to make a lot of money. Your career is something that you will do for a very long time. If you do not like what you are doing, neither a fancy title nor a large paycheck will make you happy.

One way to determine what you like is to keep an open mind about different classes while in college. Take many different courses in different areas. Continue taking classes in subjects that you find interesting and challenging, or in which you do well. Over time, you will begin to differentiate subjects that stimulate your intelligence relative to those that bore you.

If, as we hope, finance turns out to be the former, the following information will provide you with a brief overview of the level of salaries and the different types of jobs that you can expect in the field of finance. As described in section 1.3, the field of finance is divided into three separate, although interrelated subject areas: corporate financial management, investments, and financial markets and institutions. Jobs and career paths exist in each of these areas.

1.8.1 Finance Salaries

Salaries in all areas of business are constantly changing, so any precise data we would list here would most likely be out of date. Fortunately, current salary data for nearly all jobs is available online. Websites are constantly changing, so we cannot guarantee perfect results, but we have found the following site to be extremely reliable, accurate, and useful for finance career information and salary data:

www.careers-in-finance.com

Note that the salary estimates and ranges on this (and any other) site are average salaries for some of the most popular jobs in finance. Numerous factors influence salaries including position, tenure, specialized skills, geographic location, and size of the employer. Use such estimates as a rough guide to understand what to expect when you graduate.

Although salary amounts are interesting, perhaps a more useful guide is relative salaries. Specifically, how do finance salaries compare to salaries in other fields. As per the following statistics, finance salaries rank in the upper range:

- According to www.payscale.com, starting salaries for finance majors rank in the top 25% of all possible majors.
- According to U.S. News, finance is one of the top "5 Bachelor's Degrees That Prepare You for a High-Paying Career."
- According to Forbes Magazine, finance majors have the third highest starting salaries in business, behind engineering and computer science.

1.8.2 Careers/Jobs in Corporate Financial Management

As the term implies, financial management is the management of a firm's finances, specifically, the money flow through the company. Financial managers determine when and how much money a company needs to begin, sustain, or expand operations. More specifically, financial managers set, alter, and monitor policies concerning a company's cash and marketable security accounts, credit policy, inventory balances, long-term asset purchases and sales, debt market structure, dividend policies, and more.

Entry-level positions involve collecting and analyzing data and identifying strengths, areas of concerns, and trends. More senior positions often also include decision making and other management responsibilities. Although much of finance is number-oriented, people skills, the ability to communicate, both orally and in writing, and salesmanship are often the traits that lead to promotions and increased responsibilities.

The most senior financial management position in a company is the chief financial officer (CFO), who is usually second only to the CEO (chief executive officer) in terms of visibility, responsibility, and compensation. The CFO is responsible for every decision in the firm that involves or concerns money—essentially all decisions. The fortunes of many companies rise and fall on the quality of the decisions made by the CFO.

1.8.3 Careers/Jobs in Investments

Investments is a broad-based subject and career opportunities in the area are varied and many. People who work in the investments field help companies, governments, and individuals to issue financial assets (that is, raise or borrow money), assist investors to purchase securities and manage their portfolios, and ensure that financial markets operate efficiently. Some of the more popular job titles in investments include Investment Analyst, Asset Portfolio Manager, Investment Advisor/Consultant, Merger/Acquisitions Underwriter, Investment Banker, Securities Broker, and Trader.

Individuals entering this field must possess strong analytical and interpersonal skills. This is a high-work, high-risk, and high potential reward profession. Although base salaries in this area are not high, bonuses and commission opportunities can be extraordinary. Very successful individuals in investments can attain annual compensation in the multimillion-dollar range.

Most entry-level positions involve analysis of company financial statements. To succeed and be promoted, you must be skilled in your understanding of accounting, have good spreadsheet skills, and be analytically fluent. Additionally, you must be able to communicate with clients to generate sales and network to expand your business contacts and opportunities. Interest in current events and an understanding of business cycles and macro-economic trends and influences is essential. A fair amount of travel should be expected, and visits to New York, Hong Kong, Tokyo, London, and Singapore are common among senior investments professionals.

1.8.4 Careers/Jobs in Financial Markets and Institutions

Most jobs in this area are in some way, shape, or form related to commercial banks. Commercial banking is a rapidly changing and evolving industry, and today's banks are more diverse and comprehensive than ever. Job and training opportunities in this area are tremendous. Many finance majors begin in the field of banking, receive training, and make contacts, then enter either financial management or investments.

The most common entry-level jobs in commercial banking are credit analyst and commercial loan officer. A strong understanding of accounting is essential for these jobs. The ability to effectively communicate via writing is also very important, because banking often requires documenting loans or justifying credit analyses.

As the area of financial services has become increasingly more competitive and as federal banking regulations have been relaxed, banks are focusing more attention on marketing their products and services to consumers, and on high-tech applications and procedures. These trends are opening opportunities in banking to finance professionals who can develop and deliver new products or services to the markets. Bank managers and officers must be able to foresee, understand, and take advantage of opportunities and trends in the economy and in the financial markets. Those who do so will find a career in banking to be exciting, challenging and rewarding.

1.9 Purpose and Organization of Text

A main purpose of this book is to explain the concept of valuation of assets. Those of you who study finance further (we hope all of you will) will discover that almost everything in finance is, in one way or another, related to valuing assets. When you study corporate finance (this course), you will learn some methods to value the assets of a firm and its investment opportunities. You will also study how this method can be used to value the securities that firms issue, for example, bonds and stocks. When you study investments, you will concentrate on how to value stocks, bonds, futures, options, and the myriad of investment possibilities that exist in the financial markets. When you study financial institution management, you will spend a considerable amount of time on loan analysis. A loan is nothing but an asset that a bank invests in; it accepts deposits from people (which is equivalent to borrowing money from depositors) and invests this money by making loans to its clients. To determine whether to make a loan, the bank will, therefore, have to value that loan. If you study real estate finance, you will value a different category of assets, namely, real estate, including homes, apartment complexes, retail stores, and many others.

Our earlier discussion indicated that the value of an asset is determined by the future cash flows that the asset will generate. To perform the actual valuation we will, therefore, need to know two things: how to determine cash flows and, once we have determined these cash flows, how to value them. Both of these aspects are vitally important. Accordingly, this book is divided into two major sections. The first section focuses on the importance, determination, and management of cash flows, particularly the past and potential future cash flows indicated by a firm's financial statements. The second section concentrates on the principles, process, and applications of valuation in corporate finance.

Questions

1. If within five years of receiving your degree you were earning $20,000 per month ($240,000 per year), would you consider yourself to be successful? If your monthly expenses were $25,000 per month and creditors were constantly calling you for payment and threatening repossession of your assets, would you still consider yourself to be successful? In what ways is this example analogous to corporate financial management?

2. In the example concerning Bennie's Auto Parts and Service Center in the beginning of this chapter, assume that Bennie could save, on average, $850 per month with better management of his accounts receivable, $1,200 per month with better inventory management, and $750 per month in better cash management (specifically, saved bounced check fees). These savings total $2,800 per month. The time required to effect this better management would be approximately 20 hours per week. Bennie does not have this amount of time to give to proper financial management. What is the obvious solution?

3. As a follow-up to question 2, what are some of the major job responsibilities or functions of a financial manager?

4. List the three main areas (that is, fields) of finance. Briefly describe each area. How are these areas related?

5. In what major ways does a corporation differ from a sole proprietorship or a partnership? Upon which form of business organization is this book based? Do the principles of financial management described in this book apply to the other forms of business organization?

6. What are the advantages and disadvantages of the three different types of business organizations (i.e., sole proprietorships, partnerships and corporations)?

7. What should be the main goal of a financial manager?

8. Profit maximization is not the same as shareholder value (that is, stock price) maximization. How is it possible that profit maximization might not lead to stock price maximization?

9. According to the text, maximizing shareholder wealth, maximizing stock price per share, and maximizing the value of the firm's assets are one and the same. That is, if a manager maximizes the value of the firm's assets, that manager will also be maximizing shareholder wealth and the price per share of the company's common stock. Explain this relationship.

10. What is the difference between book value and market value? How would you feel about owning stock in a firm whose market value was less than its book value? Could such a relationship exist? If so, what would it indicate?

11. Describe the similarities and differences between physical assets and financial assets. Why are financial assets risky? Why would anyone purchase a financial asset?

12. Does the goal of stockholder wealth maximization necessarily imply that firms will not be socially responsible (that is, responsible for the welfare of their employees, customers, the environment, or the community in which they operate)?

13. Assume that a firm is deciding whether to undertake some action that will increase the firm's stock price but hurt the environment (that is, be socially irresponsible). How might government regulations affect the firm's decision?

14. Assume that you own $15,000 worth of stock in a company whose stock is widely held and actively traded on the NYSE. Is it necessary for you to actively monitor the manager's performance (that is, to make sure that the managers of the firm are doing their best to maximize the value of your stock)? Why or why not? Now consider a bank that has made a large loan to this company. Is it necessary for the bank to actively monitor the manager's performance? Why or why not?

Chapter 2

Financial Statement Analysis

2.1 **Chapter Introduction and Overview**

2.2 **The Objective of Financial Statement Analysis**

2.3 **Financial Statement Fraud and Earnings Management**

2.4 **Tools of Financial Statement Analysis**

2.5 **Learn by Doing**

2.6 **Analyzing Financial Ratios**

2.7 **Limitations of Ratios**

2.8 **Summary**

   Assignments

   Additional Questions and Problems

After studying Chapter 2, you should be able to:

- Appreciate the importance of business analysis.
- Explain the objective of financial statement analysis according to who is doing the analysis.
- Construct a common size income statement and a common size balance sheet.
- Calculate a comprehensive set of financial ratios and understand how ratios could be used to evaluate the financial health of a company.
- Explain the limitations of ratio analysis.
- Link firm performance to creating shareholder value.

From *Lectures in Corporate Finance*, 6th Edition by Jayant R. Kale and Richard J. Fendler. Copyright © 2013 by Kendall Hunt Publishing Company. Reprinted by permission.

2.1 Chapter Introduction and Overview

All public corporations are required to publish three financial statements: an income statement, a balance sheet, and a statement of cash flows. In this chapter, we present the tools and techniques of analyzing financial statements.

Financial statement analysis is the process of evaluating a company's past performance in order to best forecast future prospects. Good analysis uncovers a firm's historical strengths and weaknesses so the analyst can better evaluate potential business prospects and associated risks. Financial analysis, sometimes more generally referred to as business analysis, includes investigating a company's current financial position (both short term and long term), business environment, and strategies in order to evaluate performance relative to benchmarks, either internal or external to the firm. Business analysis is integral to many business decisions such as whether to expand operations, purchase new equipment, increase spending on research and development, invest in equity or in debt securities, or extend credit through short- or long-term loans. It is also used to value a business in an initial public offering (IPO) and to evaluate corporate restructurings, such as mergers, acquisitions, and divestitures.

Some consider financial statement analysis to be the "boring" part of finance. In fact, properly done, it can be both challenging and exciting. It is our desire that you find this chapter to be the latter as opposed to the former. Indeed, in light of recent corporate scandals involving financial statement fraud and manipulation, the ability to properly analyze a company's financial statements to identify areas of strength and weakness, and possibly even uncover improprieties, is more important than ever.

In this chapter we present the common tools used by financial analysts to examine a firm's financial statements. The tools we list here can be used by an analyst to identify areas of the business that are functioning properly and areas that require additional attention. The material presented here is introductory in that we describe the process of financial analysis, but do not really explain the process of financial analysis itself. That is left to more advanced courses in finance.

Financial statement analysis is deep and complex, because firms are deep and complex. There are very few exact and specific answers one can derive from financial statement analysis; instead, one identifies areas of strength and areas of concern in order to ask better questions and more precisely focus additional analysis. Nonetheless, as you learn the techniques and work through the problems in this chapter, you will gain a greater understanding of the relationships between financial statements, and as you grow in that understanding, you will begin to appreciate the importance, as well as the complexity, of good business analysis.

2.2 The Objective of Financial Statement Analysis

The main purpose of financial statement analysis is to identify a company's strengths and weaknesses. Specific objectives, however, depend on who is doing the analysis. Three groups are typically interested in the information that financial statements can reveal: creditors, stockholders, and managers.

Creditors are chiefly concerned about the ability of the firm to make interest and principal payments on borrowed funds. A creditor must assess the reason why the firm needs money or how the firm has used borrowed funds in the past. A creditor is also interested in the firm's current capital structure (that is, the ratio of total debt to total assets), and the history of debt service. Identifying the source of cash to be used to repay the loan is extremely important. In particular, the creditor must evaluate cash flow from operating activities to determine if the firm will be able to produce sufficient internal cash flow to pay its debt obligations. Finally, creditors must evaluate the quality of all assets held by the firm to determine their liquidation value in the event of bankruptcy. When a firm goes bankrupt, all assets are sold and the proceeds from the sale are divided among all of the firm's creditors. If the total value of all liquidated assets is less than the claims of all creditors, then some or all creditors will receive less in repayment than what they loaned to the firm.

Stockholders, both current and prospective, are mainly interested in the firm's future prospects. They must estimate the future earnings stream of the firm to determine the value of the company's stock. Stockholders base their investment decisions (that is, buy stock or sell stock) on the relationship between the estimated value of the stock and the current price at which the stock is trading in the stock market. Stockholders are interested in the historical performance record of the company only to the degree that history might help to determine future expectations. Another significant area of interest to stockholders is the relationship between reported earnings and cash flow. Recall from the Derrick Dickerson example that the wealth of the owners (that is, the stockholders) is a function of cash flow, not net income. Finally, stockholders are concerned about the risk and timing of the firm's future cash flows. The value of immediate, low-risk, small cash flows might be greater than the value of distant future, high-risk, large cash flows, or vice versa. Specific value can be determined only by estimating risk and timing.

Managers are interested in all of the areas of concern to both creditors and stockholders, because creditors and stockholders provide funds that the firm needs to operate and grow. Companies must be able to attract sufficient and low-cost capital to survive in a competitive environment. Management must also consider the firm's employees, the community in which the firm operates, the environment, government regulators, and the financial press. The company must appear to be friendly and attractive to all of these groups. Finally, managers must identify the strengths and weaknesses of the firm's historical operational performance and current financial position and must estimate the company's future funding needs. Strategic plans must be formulated, communicated, and effectively implemented to accentuate strengths and correct weaknesses.

2.3 Financial Statement Fraud and Earnings Management

Financial statements are meant to summarize a company's financial operations for a period of time. They should paint an accurate picture of the health of a business and should provide information concerning the firm's future prospects. Current stockholders rely on financial statements to evaluate firm and management performance; potential stockholders rely on financial statements to determine whether to invest in a firm; creditors rely on financial statements to ascertain the risks of lending money to a firm; and the country as a whole relies on financial statements to indicate the general health of the economy. Because so many people rely on financial statements, tremendous financial losses can result if financial statements are not truthful and accurate.

Financial statement fraud occurs when a company distributes financial statements that knowingly contain false information. Unfortunately, the incidence of financial statement fraud in the United States is much larger than most realize. According to a recent fraud survey conducted by a major accounting firm, 76% of companies consider fraud to be a major problem for business today and many admit having experienced fraud during the past year.

Although interesting, financial fraud is neither glamorous nor amusing. When financial fraud is uncovered, a firm is usually forced to declare bankruptcy. The stock price that was based on the fraudulent information goes to zero, the physical assets upon which creditors made loans are often found to be bogus or of much lower value than stated, retiree pensions that were based on the future performance of the firm become worthless, and, in some cases, tens of thousands of individuals lose their jobs. Financial fraud erodes the public's confidence in the reliability of financial reporting as a means to assess a firm's future prospects. This in turn erodes confidence in financial markets, which impedes economic growth for the entire country.

While the consequences of fraud are important and substantial, of perhaps greater concern than blatantly illegal financial manipulation is the legal manipulation of financial statements—in particular, of reported earnings. Whereas outright fraud is usually eventually discovered, massaged data is more difficult to uncover.

2.3.1 Playing the Résumé Game: An Analogy

Creating a balance sheet and income statement is in many ways analogous to preparing a résumé. Granted, the regulations that govern the presentation of financial data in a set of financial statements are much more stringent than those that govern the presentation of personal information in a résumé. Nonetheless, both documents attempt to present the historical achievements of the subject in a condensed format. Additionally, both documents allow the person preparing the statement discretion about the most favorable manner in which to present the data. Consider the following example.

Eleesha Erickson, a senior at State University, plans to graduate at the end of the current semester. She has just returned to her apartment from a visit to the counseling office, where she was given a set of guidelines for creating an effective résumé. Eleesha correctly realizes that before she can apply for a job, she needs to have a résumé.

The three major items that concern Eleesha as she begins to construct her résumé involve her educational achievements, her work experience, and her lack of honors. Eleesha, an English Literature major, currently has a 2.56 grade-point average. She has only worked at fast-food restaurants on a part-time basis during the summers. And she has never received an academic or athletic award or recognition.

In reviewing her transcript, she realized that in nearly all of the classes that she was forced to take outside of her major to satisfy the university's liberal arts requirements, she got Cs. Additionally, her grades in her first three years of college, while she was very active in her sorority, were miserable. Indeed, because she had to repeat many of the courses that she took during that time, it has actually taken her five years to complete her college education.

Problem 2.1: If you were Eleesha, how would you present your grades and grade point information?

Eleesha's Solution: List only her expected graduation date (as opposed to the time period she was in college) and report the grade point average for only the courses taken in her major field of study during the past two years. This allowed her to report a grade-point average of 3.5.

Eleesha had worked for two summers at a local Louisiana Fried Chicken as a fryer (a cook) and for a summer at Pizza House as a cashier. At Louisiana Fried Chicken, where Eleesha worked the weekend close-up shift, one of her major responsibilities was to dispose of all unsold chicken at the end of the night. At Pizza House, where she also worked the close-up shift, her major responsibility at closing was to reconcile sales and receipts with the final cash register balance and to pay out all tips that had been added to credit card purchases and checks.

Problem 2.2: Eleesha knew that merely listing fryer and cashier at Louisiana Fried Chicken and Pizza House was not very impressive. If you were Eleesha, how would you jazz up the description of her work experience?

Eleesha's solution: Because chicken could technically be considered as inventory at Louisiana Fried Chicken, and because her job at Pizza House involved more or less the management of cash and technically some payroll responsibilities, she input the following lines on her résumé.

Louisiana Fried Chicken, Corporation
—Inventory Control Manager

Pizza House Corporation
—Manager: Cash and Payroll

Eleesha was outgoing, friendly, and enjoyed most of what she did, however, she did not see herself as being particularly excellent at anything. She was not particularly athletic, she did not play any musical instruments, she never won a contest, and as far as she could remember, she had never won any academic or community service awards. She was just a normal, average, ordinary college student.

Problem 2.3: If you were Eleesha, what would you enter for your "accomplishments" on your resume?

Elisha's Solution: During the summer of her third year of high school, Eleesha lived in Paris with her parents, who had been transferred there on a temporary work assignment. While in Paris, Eleesha learned how to speak and read French and spent most of her time at coffee shops meeting people and reading French magazines. She figured that whereas she technically learned something while she was in France, she could list her experience as a "Literature and Culture Internship in France."

Although Eleesha had never won any type of official academic award or honor, she was voted in her sorority as the sister "most likely to succeed in talking her way out of getting a speeding ticket if stopped by a cop" during her second year in college and as the sister "most likely to succeed at skipping more than half of her classes and still getting a passing grade" during her third year in college. In fact, her sorority sisters were correct. On her résumé, under the heading Awards and Honors, Eleesha recorded the following: Voted by Sorority in 2012 and in 2013 as the Most Likely to Succeed.

2.3.2 The Field of Forensic Accounting

Although admittedly exaggerated, the preceding example illustrates the temptations that an individual might face in presenting her personal characteristics and historical achievements as she attempts to get potential employers, via her résumé, to consider her for a job. In many ways, this example parallels the temptations that managers face when they present their historical financial data. Because this data will be analyzed by creditors from whom the firm needs loans, investors from whom the firm needs equity capital, owners evaluating management's performance (and using earnings numbers to determine bonuses paid), the firm's raw materials suppliers, potential employees, and others, many managers believe that the data must "look" good.

Accordingly, the first step in the analysis of a company's financial statements must be to consider the quality of the reported numbers. Ascertaining the quality of a firm's reported income and assets is critical in the analysis of financial statements. Generally accepted accounting principles allow management considerable discretion over how and when to report certain events. Consequently, management possesses the ability to legally "manipulate" company statements. Although financial statements should present a fair and accurate picture of the company's historical performance and current condition, this legal manipulation factor can cloud the picture.

The techniques that financial managers and accountants can use to "dress up" their financial statements are varied and numerous. Uncovering the use of these techniques is obviously very important. In fact, a relatively new field of accounting and finance has recently developed called *forensic accounting*. As you may recall from science class, or perhaps from a TV show, *forensic science* is the application of scientific principles and methods from the fields of physics, chemistry, and biology to help solve legal cases, often involving foul play. Forensic science is concerned with the recognition, identification, individualization, and evaluation of physical evidence. Likewise, forensic accounting is concerned with the process of examining financial statements, tax, and business records to find irregularities that can impact major legal cases, both civil and criminal.

If, after reading this chapter, you find financial analysis to be an area that you might consider as a possible career path, we suggest you further investigate classes and degree programs in this field. As for career opportunities, forensic accounting jobs are considered to be a strong growth area, mainly due to ever more stringent state and federal regulations concerning financial reporting and disclosures. The Bureau of Labor Statistics estimates that over the next decade, job growth in this area will be about 20%, significantly faster than for many other professions. Forensic accounting salary ranges are wide and depend on whether the job is in the public or private sector. As an example, the starting salary range for an FBI forensic accountant (and those working in other federal agencies) is in the mid-five figure range. Growth in experience and responsibilities can increase salaries to the low six figures. These figures are higher in the private sector, especially for those forensic accountants who contract with law firms as an expert witness.

2.4 Tools of Financial Statement Analysis

Once the quality of a firm's financial statements has been ascertained, the numbers need to be analyzed. This involves simplifying and categorizing the data so that comparisons can be made during different time periods and between different companies. The tools most commonly used to do comparative analysis are *common size financial statements* and *ratios*. The basic purpose of these tools is to convert financial statement data into common denominator formats in order to meaningfully compare different relationships among the measures so as to identify and evaluate a firm's strengths and weaknesses.

Converting data to a common denominator format and using several different common denominator measures to analyze the item(s) being described by the data is not limited to financial statements. Assume, for example, that you own a baseball team. During the off-season you are trying to decide which free agent (J.F. Rook or O.Z. Vett) to sign. Both players will require a $7,000,000 annual salary. Last season, Rook had 142 hits and Vett had 57 hits.

Do these numbers necessarily mean that Rook is a better hitter than Vett? What if last season Rook got his 142 hits in 708 plate appearances and Vett only had 132 plate appearances (Vett was injured for the first half of the season, but is now fully recovered)? Dividing the number of hits by the number of plate appearances shows that Rook averaged 2.01 hits for every ten times at bat (a .201 batting average) and Vett averaged 4.01 hits every ten times at bat (a .401 batting average). Don't batting averages allow a better comparison of the hitters than the raw data alone?

A batting average is merely a common denominator format measure (that is, a ratio). It standardizes the number of hits for each player, allowing a more meaningful comparison. All else equal, because Vett has a higher batting average than Rook, Vett is probably a better hitter than Rook. One measure alone, however, might not be sufficient (that is, all else might not be equal). Would your opinion about which player is a better hitter change if you knew that 50% of Rook's hits last year were home runs and that all of Vett's hits were singles? Or that Rook had 142 RBIs and Vett had only 21 RBIs?

Also, additional factors other than hitting might be equally important. Would your decision about which player to pay $7,000,000 be affected by the fact that Vett has a .996 fielding average (number of errorless plays to number of total plays) and Rook has a .726 fielding average (once when Rook was playing in the outfield, a ball bounced off his head and over the fence for a home run)? Or that Rook is 22 years old and Vett is 36 years old? Or that Rook is a switch hitter (can bat either right-handed or left-handed) and Vett can bat only from the right-hand side of the plate? Or that because he is vocal about everything, many considered Rook to be a major PR problem?

We hope that the point is obvious. When analyzing a specific problem, it is important to first standardize units of measurement. Also, one measure alone is seldom sufficient. Finally, qualitative factors may be at least as, or more, important than quantitative factors.

2.4.1 Common Size Financial Statements

To create a *common size statement*, every entry on the statement is divided by a common number. For the income statement, each account is divided by net sales. For the *common size balance sheet*, each item on the balance sheet is divided by total assets. Converting the resulting figures to percentages (multiplying by 100 and adding a percent sign) results in an income statement where every account is listed as a percent of sales and a balance sheet where every account is noted as a percent of total assets.

Problem 2.4: Construct a common size balance sheet for Xicre Retail using the data in the chart below. Compute common size ratios as a percent, rounded to one decimal place. For example, record 10/220 = .04545 as 4.6%.

Xicre Retail
Balance Sheet
For the Year Ending December 31, 2013
(all figures in dollars)

	2013	Common Size (as a Percent)
Cash	1,200	_____
Accounts receivable	8,500	_____
Inventories	3,600	_____
Net fixed assets	36,700	_____
Total assets	50,000	_____
Notes payable	2,200	_____
Accounts payable	800	_____
Accruals	400	_____
Long-term debt	24,800	_____
Common stock	6,900	_____
Retained earnings	14,900	_____
Total liabilities & equity	50,000	_____

Problem 2.5: Construct a common income statement for Xicre Retail using the data in the chart below. Compute common size ratios as a percent, rounded to one decimal place. For example, record 10/220 = .04545 as 4.6%.

Xicre Retail
Income Statement
For the Year Ending December 31, 2013
(all figures in dollars)

	2013	Common Size
Revenue	200,000	_____
Cost of goods sold	154,800	_____
Gross profit	45,200	_____

Operating expenses (excl. dep)	30,800	_____
Depreciation expense	6,400	_____
Operating profit	8,000	_____
Interest	1,100	_____
Earnings before taxes	6,900	_____
Taxes	2,000	_____
Net income	4,900	_____

Viewing several years of percent format financial statements of the same company side by side reveals instant visual information about any trends the company might be experiencing. However, trends in and of themselves do not necessarily indicate strength or weakness. All they really indicate are areas that require further investigation.

Problem 2.6: The inventory and total asset accounts for Ipenama, Inc. are listed below. Compute inventory as a percent of total assets for each year.

	2010	2011	2012	2013
Inventory	$135,600	$175,600	$250,900	$320,800
Total Assets	$1,384,000	$1,626,000	$1,915,000	$2,308,000
Percent	_____	_____	_____	_____

Ipenama's inventory accounts relative to total assets are growing every year. Is this bad? Greater relative amounts of inventory might mean more storage, warehousing, shipping, or insurance costs. All else constant, these will reduce profitability. In this case, the increase in inventory as a percent of total assets would indicate a weakness. However, if higher inventory levels are generating significantly higher levels of sales, then the additional revenue might more than offset the additional costs, and profitability might be higher. In this case, the increase in inventory as a percent of total assets represents a strength.

Problem 2.7: The upper portion of the income statements of Barista, Inc., a men's retail clothing store, for the years ending December 31, 2010, 2011, 2012, and 2013 are listed in the following table. For each year, compute COGS as a percent of net sales. Then, try to think of answers to the following questions:

- In what ways might the trend in COGS as a percent of sales represent a strength?
- In what ways might the trend in COGS as a percent of sales represent a weakness?

	2010	2011	2012	2013
Net Sales	$12,186,000	$14,538,000	$17,751,000	$22,698,000
COGS	$ 9,627,000	$11,846,000	$14,484,000	$18,499,000
Percent	_____	_____	_____	_____

The trend observed is a significant increase in COGS as a percent of sales from 2010 to 2011, and then relative stability thereafter. COGS as a percent of sales represents the direct cost per dollar of revenue of the products that the company sells. Thus for Barista, a retail clothing company, for every $1 of revenue made on selling clothes in 2010, it costs the company about 79 cents to purchase the clothing. Another way to look at this is that, in 2010, Barista was able to "mark up" its clothing by about 21%. For the following three years, the markup was only about 18.5%.

All else constant, a smaller markup will result in less profitability. Assume that all other costs (operating expenses, depreciation, interest, and taxes), as a percent of sales, were 19% for all four years. This would mean that Barista made positive net profit of about 2% of sales in 2010, but actually lost money (had negative net profit) in 2011, 2012, and 2013. Perhaps Barista's competitors lowered their prices (that is markups), and the only way for Barista to maintain its market share was to match the price cuts.

On the other hand, the lower markups might have contributed to (or caused) the large growth in net sales that occurred in 2011 through 2013 (average annual growth of over 20%). If the growth rate in other costs as a percent of net sales was less than the increase in COGS as a percent of sales, then profitability would have increased. This relationship could occur if Barista experienced cost-volume savings. Perhaps increases in same store sales generated higher revenue but unchanged rent, utility, and advertising expenses.

Although there are no definitive answers to the strengths/weaknesses questions, you might have come up with different possibilities or explanations. And yours might be just as right (or just as wrong) as ours. Regardless of what possibility is posited, further investigation is needed to draw meaningful conclusions, but at least the common size constructions told us where to start.

2.4.2 Financial Ratios

Financial ratios are designed to examine the relationships between key accounts on the balance sheet and the relationships between accounts on the balance sheet and certain values on the income statement. Financial ratio analysis is the comparison of these relationships through time for a given firm (trend analysis) and the comparison of these relationships for one firm to competitors or to average ratios compiled for the industry in which that firm operates (industry comparisons). Financial ratios are generally grouped into five main categories: _liquidity_ ratios, _activity_ ratios, _debt_ utilization ratios, _profitability_ ratios, and _combination_ ratios.

Ratios within each category are defined in Table 2.1. The nature of the information conveyed by each ratio is discussed below. Note that the ratios listed in Table 2.1 are merely a partial list of all of the possible ratios that could be calculated. In the world of financial ratios there is no definitive set of ratios, nor is there a uniform definition for all ratios.

Table 2.1 List of Key Financial Ratios

A. Liquidity Ratios

1. Current ratio $= \dfrac{\text{Current assets}}{\text{Current liabilities}}$

2. Quick ratio $= \dfrac{\text{Current assets} - \text{Inventories}}{\text{Current liabilities}}$

B. Asset Utilization Ratios

1. Average collection period = $\dfrac{\text{Accounts receivable}}{\dfrac{\text{Annual credit sales}}{360}} = \dfrac{\text{Accounts receivable}}{\text{Annual credit sales}} \cdot 360$

2. Inventory turnover ratio = $\dfrac{\text{Cost of goods sold}}{\text{Inventories}}$

3. Inventory conversion period = $\dfrac{\text{Inventories}}{\text{Cost of goods sold}} \cdot 360$

4. Total asset turnover ratio = $\dfrac{\text{Sales}}{\text{Total assets}}$

5. Payables period = $\dfrac{\text{Accounts payable}}{\text{Cost of goods sold per day}} = \dfrac{\text{Accounts payable}}{\text{Cost of goods sold}} \cdot 360$

C. Debt Utilization Ratios

1. Debt ratio = $\dfrac{\text{Total liabilities}}{\text{Total assets}}$

2. Times interest earned (TIE) = $\dfrac{\text{Operating income}}{\text{Interest expense}}$

D. Profitability Ratios

1. Return on assets (ROA) = $\dfrac{\text{Net income}}{\text{Total assets}}$

2. Return on equity (ROE) = $\dfrac{\text{Net income}}{\text{Total stockholders' equity}}$

3. Gross profit margin = $\dfrac{\text{Gross profit}}{\text{Net sales}}$

4. Operating profit margin = $\dfrac{\text{Operating profit}}{\text{Net sales}}$

5. Net profit margin = $\dfrac{\text{Net profit}}{\text{Net sales}}$

E. Combination Ratios

1. ROA = $\dfrac{\text{Net income}}{\text{Sales}} \times \dfrac{\text{Sales}}{\text{Total assets}}$

2. ROE = $\dfrac{\text{Net income}}{\text{Sales}} \cdot \dfrac{\text{Sales}}{\text{Total assets}} \cdot \dfrac{\text{Total assets}}{\text{Equity}}$.

This last two equations are known as the *Extended DuPont Equation*. Note that net income/sales = net profit margin; sales/total assets = total asset turnover ratio and total assets/equity is called the firm's equity multiplier.

Liquidity Ratios—Liquidity ratios, or solvency ratios, measure the extent to which a firm can meet its short-term obligations. One of the best-known and most widely used measures of a firm's solvency is the *current ratio*. This ratio attempts to measure the ability of a firm to meet its debt requirements as they come due.

The *quick ratio,* or *acid test ratio,* is similar to the current ratio in two respects—both measure the firm's liquidity, and both have the same denominator. The numerators, however, differ. The numerator in the quick ratio includes only those most liquid assets that can be quickly turned into cash. These are sometimes called "quick assets," that is, all current assets except inventory.

These two ratios attempt to indicate the probability that a firm will become insolvent. Insolvency occurs when a firm has insufficient cash to pay its bills on time. This is often the first step on the way to bankruptcy court. In general, the larger these two ratios, the less the chance there is of a firm becoming insolvent. Note, however, that if a firm's current assets are composed of obsolete inventory or bad debt that has yet to be written off, although these ratios might appear to be healthy, the firm might actually be insolvent.

Activity Ratios—Activity ratios, or turnover ratios, measure different kinds of business activity within the firm. The general idea underlying all turnover type ratios is that unused or inactive assets are nonearning assets, and actions should be taken to either use these assets more effectively or eliminate them. This is the offset to the idea that a big current ratio or quick ratio is good. A current ratio of, say 10, would almost certainly indicate an inefficient use of assets. For this reason, the ratios in this category are also sometimes called efficiency ratios.

The *average collection period* (ACP) is used to scrutinize the liquidity of the firm's accounts receivable. This ratio is useful in assessing the speed at which bills are being collected. If the credit customers are all paying their bills on time, the average collection period will be small. If, however, the company is being lax in collecting its accounts or the firm is carrying a lot of bad debt in its accounts receivable balance (that is, it is not writing off bad debt as it occurs), the ACP will be large.

The following example is designed to illustrate the nature and costs of accounts receivable. The Crawford Company sells, on average, $1,000 of merchandise per day. All sales are for credit on terms of net 10. That is, customers are given 10 days to pay their bills without penalty. Assume that sales commence today (on Day 1). The pattern of sales and collections is shown below:

Day	Dollar Amount Sold	Dollar Amount Collected
1	$1,000	$ 0
2	$1,000	$ 0
.	.	.
.	.	.
.	.	.
10	$1,000	$ 0
11	$1,000	$1,000
12	$1,000	$1,000

For 10 days, Crawford sells merchandise for which it receives no money. On the eleventh day the firm receives payment for the merchandise sold on day one. On the twelfth day Crawford receives payment for the merchandise sold on day two. And so on. Thus, from day eleven on, inflows match outflows and Crawford's average collection period is 10 days.

The merchandise sold through the first 10 days is not free; it had to be purchased or produced at a cost. Assuming (for simplicity) a cost of $1,000 per unit, Crawford spent $10,000 for this merchandise. Where did this money come from? Probably from a loan! For how long will Crawford have to fund this inflow-outflow mismatch? If sales continue at $1,000 per day and customers continue paying in 10 days, the mismatch must be funded forever! Assuming an interest rate of 12% per year, allowing customers to pay in 10 days will cost Crawford $1,200 per year in interest.

Of course, Crawford could require all of its customers to pay cash immediately. This policy, however, might negatively affect Crawford's sales. Would you shop at a clothing store that only accepted cash? If the annual reduction in sales due to a cash sale-only policy exceeds the annual interest cost on the net 10 accounts-receivable balance, the firm should sell on credit.

Consider what would happen if Crawford had a lax collection policy and, accordingly, customers took on average 25 days to pay their bills. Now the company's accounts receivable balance would be $25,000 and the annual interest expense would be $3,000. Obviously, it is in a firm's best interest to collect its accounts as quickly as possible as long as the enforcement of collection standards does not severely reduce sales. Specifics concerning the optimal amount of credit to extend, credit terms, and collection policy, are strategic decisions that managers make on a cost-benefit basis.

Note that the denominator in the average collection period formula is credit sales per day. To compute a firm's credit sales per day, merely divide annual credit sales by 360 (for simplicity, assume that there are 360 days per year). Note that the ACP should be computed using the firm's credit sales. Unfortunately, this number is seldom reported. Therefore, if the firm's annual credit sales are unavailable, total sales may be used in the denominator instead.

The *inventory turnover ratio* is a gauge of how efficiently a firm is employing its inventory. In general, the larger the inventory turnover ratio, the more efficiently a firm is using its inventory. This ratio, however, is very industry-specific. Whereas for a fruit stand, inventory (hopefully) turns over rapidly, furniture and jewelry stores have very long turnover periods.

Note that it is generally preferable to use cost of goods sold in the numerator to calculate the inventory turnover ratio. This is because most firms carry inventory on their books at cost. If, however, cost of goods sold is unavailable, sales may be used in the numerator instead.

The *inventory conversion period* is analogous to the inventory turnover ratio. As opposed to measuring the number of times per year that inventory "turns over," it measures the average length of time (in days) that it takes to convert raw materials into finished goods into sales. That is, the time period that an inventory item is in stock before it is sold.

The *total asset turnover ratio* is used to measure how productive a firm's total assets are at producing final sales. The higher the ratio, the more efficient a firm is at using its total assets. However, similar to the inventory turnover ratio, this ratio varies from industry to industry. The turnover of total assets per year varies from a low value of around once per year for heavy manufacturing industries (for example, steel mills) to over a dozen times a year for advertising agencies that own virtually no tangible assets.

The *payables period,* or accounts payable turnover ratio, measures how promptly a company pays its trade accounts. In essence, this ratio is the liability equivalent of the average collection period. If a firm purchases $1,000 per day with credit terms of net 10, paying all of its accounts in 10 days will provide the firm with, effectively, a $10,000 interest-free loan. It might be instructive to think of one firm's accounts payable balance as another firm's accounts receivable balance.

Industry credit terms usually include a discount for early payment. Typical credit terms are 2/10 net 30, where a firm can take a 2% discount on the purchase of materials if it pays the supplier within 10 days, otherwise the entire invoice price must be paid in 30 days.

Assume, again, purchases of $1,000 per day or total purchases of $360,000 per year. As shown above, if a firm facing these terms pays in 10 days, it receives a $10,000 interest-free "loan" from its supplier. If, however, the firm pays in 30 days, the "loan" from the supplier will be $30,000. The additional $20,000, though, has a cost. The firm will lose the 2% discount, which is equal to $7,200 per year. This implies an effective cost on the $20,000 loan of 36% per year ($7,200/$20,000).

In general, the effective cost of not taking the discount is given by:

$$\frac{\text{Discount percent}}{\text{Extra days if not take discount}} \times 360$$

$$\frac{2\%}{(30-10)} \times 360 = 36\%.$$

If the firm can borrow from its bank at less than 36% per year, it should pay its supplier in 10 days, and if it needs the additional $20,000, should borrow it from the bank. If a firm has a large and growing days payable ratio, it could indicate that the firm is "borrowing" from its suppliers because it is having difficulty securing funds from other sources (that is, the bank). Obviously, this would not be a good sign.

Problem 2.8a: For credit terms of 3/15 net 60, what is the effective cost of not taking the discount?

Problem 2.8b: For credit terms of 1/5 net 45, what is the effective cost of not taking the discount?

Note that the higher the discount percent or the smaller the gap between the discount period and the non-discount period (that is, extra days if not taking the discount in the equation above), the larger the effective cost of not taking the discount.

Debt Utilization Ratios—Debt utilization ratios are gauges of the extent to which a firm finances its operations with borrowed money rather than owner's equity. Using debt to finance assets is called leverage. To visualize the benefits and risks of leverage, consider the following example.

Several years ago, Tom Crowler, using $100,000 of his own money (stockholder's equity), opened a deli. Tom's deli produces annual earnings (which, because the firm has no debt and for simplicity we assume no taxes, is equal to operating income) of $20,000.

Two years ago, Tom borrowed $100,000 to open a second deli. This doubled his operating income to $40,000. However, because Tom now had to pay interest on his debt (annual interest rate of 10% on a loan of $100,000), his net income only rose to $30,000.

The benefit of using debt to finance his second store was that for no additional personal investment, Tom increased his net annual return from $20,000 to $30,000. This increased his expected return on his $100,000 investment from 20% to 30% per year. True to one of the most basic premises in finance, however, higher expected return involves higher risk. The risk of borrowing the money to open the second store is that now Tom has to pay $10,000 per year in interest. If Tom cannot pay the interest, he will technically default on his loan and perhaps lose his stores. This could occur if in any given year his operating income falls below $5,000 per store.

Now Tom is considering borrowing another $100,000 to open a third deli. This will increase his expected total operating income to $60,000 per year; however, because he now will have to pay $20,000 per year in interest (10% of $200,000), his expected net income will only rise to $40,000 per year. Nonetheless, his return on his initial investment is now expected to rise to 40% per year.

Tom is using leverage to boost his annual return. Using leverage, however, adds risk. With three stores, if in any given year his operating income falls below $6,667 per store ($20,000/3), Tom will default on his loans. Note that the additional borrowing raised the breakeven threshold from $5,000 per year to $6,667 per year. Furthermore, note that we assumed that Tom could borrow an additional $100,000 at the same interest rate. This might not be valid. In general, the greater the amounts of debt relative to stockholder equity, the higher the interest rate. If the interest rate on the second loan were indeed higher than 10%, the breakeven threshold level of operating income per store would be even higher.

Thus, the use of leverage represents a tradeoff between risk and return. The greater the leverage, the greater the expected return, but also the greater the risk (in particular, of default). Debt utilization ratios, which are sometimes also referred to as leverage ratios, attempt to measure the risk inherent in the firm's use of debt financing.

The *debt ratio* measures the proportion of all assets that are financed with debt. In general, the higher the debt ratio, the higher the risk of default. Additionally, the higher the debt ratio the more difficult it will be for a firm to obtain additional debt at a reasonable cost when needed. A high debt ratio firm will often find that funds are only available at extremely high interest rates.

Another common debt measure is the *debt to equity ratio*, which is calculated as total liabilities divided by stockholders equity. Because:

$$\text{Assets} = \text{Debt} + \text{Equity},$$

given the debt to equity ratio, one can calculate the debt ratio or vice versa. For example, assume that a firm has a debt to equity ratio of .5. If debt was $50 and equity was $100, the debt to equity ratio would be 50/100 = .5. Because Debt + Equity = Assets, this firm would have assets of $150 and the debt ratio (Debt/Assets) would be 50/150 = .33 = 33%.

The *times interest earned (TIE) ratio* measures how many times the firm's annual operating earnings cover its debt-servicing charges (mainly interest). The larger this ratio, the less likely a firm is to default during a major downturn in sales. Interest expense represents a fixed cost that must be paid regardless of how many units a company produces or sells. With a TIE of 10, a firm's operating earnings would have to fall by more than 90% before the firm would be unable to pay its fixed interest expense. In the deli example above, with two stores Tom's TIE was 4 (40,000/10,000). Adding a third store caused the TIE to fall to = (60,000/20,000).

Profitability Ratios—The profitability ratios reflect the joint effects of the preceding three sets of ratios: activity, liquidity, and leverage. They compare a firm's earnings with various factors that are necessary to generate the earnings. These ratios can shed light on which aspects of the business are particularly profitable and which are not.

The *net profit margin* measures the percent by which (all else equal) the selling price of a firm's products can decline before the firm suffers losses. *Return on assets* (ROA) measures the after-tax profitability per dollar invested in total assets. Asset intensive businesses, such as steel mills, usually have low rates of return on their huge investments in assets, whereas service companies generally have high rates of return on their small asset investments. The *return on equity* (ROE) measures the overall results of operations from the owner's standpoint. This ratio reflects both the profitability with which total investment or total assets have been employed and how effectively the firm has used leverage. The *gross profit margin* and *operating profit margin* will be discussed in greater detail later in the chapter.

Note that the difference between a firm's ROA and ROE is attributable solely to a firm's use of borrowed funds. If a firm has no debt, these two ratios will yield identical numerical values.

Combination Ratios—Sometimes ratios are combined to produce other ratios. A trend in the combined ratio can be viewed as a combination of parts, and perhaps a single part can be identified as a strength or weakness. The most commonly used combination ratio is the DuPont equation.

Values for selected accounts from the income statement and balance sheet of the SkerMax Company are listed below:

Annual credit sales	$360,000,000
Cost of goods sold	270,000,000
Accounts receivable balance	54,000,000
Inventories	90,000,000
Accounts payable balance	36,000,000

Problem 2.9: What is SkerMax's average collection period, inventory turnover period, and payables period?

The *extended DuPont equation* is a combination ratio that defines a firm's ROE as a function of activity, profitability, and leverage. The ROE is a ratio that is closely watched by stockholders and management. If a firm's ROE declines, the extended DuPont equation can be used to identify the specific reason for the decline. The equation is:

$$ROE = \frac{\text{Net income}}{\text{Sales}} \times \frac{\text{Sales}}{\text{Total assets}} \times \frac{\text{Total assets}}{\text{Equity}}.$$

Note that the first component of the equation is the net profit margin and the second component is the total asset turnover ratio. The third component of the equation is called the equity multiplier. It indicates the impact on ROE of a firm's use of leverage. Note that because,

$$\text{Total assets} = \text{Total Liabilities} + \text{Equity},$$

another way to measure the equity multiplier is:

$$\text{Equity multiplier} = \frac{1}{1 - \text{Debt ratio}}.$$

If a firm's debt ratio increases, then (all else constant, including net income) the firm is using less equity to finance its assets and therefore its return on equity will naturally increase.

The DuPont equation shows that if a firm experiences a decrease in its ROE, the decrease can be attributed to either a decrease in the firm's profitability (inefficiencies in the management of the income statement), a decrease in the firm's asset turnover (inefficiencies in the management of the balance sheet), or a change in the firm's capital structure (that is, debt ratio).

2.5 Learn by Doing

The best way to learn ratios is to do ratios. The more ratio problems you do, the easier the formulas will be to remember. There are two types of ratio problems that will help you recall and apply the formulas: direct ratio calculations and ratio relationship problems.

2.5.1 Direct Ratio Calculations

Problem 2.10: Using the financial data below for SAS Beers, Inc., fill in the ratio chart on the following page.Ratio Relationship Problems

SAS Beers, Inc.
Balance Sheets for Years Ending December 31, 2010, 2011, and 2012

	2010	2011	2012
Cash	100	100	200
Accounts receivable	1,000	1,900	3,100
Inventories	1,400	2,900	4,700
Current assets	2,500	4,900	8,000
Net fixed assets	5,300	5,400	6,700
Land	800	800	800
Total assets	8,600	11,100	15,500
Notes payable	100	300	1,200
Accounts payable	1,200	1,800	3,100
Accruals	200	900	1,000
Total current liabilities	1,500	3,000	5,300
Long-term bank loan	4,000	4,200	4,900
Common stock	1,500	1,900	1,900
Retained earnings	1,600	2,000	3,400
Total liabilities and equity	8,600	11,100	15,500

SAS Beers, Inc.
Income Statements for Years Ending December 31, 2010, 2011, and 2012

	2010	2011	2012
Sales revenue, net	15,000	22,500	25,600
Cost of goods sold	10,600	15,000	17,300
Gross profit	4,400	7,500	8,300
Operating exp. (incl. dep.)	2,800	3,200	4,200
Operating profit	1,600	4,300	4,100
Interest expense	200	400	700
Profit before taxes	1,400	3,900	3,400
Taxes	600	1,600	1,400
Net income	800	2,300	2,000

SAS Beers, Inc.
Financial Ratios for 2010, 2011, and 2012

	2010	2011	2012
Current ratio	_____	_____	_____
Quick ratio	_____	_____	_____
Average collection period (a)	_____	_____	_____
Inventory turnover ratio	_____	_____	_____
Inventory conversion period	_____	_____	_____
Total asset turnover	_____	_____	_____
Payables period	_____	_____	_____
Debt ratio	_____	_____	_____
Times interest earned	_____	_____	_____
Return on assets (ROA)	_____	_____	_____
Return on equity (ROE)	_____	_____	_____
Gross profit margin	_____	_____	_____
Operating profit margin	_____	_____	_____
Net profit margin	_____	_____	_____

Notes:
(a) All sales are assumed to be on credit

2.5.2 Ratio Relationship Problems

Ratio relationship problems demonstrate the connections between ratios. The more you work these types of problems, the better you will learn ratios and, more importantly, you will begin to see how ratios are interconnected. Because ratio analysis involves looking at many ratios instead of just one (recall the baseball player comparison example at the beginning of this chapter), the better you understand ratio comparisons, the more natural ratio analysis becomes. Several examples of these types of problems, and how to solve them, are presented below.

Problem: If ROE = 20% and ROA = 15%, what is the firm's debt ratio?

Solution: To solve problems like this (specifically, when you are given ratio relationships but no constants, first write out all of the equation formulas, then assume total assets = 100, then solve for each variable in the equations relative to total assets = 100, and finally solve for the ratio you are asked to find. This process is demonstrated below:

- ROE = 0.20 = net income / total equity
- ROA = 0.15 = net income / total assets
- Debt ratio = total liabilities / total assets
- Also note the we always know that total assets = total liabilities + total equity

Now assume total assets = 100. Then from ROA = 15, we know that net income = 15. And now from ROE = .20 and net income = 15, we know that total equity = 75 (because 15/75 = .20). Finally, from total assets = total liabilities + equity and total assets = 100 and total equity = 75, we know that total liabilities = 25. Thus, debt ratio = 25/100 = .25 = 25.0%.

Problem: If a firm's debt ratio is 60%, what is the firm's debt to equity ratio (i.e., total liabilities / total equity)?

Solution: First write out the ratio equations:

- Debt ratio = 0.60 = total liabilities / total assets
- Debt to equity ratio = total liabilities / total equity
- And we know that total assets = total liabilities + total equity (always!)

Assume total assets = 100, then from debt ratio = .60, we know that total liabilities = 60. From total assets = total liabilities + total equity and total assets = 100 and total liabilities = 60, we know the total equity = 40. Thus, debt to equity ratio = 60/40 = 1.50.

Note that this process (assume total assets = 100) will work for any problem where you are given ratio relationships but no constants. Note also that you can assume total assets = any number you like and you will still get the same final answer (try using total assets = 500 for both of the above to see that you will still get debt ratio = 25.0% and debt to equity ratio = 1.50. We suggest using 100 because it is a very simple and easy to use math number. Of course, if you are given a constant, then you must use the constant (and not assume total assets equal 100).

Problem: If net income = 8,000, the equity multiplier = 3.0 and ROE = 0.40, what is the firm's debt ratio?

Solution: First write out the ratio equations:

- Net income = 8,000
- Equity multiplier = 3.0 = total assets / total equity
- ROE = 0.40 = net income / total equity
- Debt ratio = total liabilities / total assets
- Total assets = total liabilities + total equity

Because we are given net income = 8,000, we must use this and ROE = 0.40 to find total equity = 20,000. From equity multiplier = 3.0 and total equity = 20,000, we know that total assets = 60,000. From total assets = total liabilities + total equity, total assets = 60,000 and total equity = 20,000, we know that total liabilities = 40,000. Thus, debt ratio = 40,000/60,000 = .667 = 66.7%.

Problem 2.11: Philips, Inc. has a debt ratio of 75% and ROE = 12%. What is Phillips' ROA?

Problem 2.12: Assume that XYZ, Inc. has: Debt ratio = 60%; Net profit margin = 15%; Return on assets (ROA) = 25%. Find XYZ's total asset turnover ratio.

Problem 2.13: Assume that your firm has ROA of 17.5%, ROE of 28% and Total Asset Turnover ratio of 2.75. Calculate the debt ratio for the firm.

2.6 Analyzing Financial Ratios

There are two main ways to analyze financial ratios for a given firm: *trend analysis* and *industry comparison analysis*. The latter method involves comparing the ratios of one firm to those of a peer group of firms. The notion here is that different industries should possess distinctive financial characteristics. That is, for certain industries, certain values should be expected. For example, one would probably expect that the average asset turnover ratio in the electric utility industry would be lower than the asset turnover ratio in the temp-services industry. In fact, the average asset turnover ratio for utilities is 0.7 and for the temp-services industry is over 5.0. An analyst should attach a caution flag to a ratio for a given firm that deviates substantially from the average of that ratio across all other firms in the industry.

Trend analysis involves the comparison of the same ratio for the same firm over a period of years. Although not always available, it is best to have at least three years of ratio data to identify meaningful trends. Ratios that exhibit trends should be more carefully investigated. Is the trend good or bad? What specific factor is causing the trend? Often, comparing the trends of two or more sets of ratios can identify specific problem areas. Note the obvious trend in the following set of current ratios for the Bakker Company:

	2010	2011	2012
Current ratio	1.5	2.0	2.5

This trend is not necessarily bad, but it is curious. What is causing the current ratio to increase? Let's look at the trend in Bakker's quick ratio:

	2010	2011	2012
Quick ratio	0.8	1.3	1.8

Because the quick ratio is also increasing, the trend in the current ratio is not due to an inventory buildup, so let's look at the trend in the average collection period:

	2010	2011	2012
Average collection period	30	40	50

The trend here seems to indicate that the increase in the current ratio is due to a slower collection period. This, in turn, might indicate a strategic shift in management's policy concerning credit collections (relax credit standards to increase sales) or it may indicate a problem. One possibility is that Bakker is carrying an ever-increasing number of bad debt accounts that are not being written off. If a problem exists, management must formulate a solution or workout. Creditors and stockholders, perhaps via discussions with Bakker's management, must discover the true reason for this trend.

The process demonstrated above is how ratio analysis is conducted. Every ratio and relationship is examined, trends and/or variations from standards are identified, questions are asked, more analysis is conducted, and on and on until as clear picture as possible of the firm is formulated. Based on this picture, decisions are made. Creditors decide whether to extend a loan, stockholders decide whether to buy the company's stock, and managers decide what policies of the firm need adjustment. The process is tedious, but because often very large sums of money are at stake, the time and difficulty is worth the effort.

2.7 Limitations of Ratios

Whereas financial ratios can reveal important information about a firm, it is very important to understand the limitations of ratio analysis. Ratios are useful in theory, but their value might be limited in practice. This is not to say that ratios are worthless. Ratios can alert analysts and management to positive or negative trends or to policies that deviate from industry standards. They cannot, however, provide definitive answers, nor are they necessarily predictive of future outcomes. Ratios should be viewed merely as screening devices. They indicate areas of potential weakness or strength, revealing items that might need further investigation.

Three specific factors limit the usefulness of financial ratios. First, all financial ratios that rely on balance sheet values are computed using "snapshot in time" data. Balance sheet values are stock measures—they are the values of a firm's assets and liabilities on a specific date (perhaps December 31, 2012). The more liquid the asset or liability, the more that number will deviate from its reported value throughout the rest of the year. A firm that reports $1,000,000 in its checking account on December 31, 2012 might have a negative cash balance two days later after making payroll and paying off suppliers. A retail clothing store that reports a relatively small accounts receivable balance in March (and therefore will have a small computed average collection period) would report a much larger balance (and would therefore have a large average collection period) in December if most of it Christmas sales were credit sales.

The snapshot nature of balance sheet data also allows firms to "window dress" their statements for reporting purposes. For example, if a firm wants to spruce up its current ratio, all it needs to do is borrow long-term money on December 28 and deposit the money in its checking account. Then at fiscal year end (December 31), it can report a healthy cash balance.

You don't think this happens in the real world? Reportedly, to window-dress its current account ratios, several years ago a firm sold a corporate jet in late December and deposited the cash in its checking account for fiscal year-end. The firm then bought the jet back in early January. This happened three years in a row! And each time the firm paid more for the jet in January than what it sold the jet for in December!

Second, financial ratios are calculated with accounting data, not market values. Accounting data is based on an asset's historical cost. Market values are based on the asset's present value.

Consider, for example, a firm that purchased a piece of land 30 years ago in a major metropolitan area. The purchase price of the land was $300,000. Because land neither appreciates nor depreciates on a balance sheet (that is, it is always carried at cost), the current listed value of this land on the firm's balance sheet is still $300,000. In fact, assume that the land is actually worth (its present value) $3,000,000. Thus, every ratio that involves this firm's total assets (total asset turnover, return on assets) will be inaccurate.

Additionally, as mentioned earlier in this chapter, accounting data (particularly income statement data) can be legally (and illegally) manipulated. If net income has been inflated and is thus neither indicative of current nor future profitability, then all ratios that involve net income (for example, ROE and ROA) can be misleading.

Also, a large and growing net profit margin does not necessarily indicate positive net cash flow Creditors and stockholders would much rather see evidence of positive cash flow than positive net income. This is why construction of a statement of cash flows is just as important as computation of a firm's ratios.

The third factor that limits the usefulness of financial ratios is the lack of a standard. Consider, for example, the current ratio. What is a good current ratio value? The standard guideline offered by bankers is 2. This, it is reasoned, allows shrinkage in the value of the current assets by 50% before the firm is unable to meet its maturing short-term obligations. Another standard often used is the average current ratio of all firms in the industry. Industry average ratios for nearly every industry and ratio imaginable are computed and published annually by Dun and Bradstreet Information Services (Industry Norms and Key Business Ratios), Robert Morris Associates (Annual Statement Studies), Standard & Poor's Corporation (Rating Handbook and Industry Surveys), and Gale Research, Incorporated (Manufacturing U.S.A. Industry Analyses).

Suppose that a firm's managers find in one of these publications that the average current ratio for a firm in the industry in which they operate is 2, with the lowest current ratio in the industry being 1.5 and the highest ratio being 2.6. If the average is 2, then what would be better than average: a current ratio of 1.8 or a current ratio of 2.2? Hopefully the firm's managers are not striving to merely be average; hopefully, their goal is to be better than average, to be the best!

Now suppose that for the firm described above the managers develop a new production and sales system that, with no negative effect on total sales,

1. allows it to perfectly match cash inflows to outflows, thereby eliminating the need to maintain a cash balance.

2. allows it to sell on a cash basis only, thereby maintaining an accounts receivable balance of zero.
3. allows it to produce its product on demand, thereby eliminating the need to carry any inventory balance (assume that the product can be materialized out of thin air and requires no raw materials).

This firm would have a current ratio of zero. Is that inefficient? Would bankers not make loans to this firm because its current ratio is below 2? Would you not buy stock in this company? In fact, this is a tremendous firm. The sole purpose of assets is to produce sales. If a firm can reduce its investment in assets and produce the same level of sales, it should do so. Assets must be financed and financing costs money. The fewer assets a firm needs to efficiently produce sales, the lower the financing costs that are associated with assets and thus the higher the annual net cash flow.

Obviously, one must be very careful when using standards. Deviations from industry standards are merely curious indications of areas that should be investigated further. Additionally, as in the example above, one might find that a deviation indicates something very positive—an innovative, aggressive management.

Considering these three limitations to ratio analysis, we again stress that whereas ratio analysis might be useful for identifying potential problems (or strengths), one must use ratio analysis very carefully.

2.8 Summary

In summary, financial ratios are useful tools that can be used to evaluate the past performance of a company in order to best forecast the firm's future prospects. With the completion of this chapter, you should now possess a healthy concern for the quality of financial statement and understand the basic tools and techniques of financial analysis that analysts use to ascertain the strengths and weaknesses of a company. You should also have some understanding of how to apply and evaluate these tools and techniques from three different viewpoints—specifically, as a creditor, as a stockholder, and as a financial manager. As such, you are equipped to enter the world of financial detective work. We know that you will find the task to be challenging. We hope you also find it to be interesting and rewarding.

Assignment 2.1

1. Income statements of Labal Company for 2011 and 2012 are as follows:

   Income Statements
   Labal Company
   For the Years Ending September 30, 2011 and 2012

	2011	2012
Net sales	$1,900	$2,200
Cost of goods sold	1,196	1,410
Gross profit	704	790
Operating expenses	514	582
Operating profit	190	208
Income taxes	80	90
Net income	$ 110	$ 118

   Prepare common size income statements for 2011 and 2012.

	2011	2012
Net sales	_____	_____
Cost of goods sold	_____	_____
Gross profit	_____	_____
Operating expenses	_____	_____
Operating profit	_____	_____
Income taxes	_____	_____
Net income	_____	_____

2. Balance sheets for Labal Company for 2011 and 2012 are as follows:

   Income Statements
   Labal Company
   For the Years Ending September 30, 2011 and 2012

	2011	2012
Cash	100	200
Net accounts receivable	1,500	2,200
Inventories	3,000	3,600
Current assets	4,600	6,000

Net fixed assets	2,100	3,100
Total assets	**6,700**	**9,100**
Bank loan (line of credit)	300	400
Accounts payable	1,600	1,900
Accruals	100	200
Current liabilities	**2,000**	**2,500**
Long term bank loan	1,800	2,900
Common stock ($0.15 par)	300	300
Retained earnings	2,600	3,400
Total liabilities and equity	**6,700**	**9,100**

Compute the following ratios for Labal Company (note that you will need some data from the income statement in problem 1 to compute some of the ratios).

	2011	2012
Current ratio	_____	_____
Average collection period	_____	_____
Inventory turnover ratio	_____	_____
Total asset turnover ratio	_____	_____
Payable ratio	_____	_____
Debt ratio	_____	_____
Cash conversion cycle	_____	_____
Net profit margin	_____	_____
Return on equity	_____	_____

Assignment 2.2

1. The Pilson Company's balance sheets and income statements for the years ending March 31, 2011 and 2012 are shown below (all figures in thousands of dollars):

	2011	2012
Current assets	$2,000	$3,000
Net fixed assets	4,000	7,000
Total assets	6,000	10,000
Current liabilities	$ 500	$1,800
Long-term debt	2,000	2,300
Common stock (.25 par value)	1,500	1,900
Additional paid-in capital	1,000	2,400
Retained earnings	1,000	1,600
Total liabilities and equity	6,000	10,000
Net sales	$7,000	$9,000
Cost of goods sold	3,000	4,400
Operating expenses	2,000	2,200
Interest expense	500	600
Taxes	100	200
Net income	1,400	1,600

a. What was the total dollar amount of dividends paid by Pilson in 2012?

b. How many shares of common stock did Pilson have outstanding in 2011?

c. How many shares of common stock did Pilson have outstanding in 2012?

d. What was the per share dividend payment in 2012 (rounded to the nearest cent)?

e. What was Pilson's ROE in 2011?

f. What was Pilson's ROE in 2012?

g. Using the extended DuPont equation, explain the reason(s) for the change (if any) in Pilson's ROE from 2011 to 2012.

Assignment 2.3

1. Complete the balance sheet and sales information in the table that follows for Johnson Company using the following information (all sales are on credit):

Debt ratio	60%
Inventory turnover ratio	5.0x
Net profit margin	10%
Total asset turnover	2.0x
Quick ratio	1.0x
Average collection period	45 days
Gross profit margin	25%
Return on equity	50%

    Balance Sheet

Cash	_____	Accounts payable	_____
Accounts receivable	_____	Long-term debt	180,000
Inventories	_____	Common stock	_____
Fixed assets	_____	Retained earnings	200,000
Total assets	**$1,000,000**	**Total Claims**	_____

2. Fill in Johnson's net sales, cost of goods sold, and net profit on the lines below:

Net sales	_____
Cost of goods sold	_____
Net profit	_____

3. Compute Johnson's cash conversion cycle.

4. List and compute the components of the Extended DuPont Equation for Johnson. Prove that the DuPont ROE is equal to 50% as given in first table above.

Additional Questions and Problems

1. To which firm would the inventory turnover ratio be more important: a grocery store or an insurance company? Why?

2. In what specific ways would high inflation affect a firm's balance sheet and income statement? How would high levels of inflation affect comparison of the financial ratios of a particular firm over time?

3. Given the other ratios listed, identify the possible specific cause of the trend in the current ratio:

	2004	2005	2006
Current ratio	2.0	1.6	1.4
Inventory turnover	6x	6x	6x
ACP	30	30	30
Payables period	40	50	60

4. Calculate the effective cost of passing up the discount for each of the following credit terms:

   a. 2/10 net 20

   b. 1/15 net 40

   c. 5/20 net 60

5. Assume you are given the following relationships for the In-Fer Company:

Current ratio	2x
Quick ratio	1.5x
Current liabilities	$100,000

   Compute inventory.

Financial Statement Analysis 49

6. Assume you are given the following relationships for the En-Fer Company:

    Return on assets   20%
    Return on equity   50%

   Compute the debt ratio.

7. Assume you are given the following relationships for the An-Fer Company:

    Total asset turnover ratio   4x
    Debt ratio   20%
    Return on equity   10%

   Compute the net profit margin.

8. Assume you are given the following relationships for the Un-Fer Company (all sales are credit sales):

    Average collection period   20 days
    Accounts receivable $1,000
    Net profit margin   5%
    Total asset turnover ratio   2x
    Debt ratio   75%

   Compute the return on equity.

9. Assume you are given the following relationships for the Givens Corporation:

    Return on assets (ROA)   12%
    Return on equity (ROE)   25%
    Total asset turnover   1.5x

   Calculate Givens' net profit margin and debt ratio.

10. Last year Popsicles and Confetti, Inc. (P&C) had sales of $10 million, a net income of $1 million, assets of $8 million, a debt ratio of 25% and a gross margin of 30%. Calculate return on assets (ROA) and return on equity (ROE).

11. The International Imports Company has $1,950,000 in current assets and $800,000 in current liabilities. Its initial inventory level is $700,000 and it will raise funds as commercial paper and use them to increase inventory. If International Imports raises the maximum short-term debt allowable without violating a current ratio of 2 to 1, what will be their new quick ratio?

12. Atlanta Unlimited has a debt ratio of 75%. What is Atlanta's equity multiplier?

13. The following data apply to J.S. Billings & Sons (dollars in thousands):

Cash	$200
Average collection period	40 days
Net fixed assets	$600
Net income	$ 60
Quick ratio	2.0x
Sales	$900
Current ratio	3.0x
Return on equity (ROE)	12%

    Billings has only current liabilities, long-term debt, and common equity on the right-hand side of its balance sheet and only cash, accounts receivable, inventories, and net fixed assets on the left-hand side of the balance sheet. Find Billings':

    a. Accounts receivable balance
    b. Current assets
    c. Current liabilities
    d. ROA
    e. Long-term debt
    f. Common equity

14. Assume the Firm is 100% equity financed. Calculate the ROE, given the following information:

• Earnings before taxes	$1,500
• Sales	$5,000
• Dividend payout ratio	60%
• Total asset turnover	2.0x
• Applicable tax rate	30%

15. Geometrics Inc. would like to expand to take advantage of new product opportunities. However, the terms of existing bond indentures and term loans with insurance companies restrict total debt to 55% of total assets. Currently, the firm has $3 million in total debt and $3 million in equity. It projects $1 million in profits after taxes in the current year, and dividends of $400,000. Compute the increase in total debt that can be raised without a violation and without an equity issue by the end of the coming year (rounded if necessary).

16. Supertronics is planning a new division with its newly developed products and finds that it can operate equally well with either of two different structures. The sales, debt ratio, net fixed assets, current liabilities, and profit margin would all be the same, but there are two

alternative current asset plans. These two plans involve only different levels of accounts receivable (AR) and inventory, as follows:

Plan A	Plan B
AR with 18 ACP (days)	AR with 36 ACP (days)
Inventory turnover of 5	Inventory turnover of 10

If sales are projected at $10 million, which plan should produce the higher ROE (that is, which plan requires the least equity investment)?

a. Plan A because of less receivables.
b. Plan B because of lower current assets.
c. Plan A because currents assets are higher.
d. The equity required would be the same, but Plan A has greater liquidity.
e. Cannot be determined without an asset turnover figure.

17. Johnson Corporation sells all of its merchandise on credit. It has a profit margin of 4%, ACP (average collection period) of 60 days, accounts receivable of $150,000, $3,000,000 in total assets, and a debt ratio of 0.64. What is Johnson's ROE?

18. The Berby Company has a quick ratio of 1.4, a current ratio of 3.0, an inventory turnover of six times, total current assets of $810,000, and cash and marketable securities of $120,000. What were Berby's annual sales and its average collection period for the year?

19. Determine the times-interest earned ratio (TIE) of a firm whose total interest charges are $20,000, whose sales are $2 million, whose tax rate is 40%, and whose net profit margin is 6%. (Hint: Reconstruct the income statement from the bottom up and find EBT and EBIT).

20. Find the debt ratio for the ABC Company that will double its current return on equity (ROE) to 10% for a projected net profit margin of 14%. Currently, ABC has a debt ratio (debt to total assets) of 0.5, a total asset turnover ratio of 0.25, and a net profit margin of 10%. Although the company expects that the net profit margin will rise to 14%, the total asset turnover ratio will remain the same. The new debt ratio is?

21. The Chicago Company has determined that its return on equity is 15%. You have the following information: debt ratio = 0.35 and total asset turnover = 2.8. What is the firm's profit margin?

22. Convert the following debt to equity ratios into debt to asset ratios and Equity multipliers:

Debt-to-equity ratio	Corresponding debt-to-asset ratio	Corresponding equity multiplier
2.5	_____	_____
1.0	_____	_____
0.6	_____	_____

23. Complete the balance sheet in the table that follows for the MacClemore Company using the following information (if necessary, round figures to the nearest dollar):

Sales	$2,000,000
Net profit margin	7.5%
Gross profit	$400,000
Return on equity	24.0%
Return on assets	15.0%
Inventory turnover ratio	4.0x
Average collection period	40 days
Days payable ratio	20 days
Current ratio	3.8x

Balance Sheet

Accounts receivable	_____	Notes payable	_____
Inventories	_____	Accounts payable	_____
Fixed assets	_____	Long-term debt	_____
Total assets	_____	Equity	_____
	_____	**Total liabilities and equity**	_____

24. Complete the balance sheet in the table that follows for the OptiPlex Company using the following information (if necessary, round figures to the nearest dollar):

Sales	$4,000
Net profit margin	10.0%
Return on equity	25.0%
Total asset turnover ratio	1.0x
Gross profit margin	30.0%
Average collection period	40 days
Current ratio	3.0x
Dividend payout ratio	65.0%
Quick ratio	1.0x

Note: 90% of all sales are credit sales; 10% are cash sales. Assume a 360-day year.

Balance Sheet

Accounts receivable	_____	Current liabilities	_____
Inventories	_____	Long-term debt	_____
Fixed assets	_____	Equity	_____
Total assets	_____	**Total liabilities and equity**	_____

Chapter 3

Overview of the Financial Markets

3.1 **Introduction to Financial Markets**

3.2 **Organization of the Financial Markets**

3.3 **Measuring the Performance of the Financial Markets**

3.4 **Stock Brokerage Firms**

3.5 **Summary**

   List of Terms

   Questions

The learning objectives for the readers of this chapter are to develop an understanding of:

- The nature and role of the primary and secondary securities market;
- The difference between the capital and the money markets;
- The major financial exchanges, their classification, and the type of issues traded on these exchanges;
- The roles of the specialist and the market-maker;
- The types of buy and sell orders that can be placed in financial markets;
- The major financial markets performance indices, how they are calculated and what they measure; and
- The services and costs of full service, discount, and electronic brokerage firms.

From *Basic Principles of Finance: An Introductory Text, 1st Edition* by Joseph Woolridge and Gary Gray. Copyright © 2011 by Kendall Hunt Publishing Company. Reprinted by permission.

In this chapter we examine the financial markets—the stock and bond markets where securities are purchased and sold, and the foreign exchange and derivatives markets. We discuss the role of the primary and secondary securities market, the money and capital markets, the major stock exchanges, the over-the-counter market, and the manner in which trades take place in the markets, as well as different ways to measure the performance of the markets.

3.1 Introduction to Financial Markets

Financial markets exist so that excess monies from investors can be transferred cheaply and efficiently to businesses, governments, individuals and other entities that have profitable investment opportunities and a shortage of funds. In return for the use of these monies, the user of the funds sells an investor a *security*—a claim against the assets or cash flows of the entity. The markets in which the issuers of securities receive the funds directly from the initial sale of securities are called primary markets.

Another function of financial markets is to provide *liquidity*—the ease with which an owner of a security can sell an investment to another investor or trade it in the securities markets. Securities markets provide a marketplace where buyers and sellers of securities can complete transactions quickly and efficiently, and save investors from a costly search for potential buyers and sellers of the stock or bond. Securities markets also provide investors, issuers and other economic participants information about the current market value of their securities. The markets in which the current owners of securities receive the funds from the buyers of securities are called secondary markets.

If the security is an equity claim, such as a common stock, the investor of funds receives ownership rights in the firm in an amount that represents the percentage of the firm's stock that he owns. The stockholder also has the right to any dividends if declared by the firm and to the residual value of the firm after all business expenses and creditors are satisfied. The stockholder also has certain voting rights and participates in electing the firm's board of directors. If the security is a debt—a bond or debenture, the bondholder receives periodic payments of interest at a specified interest rate, and the repayment of principal on a predetermined date.

3.1.1 How Financial Markets Work

During the decade of the 1990's, the stock markets in the United States performed spectacularly. Fueled by the birth and growth of the Internet and the significant reduction of transactions costs, the Dow Jones Industrial Average rose from a level of 2,753 at the end of 1989 to 11,453 at the end of the Millennium. Likewise, the S&P 500 moved from 353 points to 1,469, and the NASDAQ Index rocketed from 454 to 4,069—a nine-fold increase.

All good things must come to an end. The Internet bubble burst and markets retreated severely in 2000, 2001 and 2002—the NASDAQ plummeting a total of 75%, the S&P 500 down 40%, and the DJIA dropping 27%. In 2003, stock markets around the world rallied by an average increase of from 25% to 55%. And in 2004, the DJIA increased by 3%, the S&P 500 jumped 9%, and the NASDAQ Index increased by 8.6%.

During the five year period from 2005 through 2009, investors experienced the inflating and crashing of the stock market due to the subprime housing debacle and the mortgage market collapse that began in 2006 and still hasn't played its last song. The financial sector was significantly damaged with the bankruptcy in September 2008 of Lehman Brothers, the shotgun mergers of Merrill Lynch and Bank of America, and Bear Stearns and J.P.Morgan, and the shift of Goldman Sachs and Morgan Stanley from an investment banking charter, with their principal regulator being the SEC, to a commercial banking charter, under the regulatory purview of the Federal Reserve. Stock markets around the world dropped precipitously, with the Dow Jones Industrial Average dropping over 50% from over 14,093 to 6,547. Investors familiar with the stock markets know that stock returns and prices can fluctuate substantially.

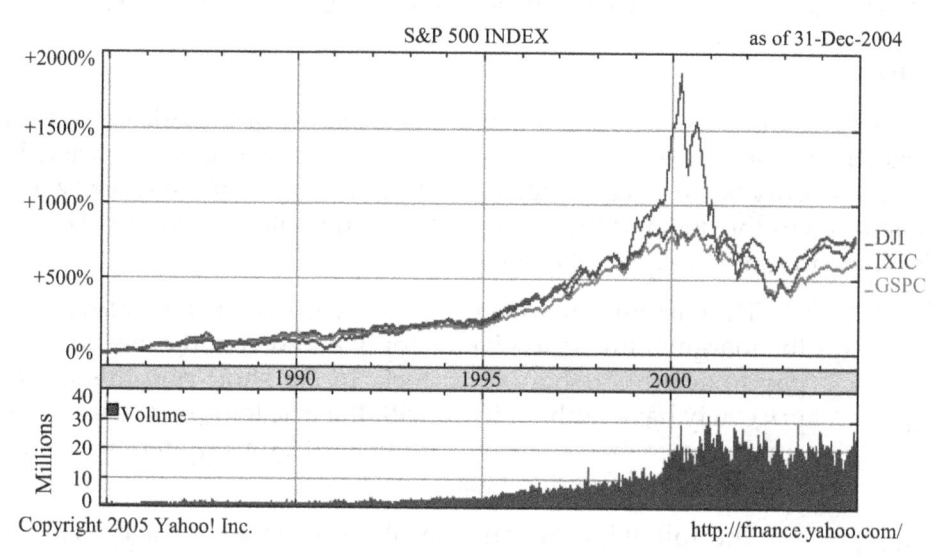

Exhibit 3-1 DJIA, S&P 500, and NASDAQ Indices: 1984–2004

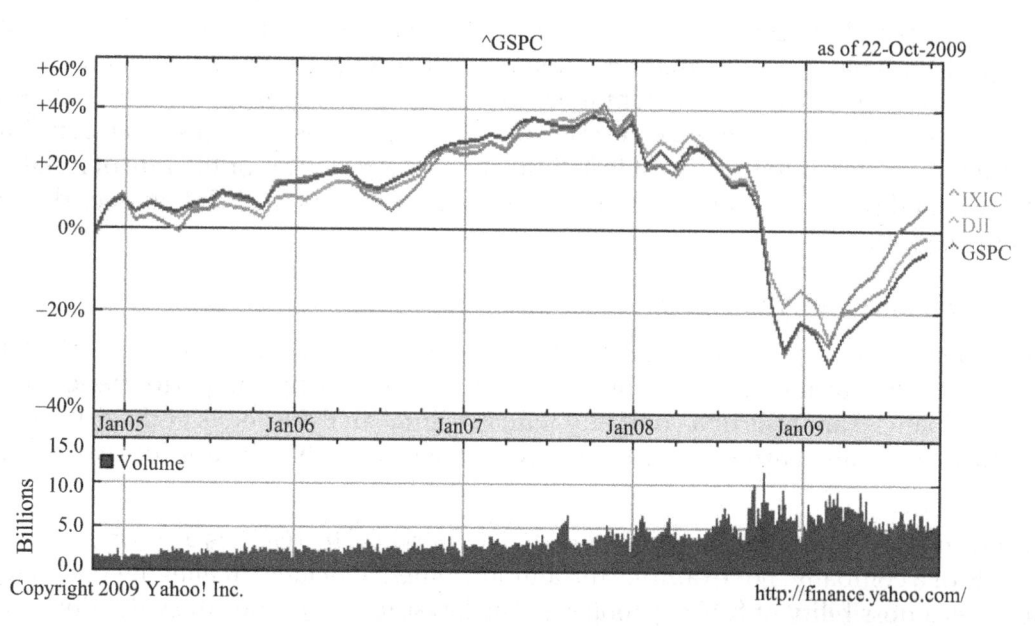

Exhibit 3-2 DJIA, S&P 500, and NASDAQ Indices: 2005–2009

Overview of the Financial Markets

Each business day millions of investors around the world trade stocks and bonds in the financial markets and stock and bond prices go up or down—often it seems for no specific reason. Perhaps you've wondered, what the principal factors are that propel these daily stock prices fluctuations.

The economics underlying the movements of the stock and bond markets are a mystery to most people. At the end of trading each day, analysts on CNBC and other financial news networks attribute price movements to any number of factors: government reports on consumer or wholesale prices; changes in interest rates; the increasingly bullish or bearish sentiment of investors; statements by Federal Reserve Chair, *Janet Yellen*; or company earnings reports exceeding or falling short of expectations. Below, we briefly examine some of those reasons.

Supply & Demand:

Like all competitive markets, the fundamental determinants of the price of a security in the secondary market are the supply and demand functions for that particular security. The market-clearing price for a security is the price at which the current supply of the security that is owned by potential sellers equals the demand for the security among potential buyers. The current price of a security is where the supply equals the demand.

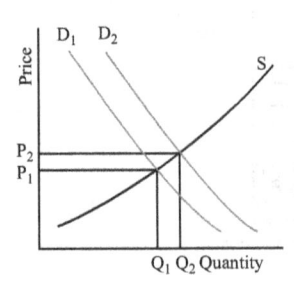

The current price of an asset, such as a stock, indicates the amount that the marginal investor, given supply and demand conditions, is willing to pay to acquire a share of a stock. In the short-run, this market-clearing price may have nothing to do with the true long-term value of a stock. The current price may be heavily influenced by a very temporary and extreme supply and demand imbalance.

The following factors contribute to investment demand for a fixed supply of shares of a stock.

Movements in Interest Rates and Economic Events:

New information about economic variables often has major impact on the bond and stock market as a whole. Variables such as inflation, interest rates, foreign exchange rates, and unemployment reports often act to drive movement in the bond, stock, mortgage, currency and derivative securities markets. For reasons that we describe in later chapters, asset prices react significantly to changes in interest rates or to the rate of inflation. When interest rates or the rate of inflation goes up, stock and bond prices go down. When interest rates or the rate of inflation goes down, stock and bond prices generally go up.

Company Financial Performance:

Investor demand for the stock of a particular company is usually affected by events that affect how a firm performs in the economy, and the effect of measuring the performance through a fundamental financial analysis of a company. Fundamental analysis looks at the expected future revenues, cash flows, and earnings of a company to determine what the appropriate value of the stock should be.

New information is continuously revealed to the market. The result is a constant changing of the prospects of a company. For example, the announcement of a lawsuit alleging patent infringement indicates a possibility of future problems. The lawsuit may reduce the valuation and lower investor demand for the stock. Conversely, positive news relating to a company that results in expectations of increased expected revenues and earnings should increase the price of the company's stock.

Industry Performance:

The expected performance of an industry in the economy often affects all of the individual companies comprising that industry. For example, Internet stocks reacted dramatically to industry performance expectations. During the 1990s, if a report was issued that the Internet is expected to grow at a higher annual rate than the market had expected previously, the majority of the stocks of companies in the Internet industry adjusted positively to the new information contained in that report. Alternatively, if an industry leader reported poor earnings or losses that were greater than anticipated, the stock prices of other companies in that industry would be negatively affected. Investors would be concerned that the factors that lowered the earnings of the industry leader will come to bear on the stock prices of the other companies in the industry.

National and World News Events:

Major news stories influence investor demand. The possibility of war in the Middle East or an international recession resulting from the devaluation of an Asian currency can dramatically influence people's attitude toward risk and investing. Negative news, such as the news relating to the terrorist attacks of September 11, 2001, causes the price of risky assets such as common stock to drop precipitously. The same negative news also causes the price of risk-free assets such as U.S. Treasury Bonds to increase substantially. This type of market reaction due to a reevaluation of risk in the market— fleeing risky securities such as stock, and redeploying funds into less risky U.S. Treasuries, is called a *flight to quality*.

3.1.2 Regulation of the Financial Markets in the United States

The principal regulator of all primary and secondary market activity in the United States is the Securities and Exchange Commission (SEC). Following the stock market crash of 1929 and the Great Depression of the early 1930s, a wave of financial regulation was implemented to curb market speculation and fraud, and to strengthen investor confidence.

The *Securities Exchange Act of 1934* created the SEC. The SEC is responsible for licensing securities professionals, collecting public disclosure information (e.g., quarterly and annual reports), and enforcing the various securities laws in the United States. This section reviews the SEC's activity in the primary and secondary markets and introduces some of the information resources available from the SEC on the Internet.

The SEC's primary objective is to provide investors with complete disclosure of all material information concerning publicly traded securities. Its goal is to create a level playing field for investors and minimize the information asymmetries that existed in the early 1900s.

Prior to the creation of the SEC, Congress initially passed *The Securities Act of 1933*. The Securities Act of 1933 is designed to regulate the *primary securities markets* by providing investors with the necessary information to make informed decisions regarding an issue of new securities. A lot of technicalities are involved, and numerous lawyers are employed in issuing a new security—a stock or bond issue, from the preparation of a registration statement and the filing with the SEC, to the distribution of a preliminary prospectus, to the sale of the securities to investors either directly or through a group of investment banks.

The Securities Exchange Act of 1934 also implemented regulation pertaining to the sale and trading of securities in the *secondary securities markets*—after the initial issuance of securities. This act regulates the activities of the various stock and bond exchanges in the United States and all of the financial institutions and finance professionals that participate in this market.

With the growth of computer technology and the Internet, the SEC has opened a database that allows immediate access to all public information electronically filed with the SEC, at its web address: www.sec.gov/. The EDGAR database is the SEC electronic public document access system; it may be accessed directly through the SEC's website.

3.1.3 Primary versus Secondary Securities Markets

The primary securities markets are the markets in which *newly issued securities* are sold to investors. The primary securities market for bonds involves the distribution to investors of newly issued debt securities by corporations, central banks, governments, and agencies. The primary securities market for stock includes the first time issuance of common stock for companies, called *initial public offerings (IPOs)*, the sale of issues of preferred stock, and the sale of additional common equity securities of corporations.

> *The **primary securities markets** involve the sale of newly issued stock and bonds and the proceeds flow from investors to the issuer of the security.*

The issuance of securities in the primary markets and the eventual sale of those securities to the public is a highly regulated process that is overseen by the SEC.

An investment bank is a financial institution in the marketplace that works with issuers to distribute new securities in the primary markets and link investors and issuers. During the securities issuance process, an investment bank performs one or more of the following three functions:

- It advises the issuer on the terms, price, and timing of the offering;
- It underwrites and purchases the securities from the issuer at a fixed price; and
- It distributes and sells the issue to the public.

The function of buying the securities from the issuer is called *underwriting*. When an investment bank buys the securities from the issuer, it accepts the risk of reselling the securities to investors, and the investment bank is referred to as an *underwriter*. In addition to underwriting securities in the primary market, investment banks advise corporations on mergers and acquisitions, optimal capital structures, and investment strategies. Investment banks attempt to act in the best interests of both investors and issuers in the primary markets.

Secondary securities markets are where financial assets that previously were issued in the primary markets are traded among investors. The key distinction between a primary market and a secondary market is that the issuer of the security does not receive funds from the buyer in a trade in the secondary market. Instead, the security changes hands, and funds flow from the buyer of the security to the seller—the previous owner of the security.

> ***Secondary securities markets** are markets where the funds flow from the buyer of a security to the seller—not to the issuer of the security.*

Liquidity is the ability to cheaply, quickly and efficiently turn an asset into cash. The secondary market provides investors with liquidity for securities. The periodic trading of a financial asset discloses information about the asset's value. Furthermore, secondary markets bring together many interested parties and reduce the search costs of buying and selling securities. This reduces transaction costs and the time required to trade financial assets. By keeping search and transaction costs low, the secondary market facilitates trading and investing in financial assets.

Trading induces additional trading. If no one trades, there is no liquidity in the market, there is no price discovery, and higher search costs. However, as long as investors are willing to participate in a secondary market, the market will facilitate trading.

To minimize search costs and to gather investors, it is helpful to have a physical central trading location. For stocks and bonds, this location is called an *exchange*. If goods and services are traded, this location is called a trading post. Nothing is made or issued at the exchange or trading post—only traded.

Stock exchanges are formal organizations, approved and regulated by the Securities and Exchange Commission (SEC). The only individuals that are able to trade on the exchange floor are *official members* of the exchange. Stocks that are traded on a given exchange are said to be *listed issues*.

> *Stock exchanges* are organizations where stocks are traded
> by the members of the exchange.

To become a member of an exchange, securities firms and individuals must buy a seat on the exchange. The number of seats on an exchange is limited—there are 1,366 seats on the New York Stock Exchange. The cost of the seat is determined by supply and demand. The highest price paid for a seat on the NYSE was $2 million in March 1998. Purchasing a seat gives its owner the right to be on the floor of the NYSE.

3.1.4 Money Markets versus Capital Markets

In *money markets*, debt securities with original maturities of one year or less are traded. Money markets serve to transfer funds from market participants with short-term excess funds to governments, corporations, and agencies that have short-term needs for funds. Investors usually purchase money market instruments as a temporary investment to park excess cash prior to its use for longer-term investments in a business or a capital asset.

Securities such as Treasury bills, federal funds, commercial paper, certificates of deposit, repurchase agreements, banker's acceptances and other short-term instruments are traded in the money market. Investors purchase low-risk, liquid money market securities with short-term excess monies. Characteristics of money market instruments are:

- They are sold in large denominations (usually $1 million and larger);
- They have a low default risk; and
- They have an original maturity of one year or less.

Interest rates on money market securities generally are lower than interest rates on assets that are traded in the capital markets, such as long-term bonds or the expected returns associated with common stock. Exhibit 3-3 below shows the interest rates on money market securities on

Exhibit 3-3   Federal Reserve Web Site, Interest Rates of 6/5/2015

Yields in percent per annum

Instruments	2015 Jun 1	2015 Jun 2	2015 Jun 3	2015 Jun 4
Federal funds (effective) 1 2 3	0.12	0.12	0.13	0.13
Commercial Paper 3 4 5 6				
Nonfinancial				
1-month	0.09	0.08	0.08	0.07
2-month	0.09	0.09	0.09	0.05
3-month	0.09	0.09	0.11	0.10
Financial				
1-month	0.09	0.09	0.09	0.13
2-month	0.12	0.13	0.12	n.a.
3-month	0.16	0.18	0.17	0.17
Eurodollar deposits (London) 3 7				
1-month	0.19	0.19	0.19	0.19
3-month	0.30	0.30	0.30	0.30
6-month	0.43	0.43	0.43	0.43
Bank prime loan 2 3 8	3.25	3.25	3.25	3.25
Discount window primary credit 2 9	0.75	0.75	0.75	0.75
U.S. government securities				
Treasury bills (secondary market) 3 4				
4-week	0.02	0.02	0.02	0.02
3-month	0.02	0.01	0.02	0.02
6-month	0.07	0.07	0.07	0.08
1-year	0.25	0.25	0.25	0.26

June 5, 2015, as taken from the Federal Reserve's web site. Short-term interest rates over the last year have been very low on a relative basis. The Federal Reserve has kept the Federal Funds rate at the level between 0% and ¼% due to the recent financial crisis.

In *capital markets*, investors buy and sell debt securities with an original maturity longer than one year, common and preferred stock, and mortgages and mortgage-backed securities. Corporations, governments, municipal entities and agencies issue the long-term securities that are traded in the capital markets. The principal purchasers of these long-term securities are financial institutions and individual investors.

The price fluctuations of long-term securities can be quite substantial. Academic studies have shown that the average price fluctuation of the shares of common stock in the United States is almost 50% per year. Price fluctuations of long-term bonds, which also can be significant, generally are dependent upon changes in interest rates. Investors, who wish to test their stock picking skills or try to earn returns in excess of those available in the money market, may relish the challenges of investing in the capital markets.

3.1.5 Foreign Exchange Markets

Each year, the world seems to grow smaller. With the Internet and news and media organizations providing instantaneous access to information from even the most remote places on earth, events that affect businesses and governments in one country has immediate and ripple effects throughout the world. Today, many U.S. corporations act on a global basis: buying raw materials for a product from different South American countries; producing components of the product in the Far East; assembling the product in Mexico; and selling the product in France or Germany or Great Britain. Many foreign corporations act in a similar manner.

It is important for financial managers of corporations to understand the foreign capital markets and to know how the foreign exchange markets operate. Many of the raw materials that a corporation buys are denominated in foreign currency. Additionally, the company may have production and assembly plants with a significant amount of employees paid in local currencies that are based in other countries. Movements in the value of foreign currency can greatly increase or decrease a corporation's revenues and profits.

Foreign exchange rates are the rates at which the currency of one country can be traded for the currency of another country. For example, on June 8, 2015, the foreign exchange rates for Euros, British Pounds, and Japanese Yen to U.S. dollars were:

1 Euro = $1.1118 U.S. Dollar

1 British Pound = $1.5274 U.S. Dollar

125.53 Japanese Yen = $1 U.S. Dollar

The exchange rates listed above as well as others are shown in Exhibit 3-4, and are called *spot exchange rates*. The spot exchange rate is the rate of exchange for the immediate delivery of currencies. Spot rates are the currency rates that are of most importance to the international traveler or tourist. Spot rates affect the real out of pocket cost for an American visitor in Europe for a glass of wine at Café Deux Magots in Paris, or a plate of Manchego cheese at Restaurante La Trucha in Madrid.

Other categories of foreign exchange rates are *forward exchange rates*. Forward rates are rates for the exchange of currencies at certain dates in the future, and can be higher than, lower than, or equal to current spot exchange rates. Forward exchange rates are used extensively by corporations and financial institutions to hedge the risk of a change in the spot exchange rates. Forward markets allow corporations to lock in exchange rates to pay for the delivery of goods or services in the future, or to receive funds for the sale of products to foreign purchasers to be delivered in the future. Forward foreign exchange rates can be used to reduce the currency risks associated with doing business in a foreign country.

The levels of spot and forward foreign exchange rates can fluctuate quite substantially, and are dependent upon many variables, including the fiscal and monetary policies of a country. Usually, a country that manages its fiscal and monetary policies on a conservative basis, meaning that it runs domestic budget and foreign trade surpluses, and does not set artificially low interest

Exhibit 3-4 Spot Exchange Rates-June 8, 2015

1 US Dollar Rates table
Top 10 Jun 08, 2015 19:33 UTC

US Dollar	1.00 USD	inv. 1.00 USD
Euro	0.886011	1.128655
British Pound	0.651784	1.534251
Indian Rupee	64.019301	0.015620
Australian Dollar	1.297923	0.770462
Canadian Dollar	1.239744	0.806618
Singapore Dollar	1.353443	0.738857
Swiss Franc	0.928411	1.077109
Malaysian Ringgit	3.761500	0.265851
Japanese Yen	124.410140	0.008038
Chinese Yuan Renminbi	6.205602	0.161145

Source: http://www.x-rates.com

rates, has a strong currency. This means that the exchange rate of the domestic currency will generally increase.

For example, during the late 1990's the United States was in a rare situation of generating budget surpluses, and in October 2000, the dollar increased in value to a level of $0.83 dollars = 1 Euro. At the end of 2009, due to increased spending associated with wars in Afghanistan and Iraq, and the costs of the subprime financial crisis, the United States was running record budget deficits and trade deficits, and had extremely low interest rates. One Euro has appreciated to $1.5038 dollars—a tremendous gain of over 70% against the dollar since 2000. This makes that plate of Spanish tapas and glass of rioja wine much more expensive in U.S. dollars for American tourists in Europe. International travelers want a strong domestic currency so their money can buy more foreign goods and services.

Conversely, corporations and businesses that produce goods and services domestically and export products generally prefer a weak currency. A weak dollar permits firms to take advantage of a depreciating exchange rate to ship more products and convert that lower exchange rate into a greater amount of dollars. A weak exchange rate also encourages investors to purchase investments that are denominated in the foreign currency. As the domestic currency depreciates, the value of the foreign investment appreciates in domestic terms.

3.1.6 Derivatives Securities Markets

A *derivative security* is a security in which the value and payoff of the derivative is based upon the value of another security. For instance, a stock option is a derivative security because the value of the option is based, among other things, upon the value of the underlying stock. And as the value of the underlying security changes, the value of the derivative security also changes.

*A **derivative security** is a security in which the value of the derivative is based upon the value of another security.*

Derivative securities consist of forwards, futures, swaps and options contracts and of more complex equity and debt securities that are embedded with these types of contracts. The markets in which derivatives trade are called derivative securities markets. Derivative securities and contracts are traded on organized commodities and stock exchanges, such as the Chicago Board of Trade and the American Stock Exchange.

Interest rate swaps and credit default swaps (CDS), two of the largest and most popular derivatives, are traded in the over-the-counter market. Credit default swaps were at the heart of the problem associated with the collapse and nationalization of the American Insurance Group, AIG. Financial regulation of the derivatives markets is being hotly debated in Washington by the financial industry, the U.S. government and its regulatory agencies.

Certain characteristics of derivative securities make them desirable as assets that can be easily structured and traded in the financial markets to manage and transfer risk. Investors who use these instruments to reduce risk are called *hedgers*. Investors who use these instruments to increase risk are called *speculators*.

3.2 Organization of the Financial Markets

There are seven major organized stock exchanges in the United States. The two largest national stock exchanges are the New York Stock Exchange (NYSE) and the American Stock Exchange (AMEX). The NYSE is the largest stock exchange in the United States.

3.2.1 New York Stock Exchange

The history of the New York Stock Exchange is deeply rooted in the history of the United States and the evolution of the economy. The NYSE began operations on May 17, 1792, when 24 individuals gathered under a buttonwood tree and declared the membership requirements and designated participation in the exchange. Over the last 200 years, the NYSE has become the center of the financial world where the market capitalization (the market value of all of the outstanding shares) of the listed companies is greater than the gross domestic product of every other industrialized nation in the world.

The New York Stock Exchange is the largest stock exchange in the world with a market capitalization in excess of $10 trillion dollars. The NYSE is an *auction market*, where the price of securities is determined by the open bids and offers made by exchange members, on their own behalf or on the behalf of their clients. Each listed security is traded at only one location called a ***trading post***, on the floor of the NYSE and all trading is monitored and facilitated by the specialist assigned to the particular issue.

*A **trading post** is the location on the floor of a stock exchange where a particular security is traded.*

The NYSE is the most liquid stock exchange in the world. The average daily trading volume has grown from 50 million shares per day in 1980 to over 5 billion shares per day in 2015. There are more than 200 billion shares on the NYSE issued by more than 3,000 companies. To be listed on the NYSE, companies must meet the exchange's listing requirements, which include a minimum number of shareholders, a minimum market capitalization of $100 million, a certain trading volume, and minimum annual earnings of $2.5 million.

The Role of the Designated Market Makers:

Designated Market Makers ("DMMs"), formerly known as Specialists, are members of the exchange who are selected to specialize in the buying and selling of shares of one or more specific stocks. Specialists are firms who are willing to buy or sell the securities that they represent whenever anyone is interested in trading in the issue. DMMs are expected to stabilize the stock price whenever possible by buying and selling stock out of their own inventory account. To be a DMM on the NYSE, a minimum trading capital requirement of $1 million is required.

DMMs can act as either *brokers* or *dealers* on the exchange. When acting as a broker the specialist acts as an agent for another member, and the specialist executes transactions for other floor brokers in exchange for a commission. When acting as a dealer the specialist acts on his own behalf, and the specialist will buy and sell out of his own account, assuming the risks associated with owning or selling the stock.

The Traditional Open Auction System

Exhibit 3-5 shows the anatomy of a trade on the NYSE in the traditional open auction system. Due to the large growth in electronic trading, this process accounts for less than 20% of trading volume today. In the traditional manner, trades are sent to a floor broker who goes to the Trading Post and tries to get the best price possible through an open auction with the DMM and other floor brokers. When the market is illiquid or trading is sporadic, the DMM is required to intervene as much as possible to minimize the temporary imbalances between market supply and demand. For this reason, the DMM often takes what is known as a *contrarian position*—when the market is selling, the DMM will begin buying, and vice versa.

Trading Systems—Super DOT and Intermarket:

The *Super DOT System* is an order routing system which provides for the electronic trades of stocks on the NYSE. This accounts for over 80% of trading volume on the NYSE. The order goes from the computer system of the member firm to the computer system of the DMM in the stock in a nanosecond. This direct placement lessens the execution time. The orders are then matched by the system with orders of similar size and price without the physical negotiation of the DMM. This especially reduces the dependence on the DMM for electronic trades. While the DMM monitors the trading through the Super Dot system, the DMM is not directly involved with the transactions.

The *Intermarket Trading System (ITS)* is an electronic communications network implemented in 1978. Its purpose is to link the NYSE with all of the regional exchanges so that investors are able to get the best price possible when they trade.

Other NYSE Members:

There are several different types of memberships in the New York Stock Exchange. Each category of membership serves a different function on the trading floor. The largest single membership group consists of floor brokers. There are two types of floor brokers: commission brokers

The Anatomy of a Trade

The New York Stock Exchange is a hectic place and often appears to be pure pandemonium. So what actually happens on the floor and how are orders routed? The New York Stock Exchange has a special section entitled "The Anatomy of a Trade," illustrated below.

Investor: Places an order to buy or sell shares of a company.

↓

NYSE Member Brokerage Firm: Checks the customer's account, quotes bid/ask information and routes the order to the trading floor.

↓

Common Message Switch/SuperDOT: CMS/SuperDOT stores and routes the order to a broker's booth or directly to a specialist.

↓

Trading Post: The order displays on the specialist's screen, an order management system.

↓

Broker's Booth: The firm's clerk receives the order. The clerk notifies the firm's floor broker that an order has arrived.

→

Specialist: Exposes the order in the agency auction market.

↓

Floor Broker: Takes the order to the trading post where the stock is traded. Competes with other brokers for the best price.

↓

Brokerage Firm: The transaction is processed electronically, crediting or debiting the customer's account with the number of shares transacted.

↓

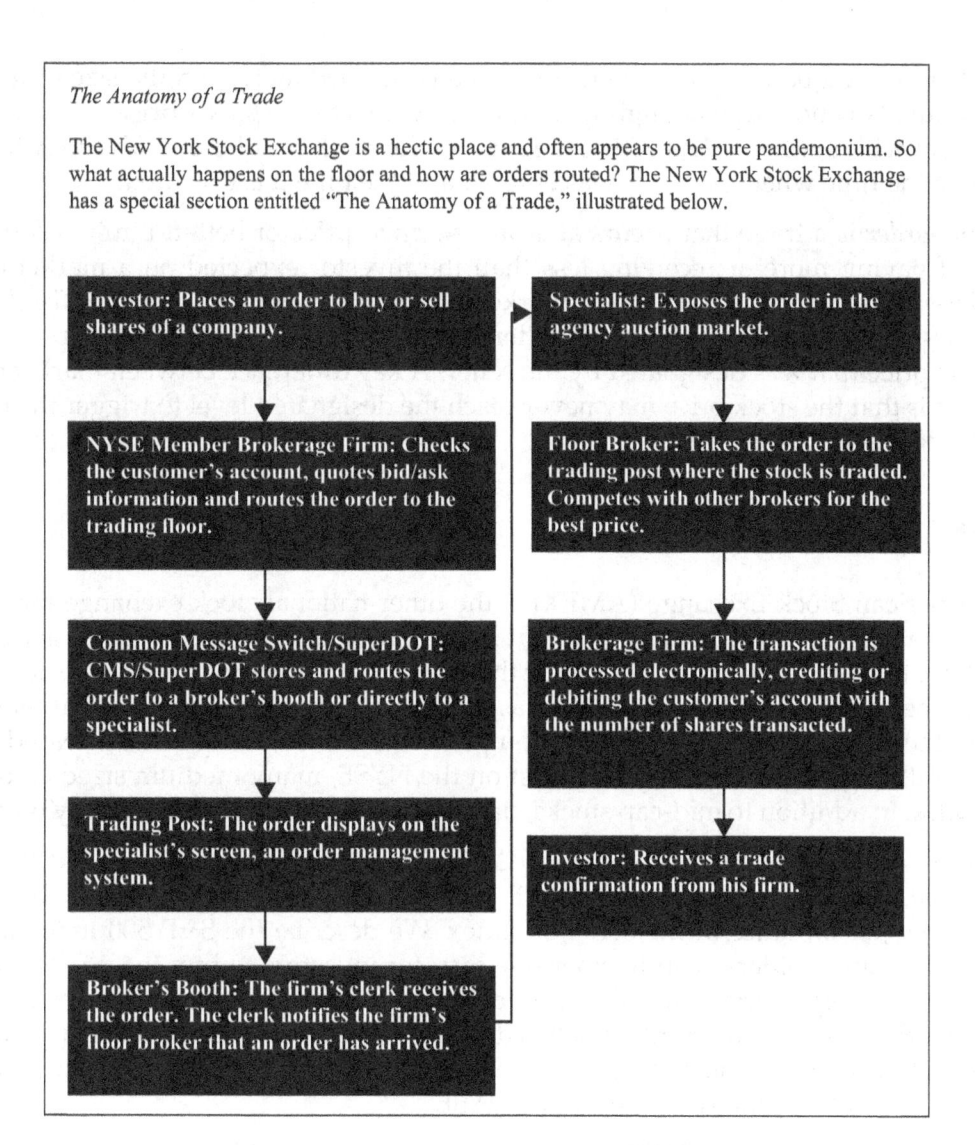

Investor: Receives a trade confirmation from his firm.

Exhibit 3-5   The Anatomy of a Trade

and independent floor brokers. Stock brokerage firms that are members of the NYSE employ commission brokers. Darting from booth to trading post, commission brokers buy and sell securities for the general public—the clients of the firm. In return for their efforts, they earn salaries and commissions.

Independent floor brokers are brokers who work for themselves. They handle orders for brokerage houses that do not have full-time brokers or whose brokers are off the floor or too busy to handle a specific order. Independent floor brokers are often referred to as *$2 brokers*—a term coined back in the days when they received $2 for every 100 shares they traded.

Types of Orders:

A *market order* is an order, either to buy or sell, which is to be executed at the best possible market price when it reaches the floor of the exchange. Most individual investors use market orders when trading because the orders are executed immediately, and the size of the trades of most individuals is not large enough to significantly affect the stock's price in the market. The main concern with market orders is that the price of the stock could move adversely to the investor between the time when the order was entered and the time it is executed.

A *limit order* is a trade that occurs at a pre-specified price or better. Limit orders avoid the problem of paying more or receiving less than the investor expected on a market order. Buy limit orders are only executed when the market price reaches or falls below the fixed limit price that was designated by the buyer. A sell order is only executed when the stock price reaches or exceeds the price that was designated by the seller. A key difference between market orders and limit orders is that the stock price may never reach the designated level to trigger the limit order, and the trade will not be executed.

3.2.2 The American Stock Exchange

The American Stock Exchange (AMEX) is the other national stock exchange that serves the capital markets of the United States. While it has not been able to attract the larger companies, such as those that are traded on the NYSE or the popular technology firms that trade in the NASDAQ over the counter market, the AMEX has carved its own niche in the capital markets. That niche is in the listing of stocks of mid-cap companies, and the trading of stock-based derivative securities. Although most large cap firms list on the NYSE, many medium sized companies list on the AMEX. In addition to mid-cap stocks, derivative trading is growing rapidly on the AMEX.

The most actively traded issue on the AMEX is a derivative security called the *Standard & Poor's 500 Depository Receipts (Spiders)*. This derivative security corresponds to a 1/10th amount in the performance of the S&P 500 index. We describe the S&P 500 Index later in this chapter. Purchasing Spiders is an inexpensive way for investors to buy the performance of the S&P 500 Index without purchasing all of the stocks in the index, or an index fund. The AMEX also has a similar derivative instrument, which is designed to represent the performance of the thirty firms in the Dow Jones Industrial Average. The trading of new financial instruments and mid-cap companies differentiates the AMEX from the NYSE.

Similar to the NYSE, the AMEX is also an auction market with one specialist appointed to trade each issue. There are 900 different companies listed on the AMEX and thousands of different options and derivative securities. The market structure of the AMEX is very similar to the structure of the NYSE. The trading floor is divided into three different areas, and within each area members trade a different type of financial instrument. One trading area is for equities, one area is for derivatives, and one is for bonds.

3.2.3 The Over-the-Counter Markets and the NASDAQ

The over-the-counter (OTC) market differs from the NYSE and AMEX in that there is no physical trading floor and no specialists. All trading takes place between brokers and dealers of securities over telephones and computer networks. The National Association of Securities Dealers (NASD) oversees all trading and regulation in the OTC market under the supervision of the SEC. The National Association of Securities Dealers Automated Quotation system, known as NASDAQ, is an electronic quotation system that provides market participants with price quotations for securities that are traded in the OTC market.

The NASDAQ is not a stock exchange like the NYSE and the AMEX, both of which have a physical location where trading takes place. NASDAQ is an automated quotation system connecting securities firms electronically through an extensive telecommunications and computer network. The computer network is used to provide quotes, route orders, and report trading activity to all participants.

Over 600 securities dealers trading almost 15,000 different over-the-counter issues are on the NASDAQ system. The requirements to become dealers, also called market makers, are: a minimum capital requirement, an electronic interface standard to quote prices and report transactions, and the willingness to make a continuous two-sided market (both buying and selling). If market makers do not continuously post bids and offers for securities, the NASD may penalize them.

The NASDAQ is not an auction market like the NYSE. Instead market makers compete against each other by posting quotes, and bid and ask prices, which attract order flows. Market demand for a specific security determines how many dealers will participate as market makers in each security. Some high volume issues, such as the stock of Intel and Microsoft, have in excess of 60 dealers quoting prices. Smaller issues with less active stock might have only one or two dealers making a market in the security.

The Bid-Ask Spread in the OTC Market:

Prices for securities that are traded in the OTC markets are quoted in a manner that is different from the price quotes on the NYSE and AMEX. Instead of a common market price determined by the auction process on the NYSE or AMEX, OTC prices depend on whether you are buying or selling the security. These prices are referred to as the *bid*—the price a dealer is willing to pay to purchase a security; and the *ask*—the price a dealer is willing to receive to sell a security.

> *Bid—the price a dealer is willing to pay to purchase a security.*
> *Ask—the price a dealer is willing to accept to sell a security.*

The difference between the two prices is called the ***bid-ask spread***. The bid-ask spread is the commission that dealers receive on a transaction if they buy at the lower bid price and sell at the higher ask price.

Bid-Ask Spread Example:

If Bank of America/Merrill Lynch makes a market in Google stock (meaning it is a dealer of Google stock), the dealer will always have two different prices at which it is willing to trade. Assume the market trading range for Google is between $628 and $645 a share. The dealer may quote a bid price of $628 a share, at which it is willing to purchase Google stock.

The dealer also posts an asking price of $645 at which it is willing to sell shares of Google. The dealer earns a bid-ask spread of $17 for every share of Google that the dealer trades at this bid-ask level.

Bidding Collusion on NASDAQ:

In 1994 an academic research study presented evidence that NASDAQ dealers may have been colluding to raise bid-ask spreads on the most active issues. This evidence was supported by the lack of odd-eighth quotes by dealers. For example, dealers would quote a stock price of $25-¼ bid,

$25-½ offered, but not $25-⅜ bid, $25-½ offered— dealers were not posting bid and ask prices at 1/8, 3/8, 5/8, and 7/8. The study created considerable negative press for the NASDAQ, and led to a number of lawsuits that required dealer firms to pay out over $100 million to investors.

The Merger between the NASDAQ and the AMEX:

In 1998 NASDAQ and AMEX merged, effectively linking together two different markets—a specialist auction market and a dealer bid-ask market. The presumed benefits are that the merger will provide the resources to upgrade the technologies on the AMEX and allows the markets to increase order execution efficiency while reducing costs. The merger will also strengthen the AMEX's options trading abilities and will allow it to compete for derivative securities business more effectively against the Chicago Board Options Exchange.

The OTC Market and Securities Other than Stock:

The trading of debt securities and derivative securities also takes place in the over-the-counter market and is done primarily by brokers who are arranging purchases for their clients, or dealers who are buying and selling for their own accounts. The size of the daily trading of debt securities in the OTC market, which securities encompass corporate bonds, municipal bonds, and government and agency debt, is larger and more profitable for financial institutions than the trading of stock. Large investment and commercial banks dominate the trading activity in these markets.

3.2.4 The Regional Stock Exchanges

In addition to the two national exchanges and the NASDAQ market, five regional exchanges trade stocks in the United States. These exchanges are: Philadelphia Stock Exchange, Chicago Stock Exchange, Pacific Stock Exchange, Boston Stock Exchange, and Cincinnati Stock Exchange.

Regional exchanges perform several functions in the secondary market. First, regional exchanges list local companies that do not meet the formal listing requirements for one of the national stock exchanges. Second, most of the actively traded issues on the major exchanges are dually listed on the regional exchanges. This allows local brokerage firms to purchase a membership on the regional exchange and trade shares of most NYSE companies without having to purchase a seat on the NYSE or trade through a member firm and forfeit some of the commission.

The trading volume on the regional exchanges is substantially lower than the volume on the NYSE. This could make the regional exchange dual listings less liquid, but because of the Intermarket Trading System, the regional exchanges receive the same quote information that is available on the floor of the NYSE.

3.2.5 International Stock Exchanges

The capital markets of countries around the world have been active in developing and broadening the role of the stock and bond markets. In the Far East, the Tokyo Stock Exchange dominates trading activity, much the same as the New York Stock Exchange does in the United States. It lists about 1700 companies with a total value of several trillion dollars. Active exchanges in the Far East are in Hong Kong—the Hang Seng, Taiwan, Shanghai, and South Korea—KOSPI.

In Europe, the London Stock Exchange is the principal exchange, and serves Great Britain and Ireland. More than 2600 companies are listed with a market value of almost a trillion dollars. Active stock markets exist in Germany—DAX, Paris—CAC, Italy—Milan BITtel, Spain—IBEX, Belgium, and Sweden—SX.

In the Americas, besides the exchanges that we described in the United States, major stock exchanges in various countries are as follows: Argentina—Merval, Brazil— Sao Paulo Bovespa, Canada—Toronto, Chile—Santiago IPSA, and Mexico—I.P.C. Most developed countries have a stock exchange and new exchanges are being established around the world with the development of newly emerging economies.

3.2.6 Electronic Communications Networks (ECNs) and After-Hours Trading

Technology has dramatically changed the markets. One of the biggest developments in the secondary markets has been electronic communication networks (ECNs). These computer-based order-matching systems, which include Instinet, Island, Archipelago, and Redibook, match bids and offers on a network, thereby giving buyers and sellers the best prices possible. The oldest ECN, Instinet, was developed in 1969 and for years functioned primarily as an after-hours market for institutions. There are nine ECNs linked to the NASDAQ system, and they control about 30% of the daily volume of trading. (See discussion at the end of this chapter.)

3.3 Measuring the Performance of the Financial Markets

Financial assets have been traded in the United States for over two hundred years. More than ten thousand different securities trade every day on the different exchanges around the United States. Perhaps ten times this amount of securities trades daily on a worldwide basis. So how does the average investor monitor all of these different securities across different exchanges throughout the world?

Investors depend on financial indices to measure everything from the price of commodities to the overnight performance of stocks that are traded on the Hong Kong stock exchange. In every major newspaper publication there is some reference to a financial index. In the United States, the most often cited indices are the Dow Jones Industrial Average, the Standard & Poor's 500 Index, and the NASDAQ Composite Index. What do these indices actually measure and how are they calculated?

Most major indices are classified as either a *price-weighted index* or a *market-weighted index*. We calculate a price-weighted index by adding all of the prices of the stocks in the index and divide that sum by a *divisor*. The Dow Jones Industrial Average (DJIA) is the world's most popular price-weighted index. First calculated in 1896, the index computed an average price of 12 industrial stocks.

The DJIA has been calculated for over one hundred years and stocks in the DJIA have changed over time. Currently, there are 30 stocks (see Exhibit 3-7) in the DJIA. The divisor has changed over time and has been adjusted for stock splits. The current value of the Dow Divisor is **0.14985889030177** as of June 12, 2015. In a price-weighted index, the index weighting of each firm is dependent on the price per share of its stock rather than the market value of the firm. Another widely used price-weighted index is the Nikkei average of 225 large Japanese stocks.

Most other major stock indices are calculated using a *market value weighting method*. With a market value index, the percentage weight of each firm is dependent on the relative market value of the firm's stock divided by the market value of the stocks of all of the firms in the index. The weighting of companies by their total stock market value allows the index to change in a manner that is directly proportional to the change in the stock market values of the companies that comprise the index. A market value-weighted index gives a more accurate measurement of the actual performance of the market since firms with a higher market value represent more of the invested dollars in the market. The most famous market value-weighted index is the Standard & Poor's 500. Other marketvalue-weighted indexes include the NASDAQ Composite, Russell 2000, Wilshire 5000, and the Morgan Stanley EAFE.

As an example of market value weighting, assume that the value of all of the stocks in the JRW Index is $10 trillion (a very big number) and the stock market value of one of its components, Big Firm, is $500 billion. Big Firm's stock represents a 5% share ($500 billion/$10,000 billion = 5%) of the JRW Index. Assume that another firm, Little Firm, is also in the index and the total market value of the stock of Little Firm is $100 million. Little Firm's stock represents a 0.001% share ($100 million/ $10,000,000 million = .001%) of the JRW Index. A one percent price movement in the stock of Big Firm will move the JRW Index much more—five thousand times more—than a similar percentage price movement in the stock of Little Firm.

3.3.1 Dow Jones Industrial Average

The DJIA is a price-weighted average of thirty stocks out of over ten thousand stocks in the United States equity markets. Although these firms represent a large portion of the market capitalization of U.S. firms, the DJIA is a small sample. All but two of the firms, Microsoft and Intel, are traded on the NYSE. The index is designed to include the largest industrial firms in the U.S. that

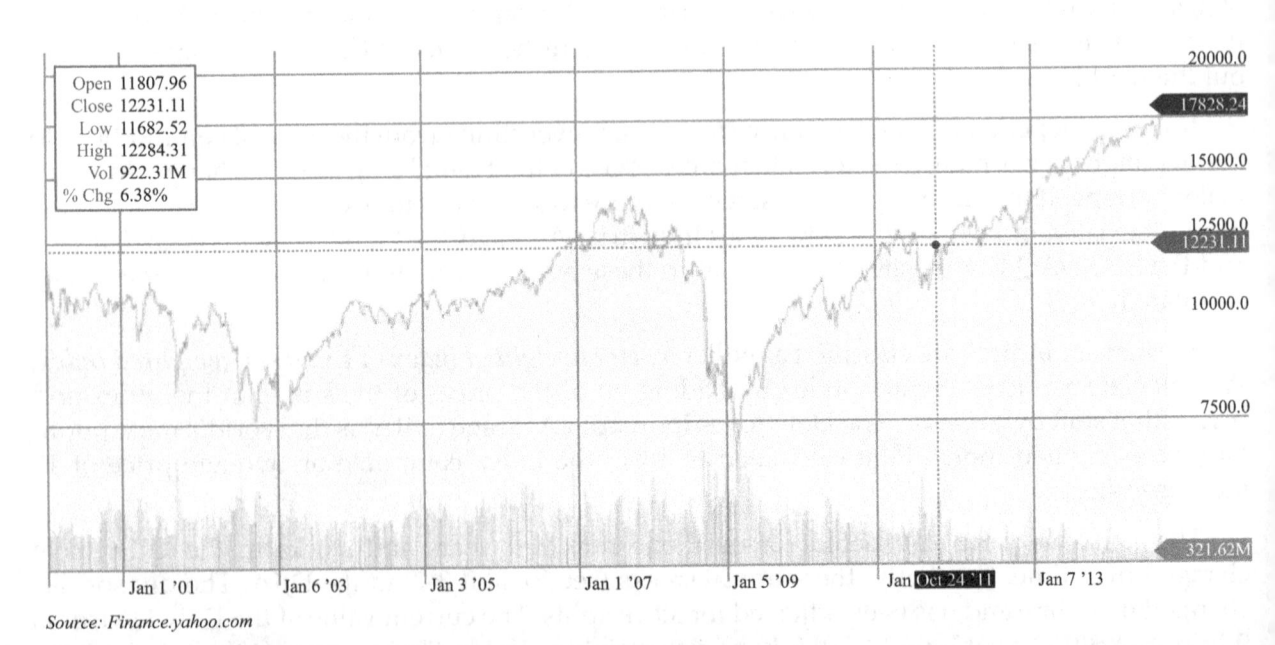

Source: Finance.yahoo.com

Exhibit 3-6 Dow Jones Industrial Average (2000–2015)

As of June 9, 2015

have a history of success and growth. The stocks are reviewed periodically by the editors of *The Wall Street Journal*, and stodgy stocks that have not done well may be replaced with new up-and-coming stocks. In 1999, four companies in the DJIA—Sears, Goodyear, Chevron and Union Carbide—were jettisoned and Home Depot, Intel, Microsoft, and SBC Communication were added.

Dow Jones calculates two additional price-weighted indices: a transportation index and a utility index, the stocks of which are not represented in the DJIA. Although it represents the performance of a small number of stocks, the DJIA correlates very closely with the S&P 500 and is a more famous measure of stock market performance.

Dow Jones Industrial Average Computation:

Exhibit 3-7 below shows the thirty stocks in the DJIA and their respective closing prices on June 12, 2015. The manner in which the DJIA is computed is to add the prices of the 30 component

Exhibit 3-7   Computation of DJIA on June 12, 2015

DJIA on June 12, 2015 =17898.84, Divisor= 0.14985889030177

Symbol	Company	Closing Price	Symbol	Company	Closing Price
AAPL	APPLE	127.1600	MCD	MCDONALD'S	95.121
AXP	AMERICAN EXPRESS	79.63	MMM	3M	158.16
			MRK	MERCK	57.90
BA	BOEING	142.825	MSFT	MICROSOFT	46.01
CAT	CATERPILLAR	87.8900	NKE	NIKE	103.86
CSCO	CISCO SYSTEMS	28.54	PFE	PFIZER	34.245
CVX	CHEVRON	99.94	PG	PROCTER & GAMBLE	78.885
DD	EI DU PONT DE NEMOURS	69.11	TRV	TRAVELERS COMPANIES	99.55
DIS	WALT DISNEY	110.03			
GE	GENERAL ELECTRIC	27.385	UTX	UNITED TECHNOLOGIES	117.675
HD	HOME DEPOT	110.720	VZ	VERIZON COMMUNICATIONS	47.225
IBM	INTL BUSINESS MACHINE	167.04	WMT	WAL-MART STORES	72.46
INTC	INTEL	31.355	XOM	EXXON MOBIL	84.0901
JNJ	JOHNSON & JOHNSON	98.370	GS	GOLDMAN SACHS GROUP	213.08
JPM	JP MORGAN CHASE	68.26	UNH	UNITEDHEALTH GROUP	117.66
KO	COCA-COLA	39.995	V	VISA	69.3690

Source: ino.com

stocks—in this case they total 2,682.30. The total is then divided by the divisor. The current value of the Dow Divisor is **0.14985889030177** as of June 12, 2015 and is listed daily in the Markets Lineup page in Section C of *The Wall Street Journal*. The divisor changes often to take into account stock splits and listing changes. Dividing the total of 2,682.30 by the divisor is equal to: *2,682.30/0.14985889030177*

3.3.2 The Standard & Poor's 500 Index

The Standard & Poor's 500 Index is a market value-weighted index that represents over $18 trillion of stock market capitalization. As such, its performance gives a better representation of the performance of the entire stock market than the performance of the DJIA. The S&P 500 Index incorporates 500 different stocks from all sectors that are listed on the three major U.S. stock markets—NYSE, AMEX, and NASDAQ.

Of the 500 companies included in the index, 460 of the companies are listed on the NYSE. The S&P 500 excludes many of the smaller firms listed on the AMEX or traded in the NASDAQ over-the-counter market. The S&P 500 Index does represent most of the dollars invested in public stocks in the United States. Three of the larger companies in the S&P 500 Index are Microsoft, GE, and IBM. The market weightings of each firm changes on a daily basis as the market values of the individual firms vary constantly.

3.3.3 NASDAQ Composite Index

The NASDAQ stock market performed spectacularly during the late 1990s as it became the preferred market of the entrepreneurs that controlled the listing of high-tech companies. Intel, Microsoft, Cisco Systems, Dell Computers, and many others are some of the companies that have stocks that trade on the NASDAQ system. The performance of the stocks of these companies and

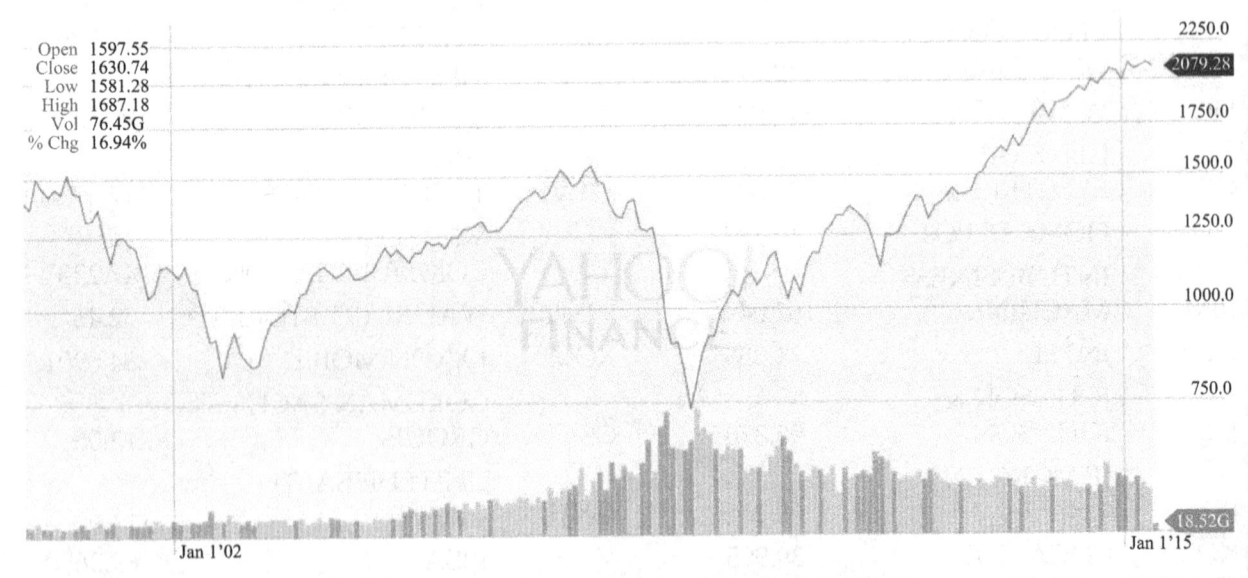

Exhibit 3-7   Chart of S&P 500 (2000–2015)

As of June 9, 2015

others carried the NASDAQ to a level of over 5,200 points in March of 2000, before plummeting over 75% in the stock market crash of the early 2000s to less than 1,200 in October 2002.

The NASDAQ competes directly and fiercely with the NYSE for domestic and international company listings. The NASDAQ Composite Index measures a market value-weighted average of the stocks of more than 5000 domestic and international companies that are listed on the NASDAQ. The Composite Index was introduced on February 5, 1971, and at that time it had a base value of 100.0.

The strong stock market performance of the high-tech sector has increased the popularity of the NASDAQ Composite and it is quoted in most major news publications alongside the S&P 500 and the DJIA. The largest companies in the NASDAQ Index are Microsoft, Cisco Systems, and Intel. Due to the tremendous returns over the past twenty years for each of these three issues, their shares are major influences on the direction of the NASDAQ Composite Index.

3.3.4 Bond Market Indices

Four investment firms, Barclay's, Merrill Lynch/Bank of America, Ryan Treasury, and Citigroup/Salomon Smith Barney, have created and compute United States investment grade bond indices. Investment grade means that the bonds are rated Baa or higher by Moodys Investor's Services, or BBB or higher by Standard & Poor's Corporation. Indices are provided for U.S. Treasury securities, U.S. corporate debt issues, tax-exempt municipal bonds, mortgage-backed debt securities, high yield bond indices, and global government bond issues. Bond market data and the performance of bond market indices is available in the Bond Market Data Bank section of *The Wall Street Journal*.

3.4 Stock Brokerage Firms

Stock brokerage firms are firms that act to buy and sell stocks, bonds, and other securities for or on behalf of clients of the firm. Broadly, stock market firms can be classified as full service brokerage firms such as Merrill Lynch/Bank of America and UBS/Paine Webber, discount stock brokerage firms such as Charles Schwab, and online stock brokerage firms such as E-Trade or Ameritrade. Below, we discuss the different types of services that each of these firms offer to investors and the difference in costs and services.

3.4.1 Full Service Brokerage Firms

A full service brokerage firm provides a broad array of financial services to investors. Those services include complete financial analysis, investment planning, and retirement planning. Full service brokers, such as Merrill Lynch/Bank of America and UBS/Paine Webber, are members of all major exchanges and usually make markets in most NADAQ issues.

Investors have access to many different financial instruments including common stock, bonds (corporate, government, municipal, and international), derivative products (options, futures, and other products), commodities, foreign currency, and just about any other publicly traded investment product. To accompany the full array of investment products, most full service brokers provide their own research and forecasts of economic, industry, and company conditions. This gives investors who are clients of the firm immediate access to information and recommendations.

Some investors allow their brokers to make all trading decisions, independent of the client's input. This arrangement is called a *discretionary account*, and only should be used when the client has complete trust in his broker.

3.4.2 Discount Brokerage Firms

Unlike full service brokers, the fees of which can be substantial, discount brokers offer basic investment services with no frills attached. Discount brokers provide fewer services to investors and have lower overhead expenses and therefore are able to charge lower commissions. Research may be limited or nonexistent and product availability may also be limited to stocks and mutual funds.

Although discount brokerage firms are offering some additional services in an attempt to compete with the full service firms, their main appeal has always been through the charging of lower commissions. Discount brokers attract investors who pick their own stocks and manage their own portfolios. These investors prefer the lower cost commissions.

3.4.3 Online Brokers and E-Trading

The growth of the Internet and services such as America Online spurred a new type of brokerage service. Electronic trading allows investors to trade stocks, bonds, and other securities through accounts that they have established with stock brokerage firms that have online services.

The pure electronic stock trading firms include Etrade, Ameritrade, and Datek, among others. Trades are placed via the telephone or the Internet without ever speaking to an individual. The fewer people that are involved in a transaction, the lower the commission rates. Electronic trading offers commission rates comparable to and even lower than the rates associated with deep discount brokerage firms. This niche grew dramatically during the Internet bubble of the late 1990s, as full service, discount, and start-up brokerage firms established online trading capabilities.

Some of the basic services that full service brokers offer are also available from electronic trading firms at a fraction of the cost. Despite the popularity of online brokers, their high costs of customer acquisition and low profitability have resulted in a decline in market valuation of these companies.

3.4.4 Brokerage Related Definitions

Round lot trades are trades executed in multiples of 100 shares.

Odd lot trades are trades that are for less than 100 shares. For example, if you received 5 shares of Disney from a relative for a birthday present and you sold them through a stockbroker, that sale would have been an odd lot sale.

Payment for order flow is a rebate paid to brokerage firms for directing trades to particular market markers.

Block trades are defined as trades of 10,000 shares or more of a given stock, or trades of shares with market value of $200,000 or more. In 1961, there were about nine block trades per day, which accounted for about 3% of the daily trading volume. In recent years there are often in excess of 3,000 block trades per day, accounting for approximately half of the daily volume.

Program trading is a computer-assisted strategy of buying and or selling a large number of securities simultaneously. Program trading is also called basket trading because the transaction usually consists of a coordinate number of trades in different securities. Since a large amount of capital is required to coordinate and execute the underlying trades, institutional investors are the principal market participants who use program trading.

An example of a program trade is if a pension fund wanted to invest $50,000,000 directly into the stocks that comprise the S&P 500 Index, and not through a mutual fund. A full service brokerage firm would design a computer trading program that would buy shares in the appropriate weightings of all 500 stocks in the S&P 500 at the same time. This coordination gives an institutional investor immediate execution instead of waiting for 500 separate orders to be filled.

With program trading, the transaction can be completed in a matter of minutes instead of taking a few hours with individual executions. Program trading is also used to rebalance portfolios while limiting market fluctuations during the time the trade is being executed.

3.5 Summary

In this chapter we examined the financial markets—the stock and bond markets where securities are purchased and sold, and the foreign exchange and derivatives markets. We discussed the role of the primary and secondary securities market, the money and capital markets, the major stock exchanges, the over-the-counter market, and the manner in which trades take place in the markets, as well as different ways to measure the performance of the markets.

Our learning objectives for the chapter included an understanding of: the nature and role of the primary and secondary securities market; the difference between the capital and the money markets; the major financial exchanges, their classification, and the type of issues traded on these exchanges; the roles of the specialist and the market-maker; the types of buy and sell orders that can be placed; the major financial markets performance indices, how they are calculated and what they measure; and the services and costs of full service, discount, and electronic brokerage firms.

List of Terms

1. **Secondary securities markets** – markets where the outstanding securities are traded among investors, the funds flow from the buyer of a security to the seller—not to the issuer of the security.

2. **Liquidity** – The degree to which an asset or security can be bought or sold in the market without affecting the asset's price. Liquidity is characterized by a high level of trading activity.

3. **Securities and Exchange Commission** – A government commission created by Congress to regulate the securities markets and protect investors. In addition to regulation and protection, it also monitors the corporate takeovers in the U.S. The SEC is composed of five commissioners appointed by the U.S. President and approved by the Senate. The statutes administered by the SEC are designed to promote full public disclosure and protect the investing public against fraudulent and manipulative practices in the securities markets.

4. **Over-the-counter market** – A decentralized market of securities not listed on an exchange where market participants trade over the telephone, facsimile or electronic network instead of a physical trading floor. There is no central exchange or meeting place for this market. Also referred to as the "OTC market".

5. **Specialist** – A member of an exchange who acts as the market maker to facilitate the trading of a given stock. The specialists holds inventories of the stock, posts the bid and ask prices, manages limit orders and executes trades. Specialists are also responsible for managing large movements by trading out of their own inventory. If there is a large shift in demand on the buy or sell side, the specialist will step in and sell out of their inventory to meet the demand until the gap has been narrowed.

6. **Market maker** – When a firm or individual quotes prices or makes a movement of prices in the market.

7. **Financial indexes** – A statistical measure of change in an economy or a securities market. In the case of financial markets, an index is essentially an imaginary portfolio of securities representing a particular market or a portion of it. Each index has its own calculation methodology and is usually expressed in terms of a change from a base value. Thus, the percentage changes is more important that the actually numeric value.

8. **Trading posts** – The located where goods and services are traded. Nothing is made or issued at the exchange or trading post – securities are only traded.

9. **Super DOT** – An electronic order routing system designed to send smaller orders, usually less than 1200 shares, from member firms directly to the specialist's post instead of being transmitted through a floor broker.

10. **Intermarket Trading System** – An electronic communications network implemented in 1978. Links the NYSE with all of the regional exchanges.

11. **Listed issues** – Being included and traded on a given exchange. Most exchanges have specific requirements which companies must meet in order to be listed and continue to stay listed.

12. **Dealer** – An individual or firm that is willing to buy or sell securities for their own account. They can also make transactions for customers.

13. **Broker** – An individual or firm that charges a fee or commission for executing buy and sell orders submitted by an investor.

14. **Contrarian** – An investor who takes the opposite stance on buying or selling a security. When the market is buying a security, the contrarian will usually sell the security.

15. **Limit Order** – An order placed with a brokerage to buy or sell a set number of shares at a specified price or better. Limit orders also allow an investor to limit the length of time an order can be outstanding before being canceled.

16. **Market order** – Buying or selling a stock at the current or market price.

17. **Spiders** – Shares in a trust that owns stocks in the same proportion as that represented by the S&P 500 stock index. Due to the acronym SPDR, Standard & Poor's Depository Receipts are commonly known as "spiders".

18. **Financial indices** – A statistical measure of change in an economy or a securities market. In the case of financial markets, an index is essentially an imaginary portfolio of securities representing a particular market or a portion of it. Each index has its own calculation methodology and is usually expressed in terms of a change from a base value.

19. **Price-weighted index** – An index of stocks in which the weight is placed on the price of the security. A stock that is more expensive takes up a greater percentage of the index weight.

20. **Market value-weighted index** – An index of stocks in which the weight is placed on the market cap or size of the security. A stock that is larger takes up a greater percentage of the index weight.

21. **Small-cap** – Refers to stocks with a relatively small market capitalization. The definition of small cap can vary among brokerages, but generally it is a company with a market capitalization of between $300 million and $2 billion.

22. **Large-cap** – Companies having a market capitalization between $10 billion and $200 billion. Are less risky than small cap stocks.

23. **Bid-ask spreads** – The amount by which the ask price exceeds the bid. This is essentially the difference in price between the highest price that a buyer is willing to pay for an asset and the lowest price for which a seller is willing to sell it.

24. **ECNs** – The amount by which the ask price exceeds the bid. This is essentially the difference in price between the highest price that a buyer is willing to pay for an asset and the lowest price for which a seller is willing to sell it.

25. **Bidding collusion** – When investors collude or work together to raise bid-ask spreads on active issues in order to take advantage of other investors.

26. **Price-weighted index** – An index of stocks in which the weight is placed on the price of the security. A stock that is more expensive takes up a greater percentage of the index weight.

27. **Market value-weighted index** – An index of stocks in which the weight is placed on the market cap or size of the security. A stock that is larger takes up a greater percentage of the index weight.

28. **Discretionary account** – When investors allow their brokers to make all trading decisions, independent of the client's input.

29. **Full service broker** – Provides a broad array of financial services to investors which can include financial analysis, investment and retiring planning.

30. **Discount broker** – Provide basic investment services (usually limited to selling and buying securities). Discount brokers are less expensive than full service brokers.

31. **Round lot orders** – Trading 100 shares of stock or round numbered amounts.

32. **Odd lot trades** – An amount of a security that is less than the normal unit of trading for that particular security

33. **Block trade** – An order/trade submitted for sale or purchase of a large quantity of securities. Also known as "Block Order". Usually 10,000 shares of stock.

34. **Program trading** – A computer assisted strategy of buying and or selling a large number of securities simultaneously.

35. **Basket trading** – A single order to buy or sell a set of 15 or more securities.

36. **Payment for order flow** – The payment by a dealer to a broker acknowledging the broker's routing of customer orders to the dealer.

37. **Decimalization** – The process of changing the prices that securities trade at from fractions to decimals. The reasoning behind this was to make prices more easily understood by investors, and to bring the United States into conformity with international practices.

38. **Minimum trading increment** – A minimum movement in a stock's price in order to facilitate trading actions.

39. **Dual-exchange** – An exchange in which a sale and a buy order can be made simultaneously.

Questions

1. **What roles does a stock exchange play in the trading of securities in the secondary market? Why is it helpful to have a central trading location?**
   Financial markets exist so that excess monies from investors can be transferred cheaply and efficiently to businesses, governments and individuals that have profitable investment opportunities and a shortage of funds. The secondary markets provide liquidity—the ease with which an owner of a security can sell an investment to other investors or trade it in the securities markets. A central trading location provides a market where buyers and sellers of securities can complete transactions quickly and efficiently and save investors from a costly search for potential buyers and sellers of the stock or bond.

2. **Why does the trading of a security disclose information about the asset's value?**
   The current prices of an asset, such as a stock, indicates the amount that the investor is willing to pay to acquire a share of stock and discloses the value an investor places on the company. In the short-run, this price may have nothing to do with the true long-term value of the stock.

3. **Who is allowed to trade on the floor of the NYSE?**
   Only official members of the exchange may trade on the exchange floor. To become a member, firms and individuals must buy a seat on the NYSE.

4. **Which are the two largest stock exchanges in the United States?**
   The NYSE and the AMEX

5. **What is the role of a specialist? Why are they important?**
   Specialists are members of the exchange who are selected to specialize in the buying and selling of shares of one or more specific stocks. They buy and sell the securities that they represent whenever anyone is interested in trading on the issue. They are important because they must stabilize the stock prices by buying and selling from their own inventory accounts.

6. **Is a specialist a dealer or broker?**
   A specialist can act as either a dealer or a broker.

7. **What are the two categories of floor brokers?**
   A dealer is an individual or firm willing to buy or sell securities for their own account. A broker is an individual or a firm that charges a fee or commission for executing buy and sell orders, they act as an agent for a customer.

8. **How is a limit order different from a market order?**
   A market order is an order to buy or sell an asset at the best possible market price. A limit order is a trade that occurs at a pre-specified price or better.

9. **Why would an investor elect to buy a derivative rather than the underlying asset?**
Investors can use derivatives to reduce risk, or hedge their positions. Investors can also use these instruments to increase risk or speculate against held positions.

10. **How does the NASDAQ differ from the NYSE?**
The NASDAQ is an over-the-counter market. It is an electronic trading platform. The NYSE is an organized exchange in that there is a physical exchange floor.

11. **Explain why collusion in trading is a bad thing. Why is it illegal?**
Collusion is when dealers collude to effect bid-ask spreads on active issues to better their positions. Collusion leads to losses among other dealers that are not colluding. It is illegal because it takes advantage of other buyers and sellers.

12. **What functions do regional exchanges play?**
Regional exchanges list local companies that cannot meet the listing requirements of national exchanges. Also, the most actively traded issues on the major exchanges are dually listed on the regional exchanges.

13. **List five factors that contribute to the fluctuation in stock prices.**
    - Movements in interest rates and economic events
    - Company financial performance
    - Industry performance
    - National and World News events
    - Supply and Demand

14. **If a large investor wants to sell a large number of shares in a particular company (greater than 100,000), what happens to price and why?**
If a trader were to sell a large block of securities, other traders in the market would take note and possibly push prices down, for if a large block is being sold that trader must obviously have little faith in a price appreciation. This would have a downward ripple effect throughout the market.

15. **What is the difference between a price-weighted index and a market value-weighted index?**
A market-weighted index weighs each stock in the index by its respective market capitalization. Larger companies account for a greater portion of the index. This is how the S&P 500 index is measured. A price-weighted index weighs each stock in the index by its respective price. Expensive companies have more weight. The DJIA is measured by price.

16. **The DJIA is comprised of 30 large companies while the S&P 500 has 500 companies in it. Is the Dow a bad measure of total market performance?**
Although it represents the performance of a small number of stocks, the DJIA correlates very closely with the S&P 500 and is a more famous measure of stock market performance.

17. **Why is it cheaper to trade through a discount broker as opposed to a full service broker?**
Discount brokers offer no-frills services and because of this, they are able to charge investors less than a full service broker.

18. **What is electronic trading? What are the advantages and disadvantages of electronic trading? Why did it grow dramatically during the stock market bubble of the 1990s?**
    Electronic trading allows investors to trade stocks and bonds through accounts that they have established with stock brokerage firms that have online services.

19. **What is program or basket trading?**
    Program trading is a computer assisted strategy of buying and or selling a large number of securities simultaneously. Basket trading is a single order to buy or sell a set of 15 or more securities.

20. **Why is it necessary for large institutional investors to use program trading?**
    A large amount of capital is required to coordinate these trades and institutional investors can afford these costs. Institutional investors must also trade in large quantities of stocks and program trading makes this possible.

Chapter 4

Time Value of Money: The Basic Concepts

4.1 **Chapter Introduction and Overview**
4.2 **The Math of Time Value of Money**
4.3 **Financial Calculators**
4.4 **Definition of Time**
4.5 **Present and Future Values: Multiple Cash Flows**
4.6 **Chapter Summary and Looking Forward**
    Assignments
    Additional Questions and Problems

After studying Chapter 4, you should be able to:

- Explain the mechanics of compounding: how money grows over time when it is invested.
- Mathematically define and be able to describe each of the variables of the single period present value and future value equations that underlie the time value of money.
- Compute the present value of a lump sum of money to be received one year from today.
- Compute the single period future value of a lump sum of money.
- Compute the present value and future value of a two-year cash flow.

From *Lectures in Corporate Finance*, 6th Edition by Jayant R. Kale and Richard J. Fendler. Copyright © 2013 by Kendall Hunt Publishing Company. Reprinted by permission.

4.1 Chapter Introduction and Overview

Maria Martinez sat at her kitchen table sipping her morning coffee, as she contemplated her life and considered her future. Today was special; it was her 65th birthday. Maria knew that she had much to be happy about, and yet she was also fearful of the future. She had worked very hard her entire life, always living within her means, and two years ago she had paid off the mortgage on her home. Her three children, whom she raised on her own after her husband died in Vietnam, had all graduated from college and were now in the early stages of their careers. She had managed to save some money for retirement, but she knew that what she had was not enough to last more than a few years after she stopped working. And the hospital where she worked as a nurse had a mandatory retirement age of 67.

A knock on her front door started her back to reality. She opened the door to find a courier with an envelope addressed to her. After she signed the receipt, she returned to her kitchen excited to open what she expected was a special delivery birthday card from one of her children. Instead, the sender was a local law firm and the envelope contained a very official looking letter and smaller envelope with four perforated sides.

Maria unfolded the letter and began to read. It said that on the day she was born, her grandparents opened a stock mutual fund account in her name with a $1000 deposit. That was the only money that was ever deposited into the fund. The law firm was named as the trustee of the account, and the account had a specific requirement that Maria could not know about the account or receive any money from the account until her 65th birthday. On that birthday, the law firm had been instructed to liquidate the fund and deliver the proceeds to Maria. The perforated envelope was her check.

As Maria stared at the perforated envelope, she started to tremble. Surely the check was for several thousand dollars and she really needed a new washer and dryer as well as a new refrigerator. A new bed would also help with back pain she had been experiencing lately, and perhaps there would even be enough for a downpayment on a new car. She tore off the four perforated strips and opened the envelope.

When Maria saw the number on the check, she nearly fainted. Surely this was some kind of cruel joke. On the amount line of the check, made payable to Maria Martinez, was for following number:

$$\$2,041,053.56$$

What do you think? Was it a joke or could this be for real? Could $1000 deposited into the stock market grow by over 200,000 percent in 65 years?

In fact, it could! As you will learn over the next several chapters, the average annual total return (price appreciation plus dividends) of funds invested in the stock market between 1948 and 2013 was 12.44% and the future value of $1000 invested at this return for 65 years is the amount on Maria's check.

We told you finance was fun. Now just imagine how happy you might be on your 65th birthday if your parents or grandparents did the same for you on the day you were born! Of course, we do not suggest that you make this hope your personal retirement plan, but the story does demonstrate a couple of very important facts concerning the "time" value of money. Money deposited in a return-generating account will grow over time, and the sooner you start saving for retirement, the better.

The notion that money has a time value is one of the most important concepts in valuation and, consequently, in finance. It is a fairly simple concept and is best illustrated as the answer to the following question. If we gave you a choice between receiving $100 today versus receiving $100 one year from now, which alternative would you choose? We are sure that your answer will be: $100 today.

Let us spend a few minutes analyzing the reason you chose to receive the $100 today. Was it because you could invest the money received today in a bank or some investment opportunity and hope to have more than $100 at the end of the year? Clearly, if there are such investment opportunities available, it makes perfect sense to choose to receive the money today. Now suppose that you are living in an environment where there are absolutely no investment opportunities and the only use of money is for spending it to buy things; that is, for consumption. In such an environment, would you still choose to receive the $100 today rather than one year later? Again, intuitively, you would still choose to receive the money earlier. The reason for this is that if you receive the money today, you could use it for consumption today or anytime later as you wish. For rational persons, consumption always brings in some benefits, or, if you prefer, utility. If the amount were to be received one year later, you would have to postpone your ability to consume by one year. Rational people prefer to have choices as to when to spend money. Thus, even in an environment with no investment opportunities, money has time value.

A practical implication of the concept of time value of money is that you cannot add sums of money that are received at different points in time. It would be equivalent to the proverbial adding of apples and oranges. For example, if an investment generates $100 at the end of one year and another $100 at the end of two years, one cannot say that the investment yields a total of $200. Similarly, note that if Maria's grandparents had invested $500 when she was born and added another $500 to the account when she turned 20 ($1000 total deposit), her check would have been for only $1,118,342.28. Obviously, the "timing" aspect of time value of money is very important.

The most significant implication of the concept of time value of money is the clear distinction between the amount of the money to be received in the future and its value today. The fact that you prefer to receive $100 today over receiving $100 one year from now implies that you place a lower value on the amount that is received at the later date. Recall that finance is all about valuing assets, and assets have value because they generate expected future cash flows. These cash flows, however, occur at different times in the future. Therefore, to compute the value of an asset or its price today, we have to be able to determine a method for assigning a value (at the current time) to cash flows that occur in the future. This chapter is intended to provide the basics of computing values of cash flows at a point in time that is different from the point in time at which the cash flows actually occur.

4.2 The Math of Time Value of Money

Time value of money is perhaps one of the most powerful concepts in the entire world. Literally trillions of dollars of securities trade hands every day and the price that all of these transactions sell for is determined using the time value of money. Time value of money (henceforth, TVM) impacts countless numbers of people, every day of their lives (regardless of whether they realize it):

- Have you ever taken out a loan (auto, house, credit card, student loan, etc.)? How is the monthly payment determined? TVM!
- How is payoff on a loan at any point in time determined? TVM!

- The total value of national debt in the United States at the end of 2014 was in excess of $18 trillion!!! Over $900 billion of debt securities trade hands in the United States every DAY!!! All debt values are determined by TVM!
- Do you own any stock? Approximately 54% of all U.S. households (i.e., over 64 million people) own stock in some form (either in individual companies, mutual funds, 401K pension or retirement accounts). The total value of all stocks in the United States at end of 2012 was in excess of $105 trillion!!! The average daily trading value of stocks in the United States is over $250 billion!!! All stock values and prices are determined by TVM!
- Insurance companies use TVM to determine what to charge for premiums.
- Lease and rental companies use TVM to determine rates.
- Basically 100% of all corporations in the United States use TVM to make capital budgeting (i.e., long-term investment) decisions. These decisions include issues such as building a new factory, bringing a new product to the market, expanding into new markets, opening new stores, R&D spending, and so forth.

Even though TVM is extremely important and amazingly powerful, derivation of the basic TVM equation is quite simple. Assume you deposit $1000 today into an account that pays interest of 10% per year. How much money would be in your account exactly one year from today? Obviously the answer is $1,100. We will call this amount FV_1, where FV is the future value and the index value, 1 in this case, is the number of years from today. The math of how you derived FV_1 is as follows:

$$FV_1 = \text{principal} + \text{interest}$$
$$= \text{starting deposit} + \text{interest on this amount for one year}$$
$$= \$1000 + (\$1000)(.10)$$

Note if we factor out the $1000 in this equation we have:

$$FV_1 = \$1000(1 + .10)$$

Now assume that you leave the money in the account for another year. How much would be in the account exactly two years from today—that is, what is FV_2? Once again:

$$FV_2 = \text{principal} + \text{interest}$$
$$= \text{starting deposit} + \text{interest on this amount for one year}$$

But now the starting deposit is FV_1, so we have:

$$FV_2 = FV_1 + (FV_1)(.10) = FV_1(1 + .10)$$

But since $FV_1 = \$1000(1 + .10)$, we now have:

$$FV_2 = \$1000(1 + .10)(1 + .10) = \$1000(1 + .10)^2.$$

Now assume that you leave the money in the account for yet another year. How much would be in the account exactly three years from today—that is, what is FV_3? Using the same process:

$$FV_3 = \text{principal} + \text{interest}$$
$$= \text{starting deposit} + \text{interest on this amount for one year}$$

But now the starting deposit is FV_2, and $FV_2 = \$1000(1 + .10)$, so we have:

$$FV_3 = \$1000(1 + .10)^2(1 + .10) = \$1000(1 + .10)^3.$$

Do you see the pattern? If you continue this on and on for any number of years from today (we will call this "n"), we have the following general equation:

$$FV_n = \$1000(1 + .10)^n.$$

Now notice that if we had started with $500 in the account at the beginning, or in fact any other amount, that amount would just replace the $1000 in the final equation. Likewise, if the interest rate for the account was instead 8% (i.e., .08 as a decimal), that value would just replace .10 in the final equation.

Thus, defining PV as the amount deposited into the account today (PV stands for present value) and r is the account interest rate expressed as a decimal (to get a decimal, divide the interest rate by 100; thus, 4.35% = .0435 or 12.44% = .1244), we have now derived the fundamental TVM equation:

$$FV_n = PV(1 + r)^n$$

Believe it or not, this very simple equation is what determines all of the values (and more) listed above! The equation is powerful and very useful. In fact, most of the rest of this book is devoted to exploring the power and usefulness of this equation and learning how businesses (and individuals) can use different forms of this equation to make important decisions.

Recall Maria Martinez from the opening story? Here is how we derived the amount on her check:

$$FV_n = PV(1 + r)^n$$
$$FV_{65} = \$1000(1.1244)^{65}$$
$$= \$1000(2041.05356)$$
$$= \$2,041,053.56$$

So, how did Maria's account get so big? She only earned 12.44% (i.e., $12.44) each year on the original deposit of $1000 = ($12.44 per year on original deposit)(65 years) = 808.60. Add to that the original deposit and you only come up with $1,808.60. So, where did the other $2,039,244.96 come from?

It came from earning interest on interest—what is called *compound interest*. Note that after one year, she had ($1000)(1.1244) = $1,124.40 in her account. So in the second year, she earned 12.44% on $1,124.40, not $1000. That is, in year 2 she earned interest on the interest that she earned in year 1 (i.e., $124.40) in addition to interest on the original principal of $1000. And so, at the end of year 2, she had $1,264.28 in her account. Then in year 3, she earned interest on the original $1000 deposit but now she also earned interest on all *cumulative* interest earned to date (i.e., 264.28). Note that the cumulative amount is growing each year. After several years, interest on interest (i.e., compound interest) becomes significantly more important than interest on principal (we call this "simple interest") and, as you will learn later. After many years, interest on interest literally explodes!!! More precisely, compound interest grows over time at an exponential rate.

Now note two very interesting principles about TVM:

1. If Maria's account had an annual return of half of 12.44% (i.e., if the annual return on the account was only 6.22%), the check she would have received would have been for only:

$$FV_{65} = \$1000(1.0622)^{65} = \$50{,}513.72.$$

Obviously, interest rates are very important in time value of money.

2. Assume that Maria's grandparents opened the account when Maria's parents were married, before they even considered having children (Los abuelos de Maria were forward thinking and wishful). And assume that Maria was born 10 years after her parents were married. Thus, on Maria's 65th birthday, the original $1000 deposit would have been growing for 75 years instead of 65 years. In this case, the check she received would have been for:

$$FV_{75} = \$1000(1.1244)^{75} = \$6{,}592{,}691.75.$$

Obviously, the "time" part of time value of money is also very important!

One final point before we move onto the next section. Recall the basic TVM equation we derived above:

$$FV_n = PV(1 + r)^n$$

Now, if we solve this basic TVM equation for PV instead of FV, we get:

$$PV = \frac{FV_n}{(1+r)^n}$$

This second equation is in fact the more fundamental form of the TVM equation for finance. Most of the time we are concerned with what some asset is worth today—that is, we want to know the asset's "present value." The price of a share of stock is the present value of the stock's expected future cash flows. The payoff on a loan today is the present value of all required future payments. And, absolutely fundamental to corporate finance, the value of a company today, as we discussed in Chapter 1, is the present value of all expected future cash flows that the company (or asset or collection of assets) are expected to generate for its owner(s).

4.3 Financial Calculators

Speaking of calculators, the financial calculator that we will demonstrate how to use is the hp 10BII. Except for some different default settings, a few different obscure computing functions, and different cases, both calculators are essentially the same.

The 'y^x' key we mentioned previously is below the 'X' key on this calculator. To use this function, enter the interest rate factor (i.e., 1+r), then press 2nd and the 'y^x' key, then enter the power you want to raise the interest rate factor to, and then press the = key. So, for the Maria Martinez check problem we did above, you would enter the following:

$$1.1244 \text{ 2nd 'y}^x\text{' } 65 =$$

and your calculator will display: 2041.05356. Then, if you multiply this number by $1000 (the amount of the deposit), you will get the amount that Maria saw on her check of $2,041,053.56.

Problem 4.1:   What is $(1.0625)^4$? What is $(1.136)^{12}$? What is $(1.274)^{29}$?

Problem 4.2:   What is $(1.16)^{.5}$? What is $(1.09)^{.3333}$? What is $(1.12)^{.083333}$?

Note that these last problems (where the power is less than one) are roots of the numbers. So, $(1.16)^{.5}$ is just the square root of 1.16, $(1.09)^{.3333}$ is the cube root of 1.04, and $(1.12)^{.083333}$ is the 12th root of 1.12. Since there are 12 months in a year, this is a calculation you will see again.

4.4 Definition of Time

Because "time" in time value of money is so important, we must have a very specific definition of how to measure time. In finance, we define year 0 as today, and this is also called the "end of year 0." Year 1 is exactly one year from today, and also referred to as the **end** of year 1. Year 2 is exactly 2 years from today and is called the **end** of year 2. And year n is the end of year n, or exactly n years from today.

Some problems will state that a cash flow occurs at the beginning of a year. But we can easily convert this into an end of the year, because the beginning of year n+1 is just the end of year n. For example, the beginning of year 4 is the end of year 3. And the beginning of year 83 is the end of year 82. We will investigate this issue more later. For now, just remember that the index on a cash flow represents the number of time periods (usually years) from today.

4.5 Present and Future Values: Multiple Cash Flows

In this section, we will analyze the concept of the time value of money when the number of cash flows is more than one as opposed to only one. You will find that the concepts of present and future values remain the same, only the calculations become a little more tedious.

4.5.1 Future Value

Suppose you deposit $100 in a bank today and another $100 in the bank exactly one year from today. If the bank pays interest of 5% per year on this account, and if interest is compounded annually, how much money will you have in your account at the end of year two (that is, exactly two years from today)?

Before solving this problem, note the phrase: "if interest is compounded annually." This phrase merely means that the rate is an annual rate. Unless otherwise stated, the interest rate, or the discount rate, is always for one year. Sometimes 5% per year will be written as 5% p. a., where p. a. stands for per annum (which is the same as per year).

If an interest rate is compounded more than one time per year (for example, semiannually, quarterly, monthly, daily, or even continuous compounding), the effective interest that you earn will be greater than the annual rate. For example, a rate of 10% p.a., but compounded monthly, will effectively produce a return of 10.4713% per year. In the particular problem above, we explicitly state that the interest will be compounded annually; that is, the frequency of compounding is one time per year. Later we will demonstrate the effect that increasing this frequency has on future and present values (there you will see how 10% p.a., compounded monthly, is equivalent to 10.4713% per year). However, annual compounding is most common and throughout this book, unless otherwise specifically stated, always assume that the frequency of compounding is one time per year.

Now let us solve the problem. To do this, let us introduce the concept of a time line. This may seem a little redundant at this stage but time lines will prove invaluable as the problems become more complicated. A time line is simply a pictorial representation of the occurrence of cash flows over time. We denote "time" on a time line with the letter t. Consistent with the definition of time above, today is defined as t = 0, one year (or period) from today is defined as t = 1 (also called the *end* of year 1), two years (or periods) from today is defined as t = 2 (the *end* of year 2), and so on to n years from today is defined as t = n (the *end* of year n).

Denoting t = 0 as today, t = 1 as the end of the first period (or year), and t = 2 as the end of the second period, the time line for our problem is drawn below.

```
    $100         $100          ?
  ├─────────────┼─────────────┤
   t = 0         t = 1         t = 2
```

We can divide this problem into two single period problems as follows. First, based on what we did in the previous section, we know that the amount we will have in the account at the end of the first year is:

$$FV_1 = (\$100)(1.05)^1 = \$105.$$

We can now add the second deposit to this amount (i.e., $100 + $105 = $205) and consider the second year as another single period case in which we deposit $205 into the account that pays an interest rate of 5%. Thus, at the end of the second year, we will have the following amount in the account.

$$FV_2 = (\$205)(1.05)^1 = \$215.25$$

Although this is the correct answer, doing multi-period cash flow problems as a series of single period calculations becomes tedious, so let us find a more direct route. Recall from the principle of additivity that amounts can be added if they are in the same year. Think of these two deposits as being independent. Now merely find the future value of each at the end of year two and add those two future values together.

For general notation purposes, define the deposit made today as C_0 (that is, the cash flow, or deposit, made at t = 0) and the deposit made at the end of year one as C_1 (the cash flow, or deposit, made at t = 1). Thus, the future value at the end of year 2 (at t = 2) of the deposit made today (at t = 0) is:

$$FV_2 = C_0(1+r)^2 = (\$100)(1.05)^2 = \$110.25$$

And the future value at the end of year 2 of the deposit made at the end of year 1 is:

$$FV_2 = C_1(1+r)^1 = (\$100)(1.05)^1 = \$105.00$$

Therefore, the future value at the end of year 2 of both of these deposits is $110.25 + $105.00 = $215.25 (same as we found above).

Note that we can put these into a single equation as follows:

$$FV_2 = C_0(1+r)^2 + C_1(1+r)^1 = (\$100)(1.05)^2 + (\$100)(1.05)^1 = \$215.25.$$

Think of this equation as "saying" that the deposit made today (i.e., C_0) will earn interest for 2 years (that is why the interest rate factor is raised to the second power) and the deposit made at the end of year 1 (C_1) will earn interest for 1 year (this cash flow's interest rate factor is raised to the 1 power).

To solidify your understanding of this concept, consider a slight change to the problem above. Suppose you deposit $100 in a bank exactly one year from today and another $100 in the bank exactly two years from today. If the bank pays interest of 5% per year on this account, and if interest is compounded annually, how much money will you have in your account at the end of year two (that is, exactly 2 years from today)?

The time line for this modified problem looks as follows:

```
              $100      $100
              +         +
├─────────────┼─────────┼─────▶
t = 0         t = 1     t = 2
```

where we still want to know how much is in the account at t = 2. The difference is that now the amounts in the account will each earn interest for a shorter period of time. The first deposit (C_1) earns interest for only one year and the second deposit earns interest for 0 years (i.e., from the end of year 2 to the end of year 2 = 0 years). Since anything raised to the 0 power is 1, we have:

$$FV_2 = C_1(1+r)^1 + C_2(1+r)^0 = (\$100)(1.05)^1 + (\$100)(1.05)^0 = \$105 + \$100(1) = \$205.00.$$

4.5.2 Present Value

What about present value of multiple cash flows? It works the same way. Assume that you have the opportunity to invest in a venture that offers $12,000 at the end of the first year and

$16,350 at the end of the second year. What is the maximum price that you would pay for this investment today if your required rate of return is 12%?

To solve this problem, we have to find the present value of the cash flow that occurs at t = 1 and the present value of the cash flow that occurs at t = 2, and then, using the concept of value additivity, add these two present values together. The sum of the present values (that is, at t = 0) of both of these cash flows is the maximum price that you should be willing to pay today because, as we have said many times already, the present value of a series of cash flows is what those cash flows are worth today.

The time line is for this problem is:

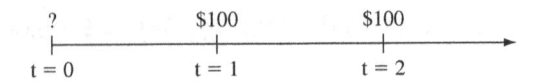

```
    ?           $100         $100
    ├────────────┼────────────┼────────▶
   t = 0        t = 1        t = 2
```

And the TVM equation is:

$$PV = \frac{CF_1}{(1+r)^1} + \frac{CF_1}{(1+r)^2}$$

$$= \frac{\$12,000}{(1.12)^1} + \frac{\$16,350}{(1.12)^2}$$

$$= \$10,714.29 + \$13,034.12$$

$$= \$23,748.41.$$

Now, solve the following problems in the space provided. Remember, if it helps you to better conceptualize the problem, draw a time line.

Problem 4.3: You plan to loan $11,000 to your friend at an interest rate of 8% per year compounded annually. The loan is to be repaid in two years. How much will your friend pay you at t = 2?

Problem 4.4: You are offered the chance to buy into an investment that promises to pay you $28,650 at the end of two years. If your required rate of return is 12%, what is the maximum amount that you would pay for this investment today?

96 Chapter Four

Problem 4.5: You deposit $5,000 in a bank account today. You make another deposit of $4,000 into the account at the end of year 1. If the bank pays interest at 6% compounded annually, how much will you have in your account at the end of two years, that is, at t = 2?

Problem 4.6: You deposit $5,000 in a bank account exactly one year from today. You make another deposit of $4,000 into the account at the end of year 2. If the bank pays interest at 6% compounded annually, how much will you have in your account at the end of two years, that is, at t = 2?

Problem 4.7: You are planning to spend a summer in Europe one year from now. You expect that the trip will cost you $15,000. Two years from now, you want to spend the summer in Asia and you expect this trip to cost you $19,000. How much should you deposit in your bank account today so that you can make both of these trips? Your bank pays you interest at 8% per year.

The answer you hopefully derived for *Problem 4.7* is $30,178.33. To better visualize what this present value means, let's trace your account balance over time for this problem. Assume you deposit $30,178.33 into the account at t = 0. At t = 1, just before you make the withdrawal of $15,000, the account will have in it:

$$\$30{,}178.33 \times 1.08 = \$32{,}592.60.$$

After you make the withdrawal of $15,000 for your European binge, you will have left in the account an amount of:

$$\$32{,}592.60 - \$15{,}000 = \$17{,}592.60.$$

This amount is left in the account at t = 1 just after the withdrawal of $15,000. At t = 2, just before your withdrawal for the Asia trip, the account balance will have become:

$$\$17{,}592.60 \times 1.08 = \$19{,}000,$$

which, not surprisingly, is exactly the amount you need for the summer in Asia.

Problem 4.8: You currently have $20,000 in your savings account. You need to have a total of $46,500 in the account exactly two years from today in order to make a downpayment on a house you will buy at that time. If the account is expected to pay interest of 8.5% p.a., what amount must you deposit into the account at the end of year 1 to achieve your goal?

Problem 4.9: You are offered an investment opportunity that requires you to pay $31,500 today and promises to give you $39,700 at the end of two years. What is the return on this investment?

Finally, let us consider two assets A and B. The discount rate is 10 percent and the cash flows from these assets are as follows:

	t = 1	t = 2
Asset A	$100	$200
Asset B	$200	$100

Which of these assets will have the higher present value? Can you answer that without performing any calculations? You can. It has to be asset B because this asset generates the higher cash flows sooner. To prove the point:

$$PV_A = \frac{100}{1.1} + \frac{200}{(1.1)^2} = \$256.20$$

$$PV_B = \frac{200}{1.1} + \frac{100}{(1.1)^2} = \$264.46$$

Now suppose that there is another asset C that generates $300 at the end of each of the next two years. What would be its present value?

$$PV_C = \frac{300}{1.1} + \frac{300}{(1.1)^2} = \$520.66$$

Notice that the sum of the present values of assets A and B is $256.20 + $264.46 = $520.66, which is exactly the same as the present value of asset C. Why? Look again at the cash flows from the three assets.

	t = 1	t = 2
Asset A	$100	$200
Asset B	$200	$100
Asset C	$300	$300

Notice that the cash flows from asset C represent the exact sum of the cash flows from A and B in each of the two periods. Therefore, recalling the principle of value additivity discussed earlier, it must be the case that $PV_A + PV_B = PV_C$.

4.6 Chapter Summary and Looking Forward

In this chapter we introduced the basic math of time value of money for one and two periods. We demonstrated how to use the fundamental time value of money equation:

$$FV_n = PV(1 + r)^n$$

to solve for the future value one year from today of an immediate cash flow, and the present value of a cash flow to be received one year from today.

Next we showed how to use a simple extension of the basic time value of money equation:

$$FV_2 = C_0(1 + r)^2 + C_1(1 + r)^1$$

to solve the same variables for two periods of cash flows. Last, we proved that the principle of value additivity applies to both individual and yearly cash flows, and also to the present values of those cash flows.

In the following chapter we will merely extend the time value of money equation to multiple years and to other than yearly (for example, monthly) cash flows. Because multiple year calculations can be tedious and complex, we will show how to use a financial calculator to assist in computing values. Never forget, however, that the simple math and ideas presented in this chapter are the foundations that underlie all time value of money calculations. This will be true no matter how complex the problems might appear or what aids (calculator, spreadsheet, and so on) they might require to determine a solution.

Assignment 4.1

1. Your neighbor is asking you to invest in a venture that will double your money in one year (you know what to do about such fantastic promises). What return (in percentage terms) is he promising you?

2. You have just deposited X dollars in your bank account that pays interest of 4.39% p.a. You discover that at the end of one year you have $7,397 in the account. What was X, that is, the amount of money that you deposited today?

3. You are going to retire after exactly one year and you plan to take a world cruise after retirement for which you will require $13,000. What is the least amount that you must set aside today at an interest rate of 8% p.a. so that you can take the cruise?

4. Assume that you need to have exactly $25,000 in your savings account exactly one year from today. Suppose that you expect to receive $4,500 exactly one year from today from your company as a bonus, and that you plan to deposit this entire amount into your savings account. What amount do you need to deposit into the account today to reach your goal, assuming that your account pays interest of 7.5% p.a.?

5. Suppose that your required rate of return is 12% p.a. and that you are offered an investment into an asset that will yield $14,739 at the end of one year. What is the maximum price that you would be willing to pay for this asset?

Assignment 4.2

1. You neighbor (from Assignment 1) comes back to you (after you spurned him the first time) with another investment opportunity. He claims that you will be able to double your money in two years. What is the annual rate of return that this investment promises?

2. You want to withdraw $3,200 from your account at the end of one year and $7,300 at the end of the second year. How much should you deposit in your account today so that you can make these withdrawals? Your account pays 6% p.a.

3. You deposit $7,448 in your account today. You make another deposit at t = 1 of $2,476. How much will be there in your account at the end of year 1 if the interest rate is 7% p.a.?

4. You deposit $7,448 in your account today. You make another deposit at t = 1 of $2,476. How much will be there in your account at the end of year 2 if the interest rate is 7% p.a.?

5. You must have $15,000 in your account exactly two years from today. Assuming an interest rate of 12 % p.a., what equal annual amount must you deposit today and at the end of year 1 to reach your goal?

Assignment 4.3

1. Your account pays interest of 4% p.a. Assume that you deposit $8,000 into the account today. You plan to withdraw some money from the account at the end of year 1. If you want the amount remaining in your account at the end of year 2 to be exactly $4,000, how much can you withdraw at the end of year 1 (so that the balance remaining at the end of year 2 is $4,000)?

2. You come across an investment opportunity that requires you to invest $10,000 today and will yield you $6,500 at the end of the first year and $5,000 at the end of the second year. If your required rate of return is 12% p.a., would you make this investment?

3. You invest $500 in an account today. You make no additional deposits into the account. One year from today there is $538 in the account. What is the nominal interest rate that you earned on your money?

Additional Questions and Problems

1. If you want to have exactly $4,000 in your account at t = 1, how much must you deposit into that account at t = 0 if the account pays interest of 6.6% p.a.?

2. If you want to have exactly $675 in your account at t = 2, how much must you deposit into that account at t = 0 if the account pays interest of 4.95% p.a.?

3. Your required rate of return is 11% p.a. and you have access to two investment opportunities. The first one costs $13,631 today and yields $15,200 at the end of the year. The second one costs $3,211 today and will yield $3,600 at the end of one year. Which, if any, investment or investments would you choose? Why?

4. Your required rate of return is 14% p.a. and you have access to two investment opportunities. The first one requires you to invest $38,439 today and will yield $42,346 at the end of the first year. The second one costs you $41,489 today and will yield you $23,100 at the end of each of the next two years. Which, if any, investment or investments would you choose? Why?

5. Assume that you deposit $2,400 into an account today and that you deposit another $2,400 into the same account exactly one year from today. If the account pays interest of 4.88% p.a., how much will you have in your account exactly one year from today?

6. Assume that you deposit $318 into an account today and that you deposit another $552 into the same account exactly one year from today. If the account pays interest of 8.18% p.a., how much will you have in your account exactly two years from today?

7. Assume that you deposit $750 into an account exactly one year from today and that you deposit another $875 into the same account exactly two years from today. If the account pays interest of 9.5% p.a., how much will you have in your account exactly two years from today?

8. Assume that you expect to receive $1,500 exactly one year from today and $2,500 exactly two years from today. At a discount rate of 6.25% p.a., what is the present value (today) of this expected future cash flow stream?

9. Assume that you expect to receive $10,000 today, $15,000 exactly one year from today, and $25,000 exactly two years from today. At a discount rate of 2.75% p.a., what is the present value (today) of this expected future cash flow stream?

10. Assume that you deposit $10,000 into an account today, $15,000 into the account exactly one year from today, and another $20,000 into the account exactly two years from today. If the account pays interest of 11.45% p.a., how much money will be in your account exactly two years from today?

11. Choose the one answer that can be correct *without using a calculator.* Your required rate of return is 10%.

    a. The present value of $432 to be received at t = 1 is $432.

    b. The t = 1 value of a t = 0 cash flow of $7,811 is $7,770.

    c. You would pay $6,600 today for an asset that yields $2,300 at the end of each of the next two years.

    d. You would pay $6,600 today for an asset that yields $3,905.21 at the end of each of the next two years.

12. You require making the following withdrawals from your account—$35,000 at the end of the first year and $47,000 at the end of the second year. If the interest rate is 10% p.a., what is the least amount that you would need to deposit into the account today so that you can make these withdrawals? Check your answer by tracing the amounts in your account over time as we did in the chapter.

13. You deposit $12,000 today in an account that pays 14% p.a. interest. You plan to withdraw $12,000 from this account at the end of the first year. How much will be left in your account:

    a. at the end of the first year after the withdrawal?

    b. at the end of the second year?

14. Your required rate of return is 13% p.a. A two-year investment requires you to pay $10,000 today and will yield $7,000 at the end of the first year and an amount $X at the end of the second year. What is the least amount that X should be for you to make this investment?

15. If the future value at the end of year 2 of $3,400 deposited today and some amount ($X) deposited at the end of year 1 in an account that pays interest of 18% p.a. is $10,000, what is X?

16. If, in an account that pays interest of 2.5% p.a., the present value of $5,000 to be received one year from today and some amount ($X) to be received two years from today is $12,500, what is X?

17. You deposited $3,500 in the bank two years ago, and the account now has $4,100 in it today. What has been the "p.a." interest rate on this account?

18. If the present value of $5,250 to be received exactly two years from today is $4,925, what is p.a. interest rate on this account?

19. A magazine subscription offer states that you can purchase a one-year subscription for $48 today and a two-year subscription for $70 today. Assuming that there will be no price changes in the future, which subscription would you choose if your required rate of return is 10% p.a.?

20. A car dealer offers you the following two payment choices on a car that you would like to buy. The price of the car is $20,000. (a) Pay the entire amount today and receive a discount of $2,850. (b) Pay $20,000 at the end of two years. Which alternative would you choose if the interest rate is 8% p.a.?

21. You have two monthly car payments of $400 each left on your car. If the interest rate is 0.75% per month, how much would you be required to pay the lender if you wanted to pay off the loan today (hint: The payoff on a loan at any time is the present value of all remaining payments)?

Chapter 5

Time Value of Money: Advanced Topics

5.1 **Chapter Introduction and Overview**
5.2 **The Basic Approach**
5.3 **The Present Value of a Perpetuity**
5.4 **The Present Value and Future Value of an Annuity**
5.5 **Time Value Calculations with a Financial Calculator**
5.6 **Present and Future Values of Single Cash Flows**
5.7 **Present and Future Values of Annuities**
5.8 **Special Topics in Time Value**
   Assignments
   Additional Questions and Problems

After studying Chapter 5, you should be able to:

- Mathematically define and be able to describe each of the variables of the multi-period present value and future value equations that underlie the time value of money.
- Differentiate between an ordinary annuity and an annuity due.
- Determine the future or present value of a sum when there are non-annual compounding periods.
- Calculate the annual percentage yield or effective annual rate of interest and then explain how it differs from the nominal or stated interest rate.
- Use a financial calculator to solve time value of money problems.

From *Lectures in Corporate Finance*, 6th Edition by Jayant R. Kale and Richard J. Fendler. Copyright © 2013 by Kendall Hunt Publishing Company. Reprinted by permission.

5.1 Chapter Introduction and Overview

Twenty years ago, when he was only four years old, Kaito Tanaka moved with his family to America. Kaito attended American schools all his life and three years ago he graduated from a major urban university in the southeastern United States. An internship that he participated in during his senior year in college provided a lead that allowed him to secure a full-time position after graduation as a computer technician for a rapidly growing, mid-sized technology firm. Things were going well for Kaito at the company. He just received a promotion and a significant raise, so he decided that it was time to buy a new car. The car he currently owned was a 12-year-old clunker given to him by his parents, and he was tired of parking three blocks from his office and walking to work in order to hide this heap from his work buddies.

Kaito woke very early Saturday morning, dressed in the sharpest clothes he owned, and parked his junker in a breakfast restaurant lot less than a block from a BMW dealership. He walked to the car lot and began browsing. Soon a salesman spotted him, and sizing Kaito up as most likely a hot shot stockbroker who just closed a major deal, he took Kaito to the luxury side of the lot. There Kaito spotted a Jerez Black Metallic, 2016 BMW M3 convertible, with Fox Red Novillo leather interior, and nearly every upgrade option available. According to the sticker, the 4.0L, 32-valve, V8 engine that generated 414 hp at 8300 rpm could go from 0 to 60 mph in just over 4 seconds. Kaito had no idea what that meant, but it sure sounded sweet.

When the salesman opened the door and Kaito got behind the wheel, his mind began to spin. This was the car he wanted, needed, had to have. With this car, Kaito was sure he could do anything he wanted and achieve any goal he set his mind to. After a spin around the block, Kaito told the salesman he wanted the car and the salesman took Kaito to see the finance manager. Kaito filled out the papers he was given, showing his income, assets (zero), and outstanding school loans (lots). When the finance manager looked at what Kaito filled out, he looked at him quizzically and said: "Son, do you know the price of this car? You are trying to buy a $78,950 automobile. How much do you think you can afford to pay monthly?"

Kaito had never thought about this, but after a few minutes, he said he was pretty sure he could squeeze out about $300 per month because that was the increase in his monthly pay due to his raise. So, what do you think? Can Kaito afford this car? Hopefully, you know that the answer is no. However, a recent survey of college graduates shows that Kaito may not be as far out of touch as you might think. Less than 20% of those surveyed who had bought a new car in the last 12 months said that they knew how the monthly payment on the car loan was determined. They merely "trusted" that the finance manager or bank loan officer "did it right."

Knowing what you can actually afford before you buy a car or house or any other asset that requires monthly payments over a long period of time, is a life skill that everyone should possess. And, as we will show you in this chapter, these calculations are merely a simple extension of the time value of money principles you learned in Chapter 6. By the way, as you will soon learn, with a 60-month (i.e., 5-year) loan at an interest rate of 5.5% p.a., the monthly payment on Kaito's BMW would be $1,508.04—significantly greater than the $300 Kaito thought he could afford. In fact, for $300 per month, with a loan with these same terms, Kaito could afford a car that costs $15,705.85. At that price, Kaito should be looking at a Chevrolet Sonic, a Ford Fiesta, or a Kia Rio 5. Dependable, yes; but most likely not the type of car that would allow Kaito to "do anything he wanted and achieve any goal he set his mind to."

Another recent survey conducted by a major financial journal found that the majority of Americans believe that if they have liquid[1] savings of $1,000,000 by the time they reach the age of 65, they will be able to retire in comfort. Assuming you agree with this statement and that you begin saving for retirement when you turn 25 years old (after you get out of school and spend a couple of years getting settled into your career, life, etc.—maybe even after you buy a car), how much money would you have to save every year to achieve your goal? Or, since most people are paid bi-weekly, a more pertinent question might be, how much would you have to save out of every paycheck to reach your goal?

By the end of this chapter, you will know how to calculate the answers these, and many other similar, questions. The process is actually quite simple and nothing more than an application of an extension to the basic TVM equations that we learned in Chapter 4. Still, it is amazing how few people know what you are about to learn. In this same survey, although people indicated that they understood the "need" to save for retirement, nearly 90% admitted that they really have no idea what the "magic number" is that will allow them to successfully transition from the working world to the retirement world. The answer of $1,000,000 is given because it just "sounds" like a really big amount! Even more alarming, only 14% of those surveyed claimed to be confident that they will have enough money to live on when they retire. Given that retirement is something that nearly everyone will someday face, these statistics are alarming.

In this chapter, there are really no new concepts from those presented in Chapter 4. However, the computations for computing present and future values, and so on, will become more complex. In fact, the time line representation that was introduced in the previous chapter (and had seemed so redundant then) will prove invaluable in solving the more complex problems in this chapter. The computational methods necessary for solving time value problems with multiple cash flows in multiple periods are conceptually very similar to those with just one or two time periods. But computationally, they are much more complex. Therefore, we will resort to the use of financial calculators in solving these problems.

In case you are super curious, if the return on the retirement fund averages 11% p.a., the annual deposit needed to achieve $1,000,000 after 40 years (i.e., from age 25 to age 65) is $1,718.73. For bi-weekly deposits, the amount is $53.08.

5.2 The Basic Approach

From the previous chapter, we know that the general expression for the future value at $t = n$, of a cash flow occurring today (at $t = 0$), C_0, is given by:

$$FV_n = C_0(1 + r)^n.$$

and the present value of a single cash flow, C_n, occurring at $t = n$, is given by:

$$PV = \frac{C_n}{(1 + r)^n}$$

---

[1] Meaning funds that can easily and quickly be converted to cash at market value, such as investments in an IRA, stocks, bonds, a pension account, or other. A house is considered an illiquid asset because it cannot be converted into cash quickly at market value.

You sometimes see this present value formula written differently. Instead of dividing the future cash flow C_n by $(1 + r)^n$, you can equally well multiply the future payment by $\frac{1}{(1+r)^n}$. The expression $\frac{1}{(1+r)^n}$ is called the present value interest factor, denoted as:

$$\text{PVIF}(r,n) = \frac{1}{(1+r)^n}$$

It measures the present value of one dollar received in period n. For example, with an interest rate of 6%, the two-year present value interest factor is:

$$\text{PVIF}(6\%,2) = \frac{1}{(1+0{,}06)^2} = 0.8900$$

It means that each dollar received in year 2 is only worth $0.8900 today, then the present value of your payment of $1,000 in year 2 must be:

$$PV = 1000 \times \text{PVIF}(6\%,2) = 1{,}000 \times 0.89000 = 890.0$$

The expression $(1 + r)^n$ is called future value interest factor, denoted as:

$$\text{FVIF}(r,n) = (1+r)^n$$

Future value interest factor table and present value interest factor table are provided in Appendices A and B.

Consider an asset that generates cash flows for two years with C_1 at the end of the first year and C_2 at the end of the second year. Then, denoting the required rate of return by r, the present value of the asset is given by:

$$PV = \frac{C_1}{(1+r)^1} + \frac{C_2}{(1+r)^2}$$

Now suppose that, instead of the asset generating cash flows for only two years, it generates cash flows for four years. The method shown above can be logically extended to the following:

$$PV = \frac{C_1}{(1+r)^1} + \frac{C_2}{(1+r)^2} + \frac{C_3}{(1+r)^3} + \frac{C_4}{(1+r)^4}$$

where C_1, C_2, C_3 and C_4 denote the cash flows at the end of years one, two, three, and four, respectively.

In the above, note that the cash flow in the third year, C_3, is discounted by $(1 + r)^3$ and the fourth one by $(1 + r)^4$. In general, the number in the power term for $(1 + r)$ equals the number of time periods from $t = 0$.

Likewise, the future value of these same cash flows at the end year four can be written as:

$$FV_4 = C_1(1+r)^3 + C_2(1+r)^2 + C_3(1+r)^1 + C_4(1+r)^0$$

In the above expression for the future value, it might appear strange that the cash flow at the end of the first year is multiplied by $(1+r)^3$ rather than by $(1+r)^4$. To see why this is so, let us draw the time line.

```
          C₁        C₂        C₃        C₄
├─────────┼─────────┼─────────┼─────────┼──────→
t = 0    t = 1    t = 2    t = 3    t = 4
```

Recall that we have to find the future value as of the end of the fourth year, that is, at $t = 4$. Count the number of periods that cash flow C_1 needs to be compounded to be at $t = 4$. It is three times and not four (from the end of year 1 to the end of year 2, then from the end of year 2 to the end of year 3, and then from the end of year 3 to the end of year 4). Therefore, in the future value equation given above, the cash flow at the end of the first year is multiplied by $(1+r)^3$ *and not* by $(1+r)^4$.

However, if there was a cash flow at $t = 0$, say C_0, then its future value at $t = 4$ would be $C_0(1+r)^4$. Another point to note is that the cash flow C_4 occurs at $t = 4$, the very point in time at which we want to determine the value. What is the value of C_4 at $t = 4$? It is simply C_4. Therefore, the cash flow C_4 is multiplied by $(1+r)^0$, and we know that anything raised to the power of zero equals one.

Let us look at the general case where the number of time periods is n and the cash flows that occur at the end of each time period are denoted by C_t, where $t = 1, 2, \ldots, n$. The general present valuation equation, therefore, is given by:

$$PV = \frac{C_1}{(1+r)^1} + \frac{C_2}{(1+r)^2} + \ldots + \frac{C_n}{(1+r)^n}$$

Another way of expressing this is:

$$PV = \sum_{t=1}^{n} \frac{C_t}{(1+r)^t}, t = 1, 2, \ldots, n.$$

Likewise, the expression for future value at time $t = n$ is given by

$$FV_n = \sum_{t=1}^{n} C_t (1+r)^{n-t}, t = 1, 2, \ldots, n.$$

Some observations from these expressions are immediately apparent. They are very similar to the ones we made in the one- and two-period cases in the previous chapter. These observations, assuming r is greater than zero, are:

a. PV is always less than FV.
b. $\frac{1}{(1+r)^n}$ is always less than one, and $\frac{1}{(1+r)^1} > \frac{1}{(1+r)^2} > \frac{1}{(1+r)^3} > \ldots > \frac{1}{(1+r)^n}$
c. $(1+r)^n$ is always greater than one, and $(1+r)^1 < (1+r)^2 < (1+r)^3 < \cdots < (1+r)^n$

d. Because $\dfrac{1}{(1+r)^n}$ is always less than one and decreases as n increases, we can say that we put a lower weight on the cash flow that occurs later. Additionally, because $(1+r)^n$ is always greater than 1 and increases as n increases, we can also say that the further out a cash flow occurs, the lower is the weight that we assign to it.

Although the above observations are important and you should know them, understand them, and remember them well, you do not really need to memorize all the equations unless you want to do long time-value problems in the most tedious manner possible. You could if you wanted to. However, in the remaining part of this chapter, we will consider several short cuts, one of the major ones being the use of a financial calculator. The purpose of introducing these equations was to convey that what we will study in this chapter is conceptually very similar to that in the previous chapter.

Now try the following problems. These require you to circle the correct answer and do not require any calculations. You should be able to do them using the concepts that we have covered so far. Circle your choice and then read below each set of answer choices to see if your answers are correct (and why).

Problem 5.1: Suppose that an asset generates cash flows of $100, $200, and $300 at the end of years one, two, and three, respectively. If the discount rate is zero, of the following answers, which is the only one that can be correct?

   a. The PV = $600 and FV at t = 3 ($FV_3$) equals $600.

   b. PV < $600, FV_3 > $600.

   c. PV = $481.59, FV_3 = $641.00.

Because the discount rate is zero, the present value and the future value is simply the sum of the cash flows. Therefore, answer (a) is the correct one.

Problem 5.2: Suppose that an asset generates cash flows of $100, $200, and $300 at the end of years one, two, and three, respectively. If the discount rate is 10%, which of the following answers is the only one that can be correct?

   a. The PV = $600, FV_3 = $600.

   b. PV = $600, FV_3 = $600.

   c. PV = $481.59, FV_3 = $641.00.

Which answer did you circle? Clearly now that the discount rate is greater than zero, (a) is incorrect. What about (b)? Were you tempted to say it is correct? It is, however, not correct. Because the discount rate is greater than zero, the present value is strictly less than, not less than or equal to as in the answer, the sum of cash flows, and FV_3 > $600 and not = $600. In answer (c), the values of PV and FV_3 are as they should be and, therefore, it can be the only correct answer.

Problem 5.3: Suppose that the discount rate is 10%. Asset A generates cash flows of $100, $200, and $300 at the end of the first three years, respectively. Asset B generates cash flows of $300, $200, and $100 at the end of the first three years, respectively. Which is the only one of the following statements that is correct?

a. $PV_A > PV_B$ and $FV_A > FV_B$.
b. $PV_A < PV_B$ and $FV_A > FV_B$.
c. $PV_A > PV_B$ and $FV_A < FV_B$.
d. $PV_A < PV_B$ and $FV_A < FV_B$.

Choosing the correct answer is little tricky here. Let us first consider the present values of the two assets. If the discount rate were zero, the present values of the two assets would be the same, that is, $600. However, the discount rate is not zero. In that case, the asset that generates the higher cash flows sooner should have the higher PV. Why? Because we know that

$$\frac{1}{(1+r)} > \frac{1}{(1+r)^2} > \frac{1}{(1+r)^3}.$$

In other words, the PV of $300 received at $t = 1$ is greater than the PV of $300 received at $t = 3$. Thus asset B should have the higher PV or $PV_A < PV_B$. Once we know this, answers (a) and (c) can be ruled out. Next consider the case of the future values of the two assets. The $300 received at $t = 1$ will have a greater FV at $t = 3$ than $300 received at $t = 3$. The former will be compounded by a factor of $(1 + r)^2$ and the latter by $(1 + r)^0$ (which equals 1). Thus, again the asset that generates the higher cash flows sooner will have the higher future value; that is, $FV_A < FV_B$. Thus, the only correct answer is (d).

Let us actually calculate the present and future values of the two assets A and B.

$$PV_A = \frac{100}{1.1} + \frac{200}{(1.1)^2} + \frac{300}{(1.1)^3} = \$481.59$$

$$FV_A = 100(1.1)^2 + 200(1.1) + 300 = \$641.00$$

$$PV_B = \frac{300}{1.1} + \frac{200}{(1.1)^2} + \frac{100}{(1.1)^3} = \$513.15$$

$$FV_B = 300(1.1)^2 + 200(1.1) + 100 = \$683.00$$

These answers confirm our answer to Problem 5.3. In addition, notice the following:

$$PV_A (1.1)^3 = \$481.59 \,(1.1)^3 = \$641.00 = FV_A, \text{ and}$$
$$PV_B (1.1)^3 = \$513.15 \,(1.1)^3 = \$683.00 = FV_B.$$

The above calculations point out another relation worth remembering. As long as the same (positive) discount rate is used for both the assets, and the assets generate cash flows for the same number of periods, the asset that has the higher present value will also have the higher future value at the end of the last period. Think about this. Does this statement seem intuitive? As long as discount (interest) rates are the same, anything that has more value today will be more valuable also in the future.

5.3 The Present Value of a Perpetuity

In the preceding section, we considered the general case when the cash flows occur over n periods. Here, we want to consider the very special and very important case when n is infinity (usually denoted by ∞) and the cash flows are the same in each period. In other words, what would be the present value of a stream of equal cash flows (C) that occur at the end of each period and go on forever? This special stream of cash flows is called a *perpetuity*. We can always write the general equation for this as follows:

$$\text{PV (perpetuity)} = \sum_{t=1}^{\infty} \frac{C}{(1+r)^t}.$$

The above equation seems impossible to solve and, consequently, useless. However, our friends (?) in mathematics have made life very simple for us. They have *proved* that the above summation *exactly* equals a very simple expression and, therefore, we have the following:

$$\text{PV (perpetuity)} = \frac{C}{r}.$$

Do you think this expression is still of any use? Are there any assets that generate equal cash flows forever? It turns out that there are. For example, in the United Kingdom, there are some bonds that have no maturity (that is, maturity is infinity) and pay a fixed coupon every period. You can see that the cash flows from owning this bond are exactly described by a perpetuity. Additionally, we will use this expression several times in the future for valuing stocks and annuities.

Let us consider an example of an asset that generates a cash flow of $1,000 per year forever, in other words, a perpetuity of $1,000. If the discount rate is 8%, the present value of this perpetuity will be

$$\text{PV (perpetuity)} = \frac{1{,}000}{0.08} = \$12{,}500.$$

Now do the following simple problems in the space provided

Problem 5.4: Suppose the value of a perpetuity is $38,900 and the discount rate is 12% p.a. What must be the annual cash flow from this perpetuity?

Problem 5.5: An asset that generates $890 per year forever is priced at $6,000. What is the required rate of return?

Problem 5.6: What is the present value today (i.e., in year 0) of a perpetuity of $1250 per year, but the first cash flow in the perpetuity begins in year 5 (that is, the perpetuity pays $0 in years 1, 2, 3, and 4 and then pays $1250 in years 5, 6, 7, 8, . . ., infinity)? The interest rate for the account is 4.25%.

5.4 The Present Value and Future Value of an Annuity

In the previous section, we considered a cash flow stream where a fixed amount was received every year forever. An *annuity* is a cash flow stream where a fixed amount is received every year (period) for a fixed number of years or periods. Examples of this should be quite easy to conceive. For example, if you rent out a property at a rent of $12,000 per year for 10 years, then you are going to receive a 10-year annuity of $12,000. Likewise, a 60-month car payment is an annuity, where the periods are months instead of years.

A little later in this chapter we are going to start using a financial calculator, which will make finding the present value and future value of an annuity very simple. However, let us first look at an annuity in a conceptual framework. We can find the present value of an annuity using three of the concepts we have studied so far: (i) present value of a single future cash flow, (ii) the present value of a perpetuity, and (iii) value additivity.

Consider an asset A that generates cash flows that are a perpetuity of $100 per year and let the discount rate be 10%. The time line for this is as below:

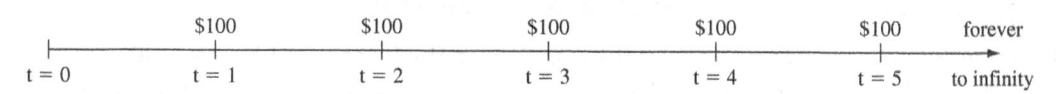

```
                $100      $100      $100      $100      $100    forever
    ├─────────┼─────────┼─────────┼─────────┼─────────┼─────────→
    t = 0     t = 1     t = 2     t = 3     t = 4     t = 5    to infinity
```

Then the present value of this asset is:

$$PV_A = \frac{100}{0.1} = \$1{,}000.$$

Now consider another asset B that also generates a perpetual cash flow of $100 per year except that the first cash flow occurs at t = 4, that is, at the end of year 4. There are no cash flows at the end of the first three years. Let us draw the time line as below for this asset:

```
                 0         0         0        $100      $100    forever
    ├─────────┼─────────┼─────────┼─────────┼─────────┼─────────→
    t = 0     t = 1     t = 2     t = 3     t = 4     t = 5    to infinity
```

What is the present value of this stream of cash flows? Note that from t = 4 onwards, the cash flow stream is a perpetuity. Therefore, we can find the value of this perpetuity at t = 3 by using the formula for the present value of a perpetuity as follows:

$$PV_3 = \frac{100}{0.1} = \$1{,}000.$$

Time Value of Money: Advanced Topics 119

We are, however, interested in finding out the value of this stream at t = 0. We know that the value of this stream at t = 3 is $1,000. Therefore, the value of this stream at t = 0 must be the present value of the $1,000 at t = 3. That is,

$$PV_B = \frac{1,000}{(1.1)^3} = \$751.31.$$

Now suppose that you buy asset A. You will receive the cash flows from this asset which are $100 per year forever with the first cash flow received at t = 1. In addition, now suppose that you sell asset B. In other words, to the person who buys asset B from you, you will have to pay $100 per year forever with the first payment of $100 to be made to the buyer at t = 4.

Let us look at the cash flows that result to you from these transactions.

	t =1	t = 2	t = 3	t = 4	t = 5	each future period
Buying Asset A	$100	$100	$100	$100	$100	$100
Selling Asset B	$ 0	$ 0	$ 0	–$100	–$100	–$100
Total	$100	$100	$100	$ 0	$ 0	$ 0

The last row gives the net cash flow to you from these transactions and the entries in the row are simply the sums of the entries in the two rows above it.

How would you describe the cash flow stream in the last row of the table above? It is an annuity of $100 per year for three years. What would be the present value of this annuity? Recall the principle of value additivity. Because this annuity is obtained by subtracting the cash flows of perpetuity B from those of perpetuity A, the value of this annuity must be the difference between the present values of perpetuities A and B. That is,

$$PV \text{ (annuity of \$100 per year for 3 years)} = PV_A - PV_B$$
$$= \$1,000 - \$751.31 = \$248.69.$$

Let us check if the answer is correct. We can do this as follows:

$$PV = \frac{100}{1.1} + \frac{100}{(1.1)^2} + \frac{100}{(1.1)^3} = \$248.69.$$

Thus, we have discovered a method for computing the present value of an annuity. The present value of an annuity of $C per year for n years equals the difference between the present values of two perpetuities, one that begins paying $C per year from t = 1 and another that begins paying $C per year from t = n + 1.

This gives the following formula:

$$\text{PV (annuity of \$C per year for n years)} = \frac{C}{r} - \frac{C}{r} \times \frac{1}{(1+r)^n}.$$

In the above, the first term on the right-hand side is the present value of the perpetuity that begins at t = 1, and the second is the present (t = 0) value of the perpetuity that begins at t = 4. By rearranging terms, we can express the above formula also the following way

The expression $\frac{1}{r}[1 - \frac{1}{(1+r)^n}]$ is called the present value interest factor of annuity, denoted as:

$$PVIF(r,n) = \frac{1}{r}[1 - \frac{1}{(1+r)^n}]$$

It measures the present value of one dollar received at the end of each period for n period. For example, with an interest rate of 10%, the three-year annuity present value interest factor is:

$$PVIFA(10\%,3) = \frac{1}{0.1}[1 - \frac{1}{(1+0.1)^3}] = 2.4869$$

It means that each dollar received at the end of each year for three year is worth $2.4869 today, and then the present value of your payment of $100 per year for three years must be:

$$PVA(10\%,3) = 100 \times PVIFA(10\%,3) = 100 \times 2.4869 = 248.69$$

What if you save each $100 you received at the end of the year? How much would you accumulate at the end of the third year assuming you can earn 10% annual interest rate? That is the future annuity value. Since we already figured out that the today's equivalent value (present value) of this three-year annuity is $PVA(10\%,3) = 248.69$, the future value of this annuity can be found by multiplying 248.69 by the three-year future value interest factor $FVIF(10\%,3) = 1.331$, which is 331.00. The general formula for the future value of an annuity of $C per year for n years equals the present value of the same annuity times the future value interest factor, that is:

$$FVA(r,n) = PVA(r,n) \times FVIF(r,n) = C\frac{1}{r}[1 - \frac{1}{(1+r)^n}](1+r)^n = C[\frac{(1+r)^n}{r} - \frac{1}{r}]$$

The expression $\frac{(1+r)^n}{r} - \frac{1}{r}$ is called future value interest factor of annuity, denoted as:

$$FVIFA(r,n) = \frac{(1+r)^n}{r} - \frac{1}{r}$$

It measures the future value of one dollar annuity. For example, with an interest rate of 10%, the three-year annuity future value interest factor is:

$$FVIFA(10\%,3) = \frac{(1+0.1)^3}{0.1} - \frac{1}{0.1} = 3.310$$

It means that each dollar saved at the end of each year for three years will accumulate to $3.31 after three years, and then the future value of your saving of $100 per year for three years must be:

$$FVA(10\%,3) = 100 \times FVIFA(10\%,3) = 100 \times 3.310 = 331.0$$

Again, we introduced these formula only to provide an intuitive understanding of how the present value and future value of an annuity are computed. Shortly, we will simply be punching buttons on a financial calculator. However, to cement this understanding, solve the following problems to see if you can obtain the given answer.

Problem 5.7: What is the future value of a three-year annuity of $700 per year? The interest rate is 8% p.a.

Problem 5.8: What is the present value of an annuity of $1,800 per year for four years? The discount rate is 12% p. a.

Problem 5.9: You want to replicate the cash flow streams from a four-year annuity of $3,000 per year. Show how two perpetuities will allow you to do this as we did earlier, in a table.

Problem 5.10: You decide to invest in two investments A and B. The cash flows from these two investments are as follows:

	t = 1	t = 2	t = 3	t = 4
Inv. A	$475	$381	$533	$291
Inv. B	$325	$419	$267	$509

What is the present value of your total investment if the required rate of return is 11%?

How did you do this problem? One method is the long way where you find the present value of each of the investments and then sum the two present values. The other is the shorter way. Notice that if you sum the cash flows from the two investments in each year, you will obtain $800 every year. Then the solution is to find the present value of a four-year $800 annuity.

Problem 5.11: Bill plans to fund his individual retirement account (IRA) with the maximum contribution of $2,000 at the end of each year for the next 20 years. If Bill can earn 12% on his contributions, how much will he have at the end of the twentieth year?

5.5 Time Value Calculations with a Financial Calculator

Several excellent financial calculators are available. All of them are basically the same in how they process calculations. There are, however, some differences in the operating procedures. Throughout the remainder of the book we will describe procedures and solutions using the **hp 10BII**. The hp 10BII is one of the most economical calculators that we know of on the market, and it is available at all retail office stores as well as at all major discount department stores.

You do not have to use the financial calculator in finance. In fact, any calculator that can compute present and future values of lump sums, annuities, and uneven cash flows will work. If you are using a different financial calculator, you can still work through this material as long as you know/learn the basic operations of your model on your own.

Note that this section of the book is meant to be an introduction to some of the uses of this very powerful machine. We strongly urge you to study the manual that comes with the calculator to derive the full benefit of owning this instrument. We are sure that as you work through the problems in this chapter, you will soon realize that more likely than not, you will continue using this calculator after the course ends—even if this is the only finance class you ever take. Kaito would have saved himself from major embarrassment if he had learned how to use a financial calculator when he was in school.

5.5.1 The Basics

Courtesy of Guan Jun Wang

Study the keys on the calculator. You will notice buttons that correspond with variables we have been using up to this time. Specifically, in the first row, PV, FV, and N. The I/YR key is the interest rate, but as a percent instead of a decimal. So, where we used r above, the financial calculator uses (r)(100) = percent. The PMT key stands for a series of payments in an annuity. If you enter PMT = 800 and N = 4, you can find the PV of an annuity of 800 per year for four years.

Most of the keys have notation on the key and below it. For example, the 'N' key has 'xP/YR' written below it. To access the function written below the key, first press the shift key (orange color), later will be referred to 2nd key.

Let us first set the calculator.

1. Press '2nd' and [DISP]. The screen will display the number of decimal places that the calculator will display. If it is not four, press '4.' We will round most problems to cents (i.e., 2 decimals), but for intermediate calculations, your final answers will be more precise if you use numbers rounded to at least 4 decimal places.

2. Press '2nd' and then press [[C ALL] key,]. If the display does not show one, press '1 and 2nd' and then [P/Y]. As a rule, we want to ensure that this number is **always** one. This says that the frequency of payment is once per time period. A time period will most often be a year, but it can also be a half year, month, day or other. Many times, the cause of your not obtaining the correct answer is that the [P/Y] is set at something other than one. So, if you start getting incorrect answers on your calculator, check the [P/Y] setting.

3. Press '2nd' and [BGN]. If the display is not END, that is, if it says BGN, press '2nd' and then [BEG/END, and delete next sentence.]. The display will read END. This tells the

calculator to assume that all the payments are at the end of the period. This is something that we have always assumed thus far. In case payments occur at the beginning of the period, this setting may be changed, or we can just rethink of beginning year cash flows as occurring at the end of the prior year. We will discuss this process more below. For now, set it at END.

Now that the basic setting is done, before you can start using the calculator to do TVM problems, you MUST learn how to properly clear TVM memory to clear TVM memory, press '2nd' and [C ALL].

5.6 Present and Future Values of Single Cash Flows

Example Problem: What is the present value of receiving $6,000 exactly 6 years from today assuming a discount rate is 14%?

After you clear TVM memory, do the following:

a. Type 6,000 and then press 'FV.'
b. Type 6 and then press 'N.'
c. Type 14 and then press 'I/YR.'
d. Finally, press 'PV.'

If you did everything correctly, your calculator should display:

$$PV = -2{,}733.5193$$

So, the correct answer is $2,733.52.

You might wonder about the minus sign before the number. The reason this happens is because financial calculators are programmed to solve the equation:

$$PV + \frac{FV_n}{(1+r)^n} = 0$$

With the values we entered above, the calculator is just telling us that:

$$-2733.5193 + \frac{6000}{(1+r)^n} = 0$$

Which is correct? So, if the future value is entered as a positive number, the present value will appear as a negative number. As a rule, we usually assume that any amount you receive should be positive, and any amount that leaves your pocket should be negative. Thus, to receive $6,000 at t = 6 you need to spend $2,733.52 at t = 0. Or, receive $2,733.52 at t = 0 and pay $6,000 at t = 6. If you want to convert a number from positive to negative or the other way round, use the key '+/−' on the calculator.

Example Problem: Suppose you deposit $150 in an account today and the interest rate is 6% p.a. How much will you have in the account exactly 33 years from today, or at the end of year 33?

After you clear TVM memory, do the following:

a. Type '–' 150, then press 'PV' then press '+/–' to convert this.
b. Type 33 then press 'N.'
c. Type 6 then press 'I/YR.'
d. Press 'FV.'

If you did everything correctly, your calculator should display:

$$FV = \$1{,}026.09$$

Note that the order of entering input values does not matter at all. If you go back and redo the prior two problems reordering a, b, and c, you will get the same final answer.

Now that you are familiar with how to enter values, in the following problems, we will simply give you the values for each of the keys. A question mark, '?,' after a key means that is the value to be computed.

Example Problem: You deposited $15,000 in an account 22 years ago and now the account has $50,000 in it. What was the annual rate of return that you received on this investment?

$$PV = -15{,}000, \; N = 22, \; FV = 50{,}000, \; I/YR = ?$$

You should get I/YR = 5.625%.

Example Problem: You currently have $38,000 in an account that has been paying 5.75% p.a. You remember that you had opened this account quite some years ago with an initial deposit of $19,000. You forget when the initial deposit was made. How many years (in fractions) ago did you make the initial deposit?

$$PV = -19{,}000, \; FV = 38{,}000, \; I/Y = 5.75, \; N = ?$$

You should find that N = 12.398 years.

For these last two problems, if you saw the following message on your calculator: **no solution** this means that you did not enter PV as a negative value. If PV and FV are positive, for any given N, there is no (positive) I/YR, and for any given I/YR, there is no N, that will make:

$$PV + \frac{FV_n}{(1+r)^n} = 0$$

So, if you ever see no solution displayed on your calculator, redo the problem with PV (or FV) as a negative.

As you can see, the financial calculator makes TVM calculations quite simple. Now try the following problems in the space provided.

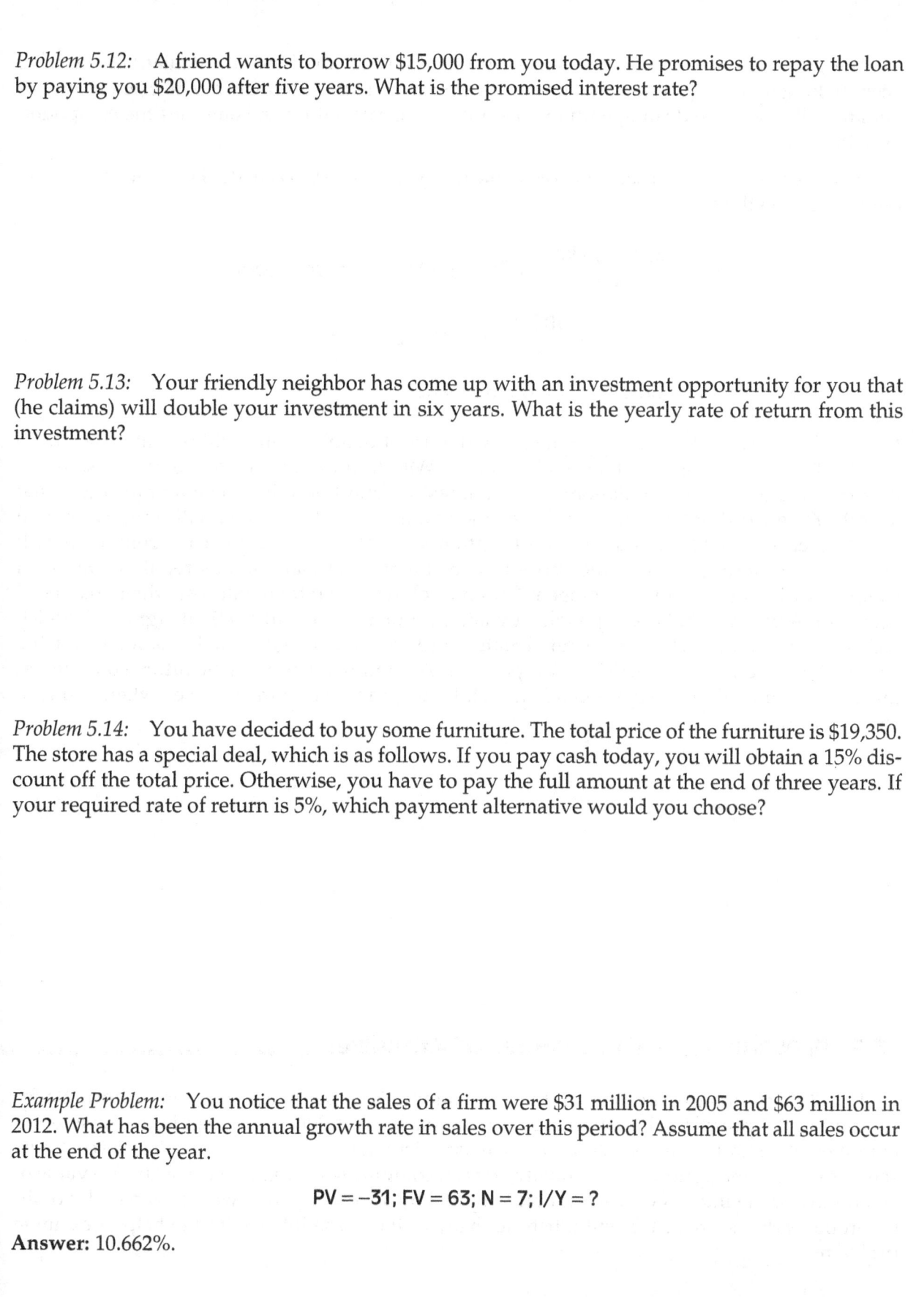

Problem 5.12: A friend wants to borrow $15,000 from you today. He promises to repay the loan by paying you $20,000 after five years. What is the promised interest rate?

Problem 5.13: Your friendly neighbor has come up with an investment opportunity for you that (he claims) will double your investment in six years. What is the yearly rate of return from this investment?

Problem 5.14: You have decided to buy some furniture. The total price of the furniture is $19,350. The store has a special deal, which is as follows. If you pay cash today, you will obtain a 15% discount off the total price. Otherwise, you have to pay the full amount at the end of three years. If your required rate of return is 5%, which payment alternative would you choose?

Example Problem: You notice that the sales of a firm were $31 million in 2005 and $63 million in 2012. What has been the annual growth rate in sales over this period? Assume that all sales occur at the end of the year.

$$PV = -31; FV = 63; N = 7; I/Y = ?$$

Answer: 10.662%.

The purpose of the above problem is to illustrate that the kind of calculations we have been making in solving time value problems are not restricted to finance. The calculator does not know that you are dealing with interest rates. The calculator just computes the compound growth rate.

A *common mistake* that some people make (not you, of course) is to do the following in computing the growth rate

$$\frac{\$63m - \$31m}{31m} = 1.032 \text{ or } 103.2\% \text{ in seven years}$$

$$\text{or } \frac{103.2}{7} = 14.743\% \text{ per year.}$$

This is *incorrect*. It ignores the compounding effect.

Problem 5.15: Recall from the opening story that most people seem to think that if they have $1,000,000 when they retire, they will be okay. We all know that prices tend to rise every year (i.e., there is positive inflation), so an interesting question might be how much will that $1,000,000 be worth when you retire? Assume you are now 25 and you will retire when you turn 65 (i.e., 40 years from today). To conceptualize what $1,000,000 40 years from today will buy in today's terms, consider the current price of a product that you buy regularly and then compute (using the historical average inflation rate), what that item will cost when you are 65 years old. A product that many people buy fairly regularly is a Starbuck Latte (grande), which has a current average price in the United States of $3.65. The average annual inflation rate in the United States from 1913 to 2013 is 3.22% per year. Assuming inflation in the future continues at this average annual rate, what will a Starbuck Latte (grande) cost in 2053 (i.e., when you turn 65 years old)?

5.7 Present and Future Values of Annuities

Recall that when we did some problems on annuities earlier where we used the formula for computing the present value of an annuity, we made the calculations simple by considering annuities of just a few years. With the financial calculator, we no longer need to restrict ourselves to short time periods. Additionally, we can compute some things, such as future value of an annuity or the interest or discount rate implied by an annuity, that we (conveniently) omitted in the earlier section. We will illustrate many of the possibilities with the help of example problems.

5.7.1 Annual Annuities

Example Problem: Suppose an investment promises to yield annual cash flows of $13,000 per year for 11 years, with the first cash flow occurring exactly one year from today. If your required rate of return is 13%, what is the maximum price that you would be willing to pay for this investment?

The maximum price that you would be willing to pay is the present value of this annuity using your required rate of return as the discount rate. To compute the PV, do the following on your calculator.

$$N = 11, I/YR = 13, PMT = 13,000, PV = ?$$

Answer: $73,930.23

The fixed cash flow from the annuity is entered as the PMT. Also, you will notice that the PV displayed has a minus sign. The reason for the negative value is for the same as we discussed earlier.

Example Problem: An asset promises the following stream of cash flows. It will pay you $80 per year for 20 years (first cash flow to occur one year from today) and, in addition, at the end of the twentieth year, you will be paid $1,000. If your required rate of return is 9%, what is the maximum price that you would pay for this asset?

Again you have to find the PV of all these cash flows. With the calculator, enter the following:

$$N = 20, PMT = 80, FV = 1,000, I/Y = 9, PV = ?$$

Answer: $908.71

The only difference between this and the previous problem is the entry for FV. If you draw the time line for the above problem, you will see why 1000 is entered as the FV. By the way, you have just found the price of an 8% fixed-coupon bond with 20 years to maturity when the market interest rates are 9%. We will do bond valuation in greater detail later.

Example Problem: You have $1,000,000 that you want to use for the first 15 years of your retirement. You need equal yearly withdrawals at the end of each year (that is, the first withdrawal will be one year from today), and at the end of the 15 years, you do not want any of the original amount left over. You could deposit the money in the bank today at 9% p.a. and make 15 equal yearly withdrawals. A retirement planner offers the following alternative. Buy an annuity of $125,000 per year for 15 years with the $1,000,000. Which alternative would you choose?

You can look at this problem in two different ways.

  a. Find the equal withdrawals that you can make from the bank account and compare them to the annuity of $125,000. To do this:

$$N = 15, PV = -1,000,000, I/YR = 9, PMT = ?$$

PMT = $124,058.88 per year for 15 years

Since this is lower than that promised in the annuity, choose the annuity.

b. Find the interest rate of the annuity and compare it to the bank's 9%. That is:

$$N = 15, PV = -1{,}000{,}000, PMT = 125{,}000, I/YR = ?$$

$$I/YR = 9.128 \text{ percent p.a.}$$

Answer: This is more than the 9% offered by the bank, so choose the annuity.

Example Problem: You plan to retire 40 years from today. After retirement, you expect that you will need $250,000 per year for 20 years with the first amount required at the end of the forty-first year. You want to start saving for retirement and plan to make 40 equal yearly deposits into your retirement account, which yields 8% p.a. The first payment into this account will be exactly one year from today. What should these equal payments be to satisfy your retirement needs?

Let X be the amount that you deposit (i.e., going out of your pocket) each year, and you have to determine what it should be. For this problem, we will create a cash flow table (this is the same concept as a time line but just in a different format—we suggest you use whatever format makes the most sense to you).

Year	Cash Flow
0	0
1	-X
2	-X
.	.
.	.
.	.
39	-X
40	-X
41	250,000
42	250,000
.	.
.	.
.	.
60	250,000

From the cash flow table, it is clear that there are two annuities, one of $X per year for 40 years beginning at t = 1 and the second of $250,000 per year for 20 years, beginning at t = 41. The first one you pay in and the second one you receive. The interest rate for the entire period is 8% p.a. The logic is that the initial $X annuity should exactly pay for the later $250,000 annuity. This would be true if the present values of the second annuity at t = 40 is equal to the future value of the first annuity at t = 40.

Let us first determine the PV of the second annuity at t = 40. To determine the PV at t = 40, on the calculator enter

$$N = 20, PMT = 250{,}000, I/YR = 8, PV = ?$$

$$PV_{40} = \$2{,}454{,}536.85$$

Now you want to find the annuity payment that has a future value of $2,454,536.85. Thus, on your calculator, enter

$$FV = 2{,}454{,}536.85, N = 40, I/YR = 8, PMT = ?$$

Answer: $9,474.91 per year for 40 years.

In the above problem, notice how the solution became apparent after the cash flow chart (or time line) is created.

Your calculator also allows you to find present values of unequal cash flows in one operation. You can have each of the cash flows occur consecutively several times. The use of this operation is illustrated in the following example.

5.7.2 Non-Annual Cash Flows

All of the problems we have done so far have assumed *annual* cash flows. What if the cash flows are monthly? Or daily? Or semi-annually? These are just a simple extension of what we learned above. The best way to compute problems like these (for example, determining a monthly car loan payment) is to input the interest rate as a per time period rate (to do this, just divide the rate by the number of cash flows per year) and let N be the total number of cash flows. Then do the problems just like we did for annual cash flows.

Example Problem: Assuming that the cost of the BMW (i.e., $78,950) was the amount that Kaito borrowed, at an interest rate of 5.5% p.a., what is the required monthly payment on a 5-year loan?

The total number of payments on the loan will be (5 years)(12 payments per year) = 60 payments. The monthly interest rate on the loan is 5.5/12 = 0.4583333. The amount borrowed in the present value and we need to compute the payment (i.e. PMT). Thus, enter:

$$PV = 78950, N = 60, I/YR = 5.5/12 =, PMT\ ?$$

To get the most accurate answer possible, after you press the '=' key for 5.5/12, immediately press the I/YR key. That is, do **NOT** retype the number on your screen. Depending on the number of decimals your screen displays, if you retype the value you see, you will be cutting off important parts of the interest rate. Over long periods of time, rounding the interest rate can result in answers that are many dollars off from the precise answer. If you press I/YR immediately after you press the '=' key, the number that will be input for your calculation is correct to the sixteenth decimal place (very precise!).

Answer: $1508.04

Example Problem: Assuming that Kaito can only afford $300 per month, at an interest rate of 5.5% p.a. and a 5-year (monthly payment) loan, how much can Kaito afford to borrow?

$$PMT = 300, N = 60, I/YR = 5.5/12 = PV\ ?$$

Answer: $15,705.85

Problem 5.16: Devin and Corey are considering buying a new home. The house they want to buy will require them to borrow $250,000. They can either take out a 30-year, monthly payment loan with an interest rate of 3.45% p.a. or a 15-year, monthly payment loan with an interest rate of 2.95% p.a.

   a. What is the required monthly payment on the 30-year loan? If Devin and Corey make all 360 payments, what is the total amount of money that they will pay for their home?

   b. What is the required monthly payment on the 15-year loan? If Devin and Corey make all 180 payments, what is the total amount of money that they will pay for their home?

Problem 5.17: Walther Buthard just turned 10 years old and his parents have decided to start paying him an allowance of $3 per day for doing chores. Motivated by a TV program he recently saw concerning the importance of starting early to save for retirement, Walther has decided that he will invest $1.50 of his allowance every day between now and when he turns 65 years old. All money will be deposited into a stock market mutual fund. Assuming that Walther does in fact deposit $1.50 per day, every day, between now and the day he turns 65 years old (i.e., assume 365 days per year and ignore leap years, so he will make 20,075 deposits in all) into his retirement account, and assuming his fund generates an average annual total return of 11.5% p.a., how much money will Walther have on his 65th birthday?

Problem 5.18: Charlene just bought her dream car, a 2016 Porsche Carrera GTS Cabriolet that cost $125,000. She paid $15,000 down and financed the balance over 72 months at 6.25% p.a. (Assume that Charlene makes all required payments are made on time.)

   a. What is the monthly payment on Charlene's loan?

   b. What will be the balance on Charlene's loan at the end of the second year (that is, immediately after Charlene makes her 24th payment on the loan)? Note that the payoff on a loan is equal to the present value of all remaining payments.

5.8 Special Topics in Time Value

There are a few "bells and whistles" kind of concepts left for us to consider in this chapter on the time value of money. These are as follows. First, thus far, we have assumed that interest is paid once a year or that discounting or compounding is performed once every year. We will now consider what happens when interest rates are compounded at a frequency of more than once a year. Second, we will also consider the special case when compounding and discounting are continuous. Next, we have thus far assumed that cash flows of annuities occur at the end of the period, we will now compute present and future values of annuities that are paid at the beginning of each period. Finally, we will analyze amortization.

5.8.1 Compounding Period Is Less Than One Year

The effect of increasing the frequency of compounding to more than once per year is best illustrated with the following numerical example. Suppose that your bank "states" that the interest on the account is 8% p.a. However, interest is paid semi-annually, that is every six months. The 8% is called the *stated interest* rate. However, the bank will pay you 4% interest (8% divided by two because the interest is paid semi-annually) every six months. In other words, the compounding frequency is two.

Suppose you deposit $100 into this account today. At the end of six months, your account balance will be:

$$\$100 \times (1.04) = \$104.$$

At the end of the year, the balance will be:

$$\$104 \times (1.04) = \$108.16.$$

If the interest had been paid once a year, the account balance at the end of the year would have been:

$$\$100 \times (1.08) = \$108.$$

Thus, with semiannual compounding, you effectively obtain more than the stated interest. So, "effectively" you have earned annual interest of:

$$\frac{\$108.16 - \$100}{\$100} = 0.0816 \text{ or } 8.16\%.$$

Viewed another way, your account balance at the end of the year will be:

$$\$100 \times (1.04)^2 = \$108.16,$$

and the *effective annual rate* (EAR) is:

$$(1.04)^2 - 1 = 0.0816 \text{ or } 8.16\%.$$

If the interest had been paid quarterly, you would have received $\frac{8}{4} = 2\%$ interest every quarter. In this case, your end-of-year account balance would be:

$$\$100 \times (1.02)^4 = \$108.2432,$$

and the effective interest rate would be:

$$(1.02)^4 - 1 = 0.082432 \text{ or } 8.2432 \text{ percent.}$$

In general, let "n" be the number of years, "m" be the frequency of compounding every year, and let "r" be the stated interest rate, then:

Effective annual rate (EAR) = $[(1 + r/m)^m] - 1$

Example Problem: What is the effective annual rate for an account that pays 4.25% p.a., with monthly compounding?

$$EAR = [(1 + .0425/12)^{12}] - 1$$
$$= 1.0433 - 1$$
$$= .0433 = 4.33\%$$

Answer: 4.33%

Example Problem: Assume you deposit $10,000 into an account today. If the account pays 8% p.a., with quarterly compounding, how much will you have in your account five years from today?

Here, the number of compounding periods = 5 × 4 = 20 and the rate per quarter = 08/4 = .02. Thus, you will "effectively" earn 2% per time period for a total of 20 time periods. Therefore, the account balance at the end of five years would be:

$$\$100 \times (1.02)^{20} = \$148.59.$$

You could compute this on the financial calculator as follows:

$$N = 20, PV = -100, I/YR = 2, FV = ?$$

Answer: FV = $148.59.

Problem 5.19: Your bank's stated interest rate on a three-month certificate of deposit is 4.68% p.a. What is the effective annual rate on this account?

Problem 5.20: You have decided to buy a car for $45,000. The dealer offers to finance the entire amount and requires 60 monthly payments of $950 per month. What are the yearly stated and effective annual interest rates for this financing?

5.8.2 Annuities Valuation with Payments at the Beginning of the Period

Consider an *ordinary* annuity of $300 per year for three years. An ordinary annuity is one where all of the cash flows are received at the end of the year (what we have assumed for all problems we have used in this chapter so far). When payments are made at the end of the period, the cash flow chart for a three year ordinary annuity is as below:

Year	Cash Flow
0	0
1	$300
2	$300
3	$300

Let us compute the present and future (at t = 3) values of this annuity the long way. Assume that the discount rate is 10% p.a.:

$$PV = \frac{300}{1.1} + \frac{300}{(1.1)^2} + \frac{300}{(1.1)^3} = \$746.06, \text{ and}$$

$$FV_3 = 300\,(1.1)^2 + 300\,(1.1) + 300 = \$993.$$

Now suppose that the annuity makes payments at the beginning of the period (this type of annuity is known as an *annuity due*). When payments are made at the beginning of the period (remember that the beginning of year n = the end of year n−1), the cash flow chart for a three-year ordinary annuity is as below:

Year	Cash Flow
0	$300
1	$300
2	$300
3	$0

Let us compute the present and future (at t = 3) values of this annuity the long way.

$$PV = 300 + \frac{300}{1.1} + \frac{300}{(1.1)^2} = \$820.66, \text{ and}$$

$$FV_3 = 300\,(1.1)^3 + 300\,(1.1)^2 + 300\,(1.1) = \$1{,}092.30.$$

Compare the expressions for PV and FV of the two annuities. Notice that if you multiply the right-hand side expression for the PV of the regular annuity, you obtain the expression for the present value of the annuity due. Similarly, multiplying the FV expression of the regular annuity yields the expression for the FV of the annuity due. In general:

$$PV(\text{annuity due}) = PV\,(\text{regular annuity}) \times (1 + r), \text{ and}$$

$$FV_n(\text{annuity due}) = FV_n\,(\text{regular annuity}) \times (1 + r).$$

Notice that this is true of the values that we have calculated.

Now attempt the following problem.

Problem 5.21: You have a rental property that you want to rent for 10 years. Prospective tenant A promises to pay you a rent of $12,000 per year with the payments made at the end of each year. Prospective tenant B promises to pay $12,000 per year with payments made at the beginning of each year. Which is a better deal for you if the going discount rate is 10%?

5.8.3 Loan Amortization

Assume that you borrow $10,000 at 10% and plan to repay it in five equal yearly installments. Your yearly repayment will be computed as

$$N = 5, \quad PV = 10{,}000, \quad I/YR = 10, \quad PMT = \$2{,}637.97.$$

In other words, you will pay $2,637.97 at the end of each of the next five years.

Every time you make a payment on a loan, part of your payment goes to principal and part goes to interest. At $t = 0$, your loan balance or principal is $10,000. At $t = 1$, just before you make your first payment, you have had a loan of $10,000 for one year. Given an interest rate of 10%, you need to pay interest of

$$\$10{,}000 \times 0.10 = \$1{,}000.$$

Thus, from your $t = 1$ payment of $2,637.97, $1,000 goes toward interest and the rest

$$\$2{,}637.97 - \$1{,}000 = \$1{,}637.97$$

goes to reduce your outstanding loan balance (i.e., goes toward principal). Therefore, just after your $t = 1$ payment, your principal balance is

$$\$10{,}000 - \$1{,}637.97 = \$8{,}362.03.$$

Then, from your $t = 2$ payment of $2,637.97,

$$\$8{,}362.03 \times 0.10 = \$836.20$$

goes toward interest and

$$\$2{,}637.97 - \$836.20 = \$1{,}801.77$$

goes toward principal.

This process is known as loan amortization and the entire *amortization schedule* for this loan is presented in the table below:

Year	Beginning Balance	Payment	Interest	Principal	Ending Balance
t = 0					$10,000.00
t = 1	$10,000.00	$2,637.97	$1,000.00	$1,637.97	$ 8,362.03
t = 2	$ 8,362.03	$2,637.97	$ 836.20	$1,801.77	$ 6,560.26
t = 3	$ 6,560.26	$2,637.97	$ 656.03	$1,981.94	$ 4,578.32
t = 4	$ 4,578.32	$2,637.97	$ 457.83	$2,180.14	$ 2,398.18
t = 5	$ 2,398.18	$2,637.97	$ 239.82	$2,398.15	0

Problem 5.22: You have borrowed $8,000 from a bank and have promised to return it in four equal yearly payments. The first payment is at the end of the first year. The interest rate is 7.5%. Create the amortization schedule for this loan.

Problem 5.23: Inigo Montoya just bought a new SUV. He borrowed $35,000 with a four-year (monthly payment) loan that has an interest rate of 5.95% p.a. Create his amortization schedule.

Problem 5.24: Referring back to Problem 5.23, what is the balance on Inigo's loan immediately after he makes the 30th payment (that is, when there are 18 payments remaining)? Prove that the amortization schedule and your answer computed as the present value of all remaining payments are the same.

Students often ask us how it is possible to remember how to do all that is presented in this chapter to solve time value of money problems. The answer is simple. Work many, many time value of money problems. The more you work, the easier this will become. We have given you many problems in the text to work with, and there are many at the end of this chapter. Additional time value of money problems can be found on the Internet (try a Google search for the term "time value of money problems"). After a while, you will see that working time value of money problems is like driving a car. At first, it seems impossible to do. There are just so many things going on at the same time that it is difficult to focus on any one thing. Soon, however, driving becomes second nature.

We have by now covered the time value of money concepts necessary to study issues of security valuation and capital budgeting in finance. The remainder of the book will cover these two areas. Once you understand the material on time value of money, you will find the rest of the book to be exceedingly easy as far as solving problems is concerned.

Assignment 5.1

1. Investment A requires you to pay $30,000 at t = 0, and you will receive $49,000 after five years. Investment B costs $73,000 and provides a cash flow of $128,000 after seven years. What is the rate of return for each of the two investments?

2. You plan spend the next four summers vacationing abroad. The first summer trip, which is exactly one year away, will cost you $22,000, the second, $27,500, the third, $33,000, and the fourth $35,000. You want to save for these vacations. How much should you deposit in your account today so that you will have exactly enough to finance all the trips? The account pays interest at 6% p.a.

3. You make the following deposits into an account that pays interest at 8% p.a. Open the account today with a deposit of $11,000, then $13,000 at the end of the first year, $17,400 at the end of the second year, $12,800 at the end of the third, $9,600 at the end of the fourth, and $17,200 at the end of the fifth year. How much will you have in your account at the end of 10 years?

Assignment 5.2

1. You deposit $28,000 in an account today. You plan to make 10 withdrawals from this account with the first withdrawal at the end of the first year. At the end of 10 years, you want the account to have a balance of $30,000. If the account pays interest of 6% p.a., what will be the size of each of the yearly withdrawals?

2. You deposit $2,500 per year for 20 years in an account that pays 8% interest. At t = 21, you make the first of the 25 equal yearly withdrawals from this account. What can be the maximum amount of these withdrawals?

3. You plan to retire in 25 years. When you retire, you will need $150,000 per year for 25 years with the first payment needed at t = 26. You expect to receive $25,000 from a trust at t = 14, which you will deposit in your retirement account. At t = 11, you plan to take a world cruise that will cost you $60,000, to be paid out of the retirement account. You open your retirement account today with an initial deposit of $5,000. You plan to make 25 equal yearly deposits beginning at the end of the first year into this account. If the account pays interest at 7% p.a., what should be these annual deposits?

4. An asset yields the following year-end cash flows. $12,000 per year for years 1–3, $17,000 per year for years 4–7, $21,000 per year for years 8–15, $24,000 per years for years 16–20, and then $30,000 per year from year 21 forever. Use a discount rate of 12% to determine the present value of these cash flows.

Assignment 5.3

1. The stated interest rate for a bank account is 7% and interest is paid semi-annually. How many years will it take you to double your money in this account?

2. Bank A pays interest annually of 10% p.a. Bank B has a stated interest of 9.8% p.a. and the interest is paid semi-annually. Bank C has a stated interest of 9.6% p.a. and pays interest quarterly. Bank D has stated interest of 9.5% p.a. and pays interest monthly. Bank E has a stated interest rate of 9.4% p.a. and compounds the interest continuously. Compute the effective rate of interest for each bank.

3. You will retire 20 years from now and will need $140,000 per year for 10 years beginning at t = 21. You plan to make 20 equal yearly deposits into a retirement account with the first deposit to be made today. The account pays interest at 9% p.a. What should be the size of these deposits?

4. You borrow $40,000 at 8% p.a. and promise to repay it in six equal yearly installments. What will be these installments? Present the amortization table for this loan repayment.

Additional Questions and Problems

1. All else constant, for a given nominal interest rate, an increase in the number of compounding periods per year will cause the future value of some current sum of money to:

   a. Increase

   b. Decrease

   c. Remain the same

   d. May increase, decrease, or remain the same depending on the number of years until the money is to be received.

   e. Will increase if compounding occurs more often than 12 times per year and will decrease if compounding occurs less than 12 times per year.

2. Consider three investment alternatives: a perpetuity, an ordinary annuity, and an annuity due. All three have the same payment amount. The annuity due and the ordinary annuity have the same number of payments, and the number of payments is greater than one. The interest rate is positive and the same for all three investments. Given this information, which of the following statements is correct?

   a. The present value of the perpetuity is less than the present value of the ordinary annuity.

   b. The future value of the annuity due is less that the future value of the ordinary annuity.

   c. The perpetuity and the ordinary annuity have the same present value.

   d. The ordinary annuity and the annuity due have the same present value.

   e. The present value of the ordinary annuity is less than the present value of the perpetuity.

3. How long does it take for an investment to quadruple in value if the investment yields (that is, pays interest of) 8.5% per year?

4. The average price of a movie ticket at the end of 1988 was $5.50 and the average price of a movie ticket at the end of 1990 was $6.00. At what annual rate did ticket prices grow?

Time Value of Money: Advanced Topics

5. Suppose that I am trying to borrow money from you to finance my business. And suppose that I promise to repay you in two installments, one payment in two years of $5,000 and one payment in four years for $10,000. If your opportunity cost of funds is 10%, how much are you willing to lend me?

6. Consider the problem of calculating a loan amortization schedule. The portion of the payment that goes toward the payment of interest is _____ than the previous period's interest payment, and the portion of the payment that goes toward the repayment of principal is _____ than the previous period's principal payment.

   a. greater; less

   b. lower; less

   c. greater; greater

   d. less; greater

   e. None of the above

7. The number of years it would take $.83 to double, assuming an annual stated rate of 7.9560931% p.a., would be least under which compounding assumption?

   a. Continuous

   b. Daily

   c. Monthly

   d. Quarterly

   e. Annual

8. What is the effective annual rate of interest for a loan that has an 18% annual percentage rate, compounded monthly?

9. If I invest $100 today in an account that earns 10% per year, compounded semi-annually, how much will I have in this account at the end of 20 years if I make no withdrawals?

10. Which of the following statements is most correct?

    a. A five-year $100 annuity due will have a higher present value than a five-year $100 ordinary annuity.

    b. A 15-year mortgage will have larger monthly payments than a 30-year mortgage of the same amount and same interest rate.

    c. If an investment pays 10% interest compounded annually, its effective rate will also be 10%.

    d. Statements a and c are correct.

    e. All of the statements above are correct.

11. Frank Lewis has a thirty-year, $100,000 mortgage with a nominal interest rate of 10% and monthly compounding. Which of the following statements regarding his mortgage is most correct?

   a. The monthly payments will decline over time.

   b. The proportion of the monthly payment that represents interest will be lower for the last payment than for the first payment on the loan.

   c. The total dollar amount of principal being paid off each month gets larger as the loan approaches maturity.

   d. Statements a and c are correct.

   e. Statements b and c are correct.

12. Compute the present and future values of a 10-year annuity with payments of $5,000 per year using discount rates of 0, 5, 10, 15, 20, 25, 30, 35, 40, 45, and 50% p.a. Plot them on the same graph with the discount rates on the horizontal and PV and FV on the vertical axis.

13. If you deposit $650 each year (first deposit made at t = 1), into an account that pays 6% interest per year, compounded annually, what will be the balance in the account after you have made 15 payments, assuming that you make no withdrawals from the account?

14. If you deposit $725 each year (first deposit made at t = 0) for 18 years into an account that pays 7.4% interest per year, compounded annually, what will be the balance in the account at the end of year 25, assuming you make no withdrawals from the account? (Note that after you stop making deposits, the balance in your account will continue to earn interest until the end of year 25.)

15. If you deposit $1 per month in an account that pays 12% interest, compounded monthly, what will be the balance in the account after two years if you make no withdrawals?

16. If you deposit $100 in an account each quarter for two years, beginning next quarter, what will be the balance in the account at the end of two years if interest is 12%, compounded quarterly, if you make no withdrawals?

17. In 1950, a Jack-in-the-Box hamburger cost 24 cents. In 1994, a Jack-in-the-Box hamburger cost 79 cents. What is the effective annual increase in the price of a Jack-in-the-Box hamburger from 1950 to 1994?

18. In 1955, an order of McDonald's french fries cost 10 cents. If McDonald's had increased the cost of its fries to keep up with inflation, an order of fries would have cost 55 cents in 1994. Given this information on the price of fries, what is the effective annual rate of inflation over the period from 1955 to 1994?

19. Assume that you deposit $2,000 each year for the next 20 years, starting one year from today, in an account that pays 9.6% interest per year, compounded annually. If exactly 10 years

from today you withdraw $5,000 from the account, how much will be in your account on the day you make the last deposit (that is, at the end of year 20)?

20. A security pays you $40 every six months for 30 years and, additionally, at the end of the 30 years, pays you $1,000. The present value of this security is $1,111. What is the stated *p.a.* rate of return? What is the effective *p.a.* rate of return?

21. You loan your friend $100,000 today. She will pay you $10,000 per year for the first five years and will make five more equal yearly payments. If the interest rate is 12% p.a., what should be the size of these payments?

22. You loan your friend $100,000. He will pay you $12,000 per year for 10 years and a balloon payment at t = 10 of $50,000. What is the interest rate that you are charging the friend?

23. You have borrowed $35,000 at 12% p.a. and plan to repay it in seven years with equal yearly installments. What is the size of these installments? Just after you make the fourth payment, what will be the remaining loan balance?

24. You borrowed some money at 11% p.a. You repay the loan by making first six yearly installments of $10,000, then three yearly installments of $12,000, and then four yearly installments of $15,000. How much had you borrowed?

25. You have just had a second child. You expect that the child will go to college after 18 years. College will be for four years, and each year will cost you $33,000. The payments are to be made at the beginning of each college year—that is, the first payment will be at t = 18. Your first child will go to college after 12 years and college will cost $25,000 per year for four years with the first payment due at t = 12. You had started saving for the first child's education when the child was born six years ago. You have $20,000 in that account today and plan to make 10 more equal yearly payments beginning t = 1. To have exactly enough money for education of both children, how much should you deposit each year? The account pays interest at 8% p.a.

26. A factory generates $800,000 per year for the next 10 years. If the discount rate is 12%, what is the factory worth today? What will the factory be worth at the end of five years?

27. Assume that I want to have $15,000 in my savings account exactly five years from today. I just deposited $3,500 into the account (that is, at the end of year 0) and I plan to deposit $3,500 into the account exactly two years from today (that is, at the end of year 2). I plan to make another deposit into the account exactly one year from today, but I am not sure how much that amount must be to achieve my goal of having $15,000 in the account exactly five years from today. If the interest rate I earn on money deposited in this account is 7.25% p.a., how much must I deposit at the end of year 1 (given my initial and other planned deposits) to achieve my goal?

28. Today is your 25th birthday and you have a dream of retiring on your 40th birthday. You want to put aside however much is necessary on your 26th through 40th birthdays (15 pay-

ments) to have enough to retire. You've estimated that you will live until you are approximately 80, and you want the first withdrawal to occur on your 41st birthday, with the last payment occurring on your 80th birthday. You think that you will need $75,000 per year to spend during retirement. You estimate constant interest rates of 9%. How much must you put aside each year in order to have sufficient money to retire at age 40?

29. You expect to receive $5,000 at the end of each of the next six years (first payment to be received one year from today). You will deposit these payments into an account that pays 9% p.a., compounded monthly. What will be the future value of these payments at the end of the year 10?

30. Twelve years ago, Leon borrowed $1,500,000 to purchase a new home. The loan had an interest rate of 6.25% p.a. and a term of 360 months (i.e., required 30 years of monthly payments with the first payment due one month after Leon closed on the loan). Every month since taking out the loan, Leon paid $1,500 in addition to the required monthly payment (for example, if the required payment was $2,000, Leon actually paid $3,500 every month on the loan). Given Leon's payments, what is the current balance on the loan (i.e., the payoff immediately after Leon made the 144th payment)?

31. Terry just celebrated her 30th birthday and she has decided to quit smoking. Terry currently smokes two packs of cigarettes per day at an average cost of $4.50 per pack. To reward herself for quitting, Terry plans to invest all that she will save each day (i.e., $9.00) into a savings account that currently pays 11.25% p.a., with daily compounding. Assuming her first deposit into the account is made tomorrow, and assuming that there are 365 days per year, how much money will be in Terry's savings account on her 65th birthday (i.e., 35 years or 12,775 days from today)?

32. John Keene recently invested $3,250 in a project that is promising to return 8.75 percent per year. The cash flows are expected to be as follows:

Year	Cash Flow
1	$800
2	$950
3	???
4	$875

Note that the third year cash flow is unknown. Assuming the present value of this cash flow stream is $3,250 (that is, CF0 = −3250), what is the missing cash flow value (that is, what is the cash flow at the end of the third year)?

33. Steven just deposited $11,000 in a bank account that has a 7.25% nominal interest rate, and the interest is compounded monthly. Steven also plans to contribute another $12,500 into the account one year (12 months) from now and another $15,000 into the account two years from now. How much will be in the account five years (i.e., 60 months) from now?

34. If a five-year ordinary annuity has a present value of $1,000 and if the interest rate is 10% p.a., what is the amount of each annuity payment?

35. Assume that your required rate of return is 12% and you are given the following stream of cash:

Year	Cash Flow
1	$10,000
2	$15,000
3	$15,000
4	$15,000
5	$15,000
6	$20,000

    If payments are made at the end of each period, what is the present value of the cash flow stream?

36. Suppose you put $100 into a savings account today, the account pays an interest rate of 6% p.a. compounded semi-annually, and you withdraw $100 after six months. Thereafter, you make no additional deposits or withdrawals. What would your ending balance be 20 years after the initial $100 deposit was made?

37. You have just taken out an installment loan for $100,000. Assume that the loan will be repaid in 12 equal monthly installments of $9,456, and that the first payment will be due one month from today. How much of your third monthly payment will go toward the repayment of principal?

38. You plan to deposit money in a savings account that earns 7% annually. You will make five equal deposits of $10,000 each. The first deposit will be made today. No deposits will be made after the fifth deposit. What will be the accumulated sum available at the end of 10 years? (Round your answer to the nearest $1)

39. Your uncle has agreed to deposit $3,000 into your brokerage account at the beginning of each of the next five years ($t = 0$, $t = 1$, $t = 2$, $t = 3$, and $t = 4$). You estimate that you can earn 9% a year on your investments. How much will you have in your account four years from now (at $t = 4$)? (Assume that no money is withdrawn from the account until $t = 4$.)

40. You are considering buying a new car. The sticker price is $15,000 and you have $2,000 to put toward a downpayment. If you can negotiate a nominal annual interest rate of 10% and you wish to pay for the car over a five-year period, what are your monthly car payments?

41. You have a $175,000, 30-year mortgage with a 9% nominal rate. You make payments every month. What will be the remaining balance on your mortgage after five years (that is, immediately after you make the 60th payment)?

42. You bought a new car three years ago. The sticker price was $13,876 and you put $2,000 toward a downpayment. The nominal annual interest rate on the loan used to finance the remaining balance was 10% and the term of the loan was five years (with monthly payments required). What is your current payoff on the loan (that is, balance immediately after the 36th payment)?

43. You plan to deposit money in a savings account that earns 7% annually. You will make five equal deposits of $7,130 each. The first deposit will be made today. No deposits will be made after the fifth deposit. What will be the accumulated sum available at the end of 10 years?

44. You have a $175,000, 30-year mortgage with a 9% nominal rate. You make payments every month. What will be the remaining balance on your mortgage after six years (that is, immediately after the 72nd payment)?

45. You will need to pay for your son's private school tuition (first grade through twelfth grade) a sum of $8,000 per year for years 1 through 5, $10,000 per year for years 6 through 8, and $12,500 per year for years 9 through 12. Assume that all payments are made at the beginning of the year, that is, tuition for year 1 is paid now (that is, at t = 0), tuition for year 2 is paid one year from now, and so on. In addition to the tuition payments, you expect to incur graduation expenses of $2,500 at the end of year 12. If a bank account can provide a certain 10% p.a. rate of return, how much money do you need to deposit today to be able to pay for the above expenses?

46. You have $10,000 on your credit card. You plan to make monthly payments of $200 until the balance is paid off. The interest rate on your credit card is 18% p.a., compounded monthly. A letter in the mail informs you that you are approved for a new credit card and balance transfers are subject to a 12% p.a., compounded monthly. How many months sooner will you pay off your bill?

47. Today, Mark invested $2,000 into an account that guarantees 6.85% p.a., compounded monthly and Madonna invested $2,000 into account guaranteeing 7.85% p.a., compounded quarterly.

    How long will it take (in years) for the value of Madonna's investment to be two times as much as Mark's?

48. (DISCLAIMER: All characters appearing in this work are fictitious. Any resemblance to real persons, living or dead, is purely coincidental). The Obamas have asked for your help in planning for the college education of their second child, Sasha. They expect that she will start college 15 years from today. At that time they would like to have on deposit sufficient funds to make quarterly withdrawals of $12,500 per quarter to pay for college costs. Because (they hope) college will last four years, there will be a total of 16 quarterly withdrawals, with the first one to be made on the day Sasha starts college. They plan to accumulate the necessary funds by making quarterly deposits into an account that pays 5%, compounded quarterly. There is, however, one complication. Their first child, Malia, will start college 12 years from today. Thanks to royalties from a book that Mr. Obama wrote, they already have sufficient funds to pay for all of Malia's college costs. However, they estimate that they

will not be able to make any deposits toward Sasha's education while Malia is in college due to the high cost of security that they believe they will have to pay after Mr. Obama completes his current "temporary" job. Thus they will only be able to make a total of 48 quarterly deposits into Sasha's college account, with the first deposit one quarter from today and the last deposit on the day Malia starts college. What should be the amount of these quarterly deposits?

Chapter 6

Financial Securities

6.1 Chapter Introduction and Overview

6.2 Stocks and Bonds

6.3 Securities Markets

    Additional Questions and Problems

After studying Chapter 6, you should be able to:

- Describe the basic nature of a financial security.
- Understand the difference between a debt security and an equity security.
- Define several different types of debt securities.
- Describe the basic rights and privileges of shareholders.

From *Lectures in Corporate Finance*, 6th Edition by Jayant R. Kale and Richard J. Fendler. Copyright © 2013 by Kendall Hunt Publishing Company. Reprinted by permission.

6.1 Chapter Introduction and Overview

In Chapter 3, we present an overview of the financial markets where financial securities are bought and sold. In this chapter, we describe the properties of two major financial securities: bonds and stocks. You may find some overlap between these two chapters.

Suppose that you are an entrepreneur and have developed an innovative new product that you believe will sell very well in the market. You do not, however, have the financial resources to buy all the assets required to manufacture this product. What do you do? You contact some entity that has the financial resources but not the product idea (for example, a bank or a venture capitalist) and ask it to lend you the money necessary to manufacture the product. If they believe that your idea is good, these financiers will provide you the money.

What do the providers of these funds receive in return? They receive your promise that they will be paid out of the cash flows that your firm will generate. In the financial world, promises have to be written down and the roles and obligations of all the parties under all conceivable scenarios have to be specified. All the parties have to agree to these by affixing their signatures. The promise then becomes a *contract*. A *financial security* is simply a contract between the provider of funds and the user of these funds that clearly specifies the amount of money that has been provided and the terms and conditions of how the user is going to repay the provider.

Let us continue with the example of your firm. Assume that you start your firm by borrowing money, say $7.5 million, from a bank at 8% interest p.a. Your contract with the bank stipulates that you will repay the bank in 10 equal yearly installments. From the previous chapter, we know that this means that you will have to pay the bank approximately $1.118 million every year. The loan that the bank has given you is a financial security.

An Aside: *The bank, on the other hand, by lending you money, has made an investment of $10 million in your firm. In fact, a bank's loans are its assets. Did you know that banks regularly sell these loan assets to other banks and investors?*

You will make the required payments on the loan out of the revenues that you generate from your firm. After paying the bank and all the other expenses related to manufacturing and selling your product, whatever is left over is your income from this venture. You are the owner. If the firm does well, there will be a lot of money left over for you and, if the firm does poorly, so will you. In fact, if the firm were to do so poorly that there was no hope that you would ever be able to repay the loan, you would be bankrupt and the assets of your firm would belong to the bank and other persons to whom you owed money. The loan that the bank has given you is a financial security.

Now assume it is 10 years since you started the firm. Your original $7.5 million has just been paid off; however, you have just borrowed another $8 million from the bank to buy some new equipment to replace some machines that have worn out. Suppose that your product has done very well and your firm has flourished over the past 10 years. You, however, are kept so busy with the work that you have no time to enjoy the fruits of your creation.

Let us suppose that your firm is generating a total of $5 million per year as net cash flow. You expect that it will continue to do so (for convenience in computation) forever. Assuming a discount rate of 10%, the present value of this perpetuity is $\frac{\$5m.}{0.1} = \$50$ million. In other words, the value of the firm (that is, the market value of the firm's assets) is $50 million. Suppose that all your liabilities, including the new loan to the bank, amount to a total of $10 million (your $8 million long-term loan and $2 million in current liabilities). Because you are the owner of the firm, the difference between what the firm is worth and what you owe, $50 − $10 = $40 million, is your wealth or *equity*.

Is this equity of $40 million in your bank account? No. In fact, this "wealth" is really only "theoretical" wealth—value that exists in theory but that cannot be immediately spent. If you are tired of running the company and would like to ease up, what can you do? You can sell the company in its entirety and if you receive the fair price for it, you will have your $40 million. On the other hand, you might not want to sell off your entire ownership in the firm. In that case, you could sell only a portion of your ownership in the firm. You can do this by either taking on a partner or taking the company public.

Taking the company public requires you to obtain authorization from the Securities Exchange Commission (SEC) to issue shares to the public. You obtain authorization for, say, four million shares. Because the value of your ownership is $40 million, each of these shares is worth $10. If you wanted to sell, say, half of your equity ownership in the firm, you would sell two million shares to the public and retain the remaining two million. From the sale of the shares, you should receive $20 million. What do the people who buy these shares obtain in return? They are now part owners of the firm. Whatever cash flows are left over after paying all other obligations would now be divided among all shareholders. You would be entitled to half because you owned half of the outstanding shares. Others would receive an amount proportionate to their ownership. Note that the equity shares that you have sold are also contracts, as we have defined above, and, hence, are financial securities.

In general, the securities that a firm issues to investors are contracts with investors that specify the exact nature of the claim that investors owning a specific security have on the cash flows of the firm. As an aside, think of the dealings that firm has with its suppliers, or its customers, or its workers, or its management, or with the government (for taxation). In each case, these dealings are nothing but contracts. In fact, you can think of a firm as a set of several such contracts. A better and more popular description is that a firm is a "nexus" of all such contracts. In this chapter, however, we will focus on only the most common financial securities issued by firms, specifically, corporate bonds, preferred stock, and common stock.

6.2 Stocks and Bonds

If you open the business section of the daily newspaper, you will be inundated with a myriad of different financial securities. Some of these securities represent contracts between the firm and investors (for example, stocks and bonds). Others are contracts between two investors and the firm is not involved. For example, a call option on the stock of ABC Corp. is a contract between the buyer and the seller of the option (also the option exchange). ABC Corp., despite the fact that the option is written on its stock, has nothing to do with the option; it is not a party to the option contract.

We are concerned here with only the former types of securities—those that are contracts between the firm and investors. These securities basically represent a contract under which the firm borrows capital from investors and, in return, depending upon the type of contract or security, promises a specific claim on the firm's future cash flows.

The above explanation about what securities are and why corporations issue securities serves a very important purpose. To an *investor* who owns a financial security, the security is nothing but a *stream of expected future cash flows*. Based on what we have studied in the previous chapters, then, the *value* of any security to the investor is the present value of all the *expected future cash flows* from owning the security discounted at the appropriate discount rate, or *required rate of return*. We will next describe the commonly observed securities in terms of the cash flows that these securities promise. Then, after describing the markets in which these securities trade, we will investigate the main issues concerning determining the required rate of return for individual securities.

There are two basic classifications for the securities that a firm issues to raise capital—*debt* and *equity*. Securities in the debt category usually promise fixed payments to the investor. These payments have to be made to the investors before anything can be paid to owners of equity securities. If the cash flows of the firm are very high, owners of debt securities still receive only the amount that was promised to them. They do not share in the cash flows over and above these fixed payments. In other words, debt investors are not the owners of the firm. However, if the cash flows to firms are so low that the firm is unable to meet its obligatory payments to owners of debt securities, the firm is held to be in default. The extreme case of default is when the value of the firm is so low that there is no possibility of ever satisfying its debt obligations. In this case the firm is bankrupt and the ownership of the assets of the firm goes to the owners of the debt securities.

Equity investors, those who own shares in the firm, are, unlike debt investors, owners of the firm. They receive the cash flow left over after the firm has made all its obligatory payments such as those to debt securities. Note that, by its very design, the cash flows to an equity security are not fixed. The higher the firm's cash flows are, the higher are the cash flows to equity securities. On the other hand, if the cash flow to the firm is less than what the firm owes to its debt securities, the equity investors obtain nothing. The following numerical example will make this clear.

Suppose that a firm has outstanding debt securities on which the obligatory payment is $300,000 per year. The following table provides the cash flows to debt and equity investors for different levels of the firm's cash flow.

Firm cash flow level	$500,000	$300,000	$100,000	$0
Cash flow to debt	$300,000	$300,000	$100,000	$0
Cash flow to equity	$200,000	$ 0	$ 0	$0

Notice that equity obtains a payout only when the firm's cash flow is greater than the amount due to debt. If the firm's cash flow is less than the amount due to debt, the entire cash flow goes to debt. Figure 6.1 is a graphical representation of this relationship.

In the graph, the horizontal axis represents the level of cash flows to the firm and the vertical axis the cash flows to debt and equity. D denotes the cash flow due to debt. As long as the firm's cash flow is less than D, the entire cash flow goes to debt. When it is greater than D, the debt-owners receive D and the residual cash flow goes to equity. For this reason, equity is commonly known as the *residual claim*. Note also that the cash flow to debt or equity security owners can never be negative. This is due to a legal feature called *limited liability*. According to it, limited liability investors can never lose more than what they have invested.

Now that we have the basic idea about the two types of claims that firms issue, we can specifically describe the securities that a firm issues.

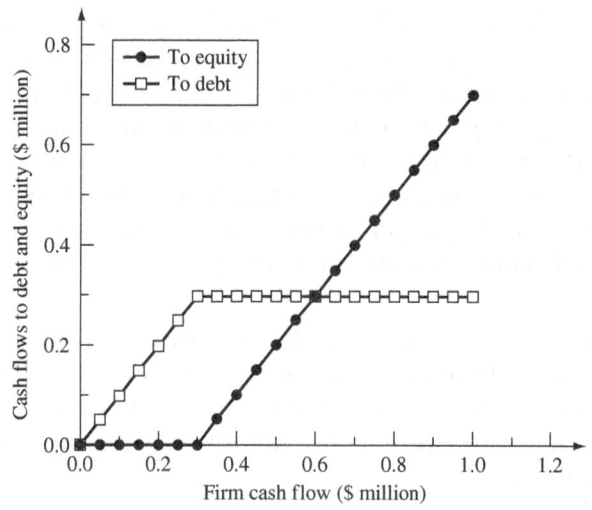

Figure 6.1 Debt and Equity Claims (D $300,000)

6.2.1 Debt Securities

Recall that owners of debt securities usually have a claim on a firm's cash flows prior to that of equity-holders. Additionally, the payment to debt-holders is fixed beforehand. If the firm does very well in terms of generating cash flows, the debt-holders still obtain only their promised cash flows. Most importantly, debt-holders of a firm are not owners of the firm. They are creditors. Therefore, they do not get to vote on matters pertaining to the operations of the firm. However, if the firm is in financial distress, that is, there is a significant chance that it will go bankrupt in the near future, the debt-holders, as per the usual debt contracts, have more of a say in the day-to-day running of the company. The reason for this is not all that difficult to see. As the cash flows of the firm become low, the cash flows to debt-holders begin to depend more and more on the cash flows of the firm. For example, in the previous numerical illustration, when cash flows to the firm are $300,000 or less, the cash flows to the debt-holders are completely determined by the cash flows to the firm. When this is the case, a firm is in financial trouble (or distress), and it is natural that debt-holders will want a say in the operations of the firm.

Fixed-Coupon Bonds—These are debt securities under which the firm pays a specific (fixed) amount called the *coupon* to the investor every period until the bond matures, and, at maturity, pays the *face value* of the bond. The most common face value, also referred to as par value, for a corporate bond is $1,000, however, bonds with par values other than $1,000 do exist, but they are significantly less common than $1,000 par value bonds.

For example, if a firm issues an 8% 30-year bond with annual coupon payments, the coupon is 8%, the maturity is 30 years, the face value is $1,000 (always assumed if no other face value is specifically mentioned), and the coupon is paid annually. The cash flows associated to this bond come in two parts—periodic coupon payments and the repayment of face value at maturity. Coupon payments are computed by multiplying the face value by the coupon rate. The *coupon rate* of a bond is **not** the required rate of return; it simply establishes the amount of the periodic coupon payment. So, from this bond, an investor will receive the following cash flows in the future: an annuity of $80 (8% percent of face value) for 30 years and $1,000 at the end of 30 years.

The coupon payment on the bond need not be annual; it can be paid semi-annually or quarterly. Suppose that the bond described above paid coupons semi-annually, the cash flow stream would be: $40 (0.5 × 8% of $1,000) every six months for 60 (30 years × 2) six-month periods and $1,000 at the end of 60 six-month periods. If it paid quarterly, the cash flow stream would be $20 every three months for 120 three-month periods and $1,000 at the end of 120 three-month periods. Notice that when mentioning the repayment of face value of maturity, I changed the wording from "end of 30 years" to the number of six- or three-month periods depending on how often the coupon is paid. This is an important aspect to note at this time. It will have implications when we value bonds.

Zero-Coupon Bonds—A zero-coupon bond is a debt security that promises only one payment at maturity. This payment is fixed. In other words, a zero-coupon bond is a fixed-coupon bond with a zero coupon rate. Suppose that a firm issues a zero-coupon bond that matures in 30 years. Then the only payment that the firm has promised to the investors who bought these bonds is $1,000 (the face value) at the end of 30 years.

Variable-Rate Bonds—These bonds pay periodic coupons, but the coupon, unlike the fixed-coupon bond, is not fixed. As the name suggests, the coupon is variable. The size of the coupon is usually tied to the level of prevailing interest rates. The interest rate to which the coupon rate is tied to is also specified in the contract.

Consols (that is, Perpetual Bonds)—A consol is a fixed coupon-paying bond that has no maturity. In other words, the issuer of the bond agrees to pay a fixed coupon payment every period forever. If you recall, we had alluded to this security in the previous chapter.

Income Bonds—Income bonds have some features of both fixed-coupon and variable-rate bonds described earlier. On the one hand, income bonds, similar to fixed-coupon bonds, carry a promise to pay a fixed coupon. However, the firm is required to pay the coupon only when its earnings are sufficiently high. In other words, if the firm's earnings are sufficiently low, it can postpone or omit the periodic coupon payment. The omission of this payment does not put the firm in default as it would if it did not make the coupon payment in a fixed-coupon or variable-rate bond.

Convertible Bonds—As the name implies, a convertible debt security allows the security holder to convert it to another security, usually equity, according to some pre-specified terms. For example, ABC Corp. may issue a convertible bond that carries a 7% coupon paid annually, has a 30-year maturity, has a face value of $1,000, and carries the feature that after five years, the owner of the bond can exchange it for 50 shares of ABC stock. Now suppose that after five years, the cash flows from this bond are worth $1,000 and ABC's stock is trading at $30 per share. In this case, the convertible bondholder will have a strong incentive to convert the bond into 50 shares of stock. On the other hand, if the price of the stock is $15 per share, the bondholder will not. As you can see, when you purchase a convertible bond, you are buying a security that is a (sort of) combination of debt and equity.

Callable Bonds—A callable bond is like a fixed-coupon bond except that the issuer of the bond, that is, the firm, has the right to repurchase it at a predetermined price. Suppose that ABC Corp issued a 30-year bond with a 7% coupon paid annually and specified that after five years it, that is, ABC Corp., had the right (that is, it could if it wanted) to call (that is, buy back from the owners of the bond) the bond at $1,100. Whether ABC will call this bond after five years depends primarily on a very simple criterion: What is the market price of the bond at that time? If the price is more than $1,100, it makes sense to call. If it is not, there is no reason to call the bond.

The above is a selective list of the different types of debt securities that trade on U.S. financial markets. U.S. corporations are very creative about designing debt securities, and new borrowing-based securities are created more often than you might think. The chances are, however, that those securities will be some combination of two or more of the above debt securities. For example, we described convertible and callable bonds separately. U.S. corporations, however, issue bonds that are usually both convertible and callable. In addition to the above, you will encounter other features of debt contracts. These features include sinking fund provisions, level of security (that is, backed by assets of the firm), level of subordination (that is, between two classes of debt which class has the priority in terms of cash flows of the firm), and others.

6.2.2 Equity Securities

Contrary to debt, equity securities are much more uniform across corporations. As mentioned earlier, equity-holders have "residual" claim on a firm's cash flows. That is, they receive the cash flow that is "left over" after all other payments have been made. Equity-holders are the owners of the firm. As owners, they have a say in the operating decisions of the firm; that is they have *"control"* privileges. Equity-holders have the right to vote on matters of importance facing the firm. These are called equity *voting rights.* Suppose that the management of a company wanted to make an important change, say changing the firm's auditors.

To make this change, the management has to call a *general shareholder meeting* and propose this change and the change is effected only if a majority of the shareholders vote in favor of this change. Attendance at a shareholder meeting might not be required; all shareholders are sent *proxy ballots* before the meeting and shareholders can, thus, vote in absentia.

In practice, for most corporations (think of General Motors, which has millions of shareholders) it is impractical for shareholders to keep tabs on what the manager is doing. Therefore, the control (arising out of ownership) aspect of equity ownership is in the form of a *board of directors* whose responsibility is to ensure that the management takes actions that maximizes the welfare of shareholders. In other words, the board is supposed to look out for the interests of the shareholders. Shareholders elect board members, and the board represents shareholders, similar to the way your local politician is supposed to represent you.

Usually, the only way in which equity securities can differ from company to company is in the level of voting power. For example, voting on a share may be cumulative or may be non-cumulative (or straight). Cumulative voting exists (and is mandated in some states) because it allows minority shareholders to have more of a say in the election of board members. The easiest way to explain this is with the help of an example.

Suppose that a corporation has only two shareholders A and B. A owns 20 shares and B owns 80 shares. The firm has to elect five members to the board. A is a minority shareholder and wants to be on the board of directors. B, however, does not want A to be on the board. Each shareholder nominates five candidates. (Because B does not want A, their list of nominations has to be different by at least one candidate.)

Under non-cumulative or straight voting, A can cast 20 votes per candidate and B can cast 80 votes per candidate. Thus, all of B's candidates will win. In other words, B can freeze out the minority shareholder A. Under cumulative voting, on the other hand, the number of votes per share is determined by the number of directors to be elected. Because five directors are to be elected, each share has five votes. Therefore, A has $20 \times 5 = 100$ votes and B has $80 \times 5 = 400$ votes. Each shareholder can distribute these votes across the candidates as he or she wishes. For example, a shareholder can cast all his or her votes for just one candidate. Thus, with 100 votes, A can be guaranteed election to the board. There is no possible way that B can divide 400 votes over five candidates such that all five have higher votes than A.

The nature of the equity security/contract provisions is fairly uniform across firms. The uniformity is because, as explained below, the owners of equity shares are not guaranteed any cash flows. Additionally equity, being a residual claim, generates cash flows only if all other claims on the firm's cash flow have been met. Thus, there is no question of creating different types of equity claims by structuring different streams of cash flows (as was the case with debt securities).

The owner of a share of stock can expect cash flows of two types. The first is in the form of dividends that the firm pays its shareholders. Recall from your analysis of income statements that dividends to equity-holders are paid from net income after tax, that is, after all other payments have been made. Thus *dividends* are a *residual cash flow*. It is also true that the firm is not required to pay a dividend or to keep the level of periodic dividends constant. In other words, to the equity holders, there is no guaranteed cash flow from dividends. The other type of cash flow that equity holders can receive is from the *sale of their shares.* Again note that the price that they receive is the prevailing market price of the stock. In other words, there is no guaranteed cash flow here either.

6.2.3 Preferred Stock

The debt and equity securities described above account for a very large portion of the corporate financing activity in the United States. The rest is primarily composed of a security that has some features of both debt and equity. This security is preferred stock. Cash flows to preferred stock are made after the payment to debt holders but before equity holders can be paid. Thus, preferred stock has a claim priority between debt and equity. A typical preferred stock has no maturity and in this sense is similar to equity. Preferred stock has a stated par value and, usually, a stated fixed dividend. These two features make it seem more like a debt security. Even though the level of dividend payments is fixed, non-payment of preferred stock dividends by the firm does not constitute default as it would if coupon on bonds were not paid. Dividend payment on preferred stock is at the discretion of the board of directors. It should, however, be noted that corporations very rarely forgo preferred stock dividend payment. As far as the control and ownership aspect is concerned, preferred stock is usually non-voting.

6.3 Securities Markets

There are actually many different types of markets in a financial market system associated with an economy such as ours. For example, there are *money markets* and *capital markets.* Money markets are the markets where financial assets trade that are close substitutes for cash and mature in one year or less. Money market securities include Treasury bills, negotiated certificates of deposit (CDs), bankers' acceptances, and commercial paper. Capital markets, on the other hand, are the markets for intermediate-term and long-term debt and corporate stocks. Capital market securities include Treasury notes and bonds, mortgages, municipal bonds, corporate bonds, preferred stock, and common stock. To a financial manager of a corporation, the last three capital market securities are of greatest interest.

Other types of markets are *spot markets* and *futures markets.* In spot markets, securities are bought and sold for "on-the-spot" delivery. For example, if you purchase 100 shares of GM stock through a broker, you have made a spot market transaction. As soon as the transaction is complete, money changes hands and 100 shares of GM stock are credited to your account. In futures markets, full payment for and delivery of the asset takes place at some future date, such as six months or one year. A particularly interesting futures market concerns the sale and delivery of agricultural products, such as corn. In the corn futures market, a farmer can actually sell bushels of corn at a pre-determined price before he even plants the seeds. This "futures contract" to sell corn at a set price will allow him to borrow money for his seeds and other planting needs. Futures contracts are usually used as insurance against some unforeseen event, but they can be used for speculative purposes. When used as insurance, futures are referred to as a *hedge*. Financial managers can use futures contracts to hedge against unfavorable interest rate or foreign exchange movements.

The financial markets that are of greatest interest to a financial manager are *primary markets* and *secondary markets.* Primary markets are the markets in which companies raise money. In a primary market transaction, one participant is a company and the other is an investor. Every security sells only once in the primary market. A subset of the primary markets is the *initial public offering* (or IPO) market. In this market, firms "go public" by issuing shares to investors for the first time. Secondary markets are where already issued securities that is, seasoned issues) trade among investors. Trading in the secondary markets does not specifically involve the company whose security is traded, in that the company does not receive any money from the transactions. Investors merely trade securities back and forth among themselves.

Secondary market trading, however, is extremely important to a company. First of all, if secondary market trading did not exist, few investors would buy securities from companies (that is, in the primary market) in the first place. Without secondary markets, investors would be "stuck" with the original security until it matured. In the case of corporate bonds, this is usually 30 years from issue, and common stock never matures. Investors would not be able to liquidate their securities regardless of personal needs. Would you buy a share of Google stock, a stock that currently pays no dividends, for $633 per share if you knew that you would never able to sell the stock? We wouldn't, and we are sure you wouldn't either. Thus, without secondary markets, companies would not be able to raise money in the primary market. Second, secondary markets set prices for primary market transactions. If Google decided that it wanted to sell 10 million shares in the primary market, how would Google know what price these shares would probably sell for? The answer is whatever shares of Google stock are currently selling for in the secondary market, assuming that Google will spend the money raised wisely. New shares of Google are essentially the same as seasoned shares that are already actively trading. (Note that IPO shares do not yet have a secondary market, so determining what these shares will sell for is extremely difficult.) Finally, secondary markets provide instant evaluation and feedback to a financial manager. Recall that the goal of a financial manager is to maximize shareholder wealth and that shareholder wealth is represented by the market value of a firm's equity (which is merely price per share times the number of shares outstanding). If, all else constant, the price per share of a company's stock is declining while other company stock prices are rising, the financial manager is receiving a bad evaluation from the market. Likewise, if a firm's manager announces some change in policy that, all else constant, causes the company's stock price to rise, the new policy is probably a good idea.

Because the primary and secondary markets for stocks and bonds are of significant importance to financial managers, we will describe these markets in greater detail. We will also explain some of the measures that are used to describe the performance of the overall market.

6.3.1 Bond Investment Risk

Recall that a fixed income security, for example a corporate bond, is actually a contract between a lender and a borrower that specifies the exact payment stream and the term required to repay the debt. For example, a bond with a $1,000 par value, an 8% coupon rate and a term to maturity of five years, promises to pay to the investor the following cash flow stream:

Year	Cash Flow
1	$ 80
2	$ 80
3	$ 80
4	$ 80
5	$1,080

Due to the exact contractual nature of a bond, the only risk inherent in this cash flow stream is the probability that the issuer might default on the payments. That is, that a specific payment or payments might be made late or may not be made at all. Such risk is referred default risk.

Fortunately for investors, several independent companies (for example, Standard and Poor's) rate, or grade, bonds according to their default risk. A typical grading scheme is:

AAA	—	Lowest probability of default
AA	—	↓
A	—	
BBB	—	Higher probability of default
BB	—	↓
B	—	
CCC	—	Highest probability of default
CC	—	Currently in default of some or all terms of the contract

A particularly important segment of the bond market is called the junk bond market. Junk bonds are bonds that are rated BB and below. These are highly speculative bonds with high default risk premiums. All else constant, corporate bonds with the same grade should have about the same default risk premium.

A second risk factor for fixed income securities has to do with the term, or length, of the loan. There is more risk inherent in lending long term than short term. This relationship is mainly a function of the difficulty associated with forecasting long-term versus short-term default risk and inflation rates. The return associated with this second risk factor is known as the *maturity risk premium.* The maturity risk premium is higher for 10-year bonds than for two-year bonds. In fact, the maturity risk premium is easy to observe. Which interest rate is higher: a 15-year mortgage or a 30-year mortgage? A three-year car loan or a six-year car loan? If you look these up, you will find that the shorter-term security has a lower interest rate.

Another risk that bond investors face is the interest rate risk. To illustrate this, let's suppose you bought a $1,000 par value bond that carries a 5% coupon rate. Suppose after a year you decide to sell your bond, and at that time, the prevailing market interest rates soar and new bonds are being issued with 7% coupon rate. What will happen to your bond price? To entice someone to buy your bond, you will have to discount your bond price. Interest rates and bond prices have what's called an "inverse relationship" – meaning, when one goes up, the other goes down.

6.3.2 Risk for Equity Securities

Whereas the expected future cash flows for a bond are explicitly stated in the bond contract and non-payment results in company default, the expected future cash flows to equity are completely uncertain. Recall that equity is a residual claim. Equity holders get what is "left over" after all creditors have been paid. In a particularly bad year for a firm when revenues are low, the cash flows to equity holders can be zero. In a good sales year, the cash flows might be very big.

Additional Questions and Problems

1. Describe a *financial security* in terms that a friend who is majoring in history could understand.

2. Assume that you own 100% of a private company that has no debt and an equity value of $1,000,000. Describe two ways that you could "extract" some of the equity (say, $500,000) from your company.

3. Complete the following sentences:

   - "To an investor who owns a financial security, the security represents a stream of _____ _____."

   - "The value of any security to an investor is the _____ of the _____ from owning the security discounted at the _____ _____."

4. What are the two basic classifications for the securities that firms issue to raise capital? In what way(s) are these types of securities similar? In what way(s) are these types of securities different?

5. Suppose a firm has outstanding debt securities of $100 million with an obligatory payment of $8 million per year. What is the cash flow to debt and the cash flow to equity if the firm cash flow level is:

   a. $40 million

   b. $20 million

   c. $10 million

   d. $5 million

   e. $0

6. The shareholders of Filbun, Inc. are about to vote for five new board members. The company has 10,000,000 shares of stock outstanding. Assume that 90% of Filbun's shareholders support candidates A, B, C, D, and E and the rest of Filbun's shareholders support candidate F. Show how, under cumulative voting, the minority shareholders will be able to elect candidate F to the board.

Chapter 7

Valuation of Bonds and Stocks and the Cost of Capital

7.1 Chapter Introduction and Overview
7.2 The Cost of Capital
7.3 Bond Valuation
7.4 Preferred Stock Valuation
7.5 Valuation of Common Stock
   Assignments
   Additional Questions and Problems

After studying Chapter 7, you should be able to:

- Describe the concepts that underlie the cost of capital.
- Explain the key features of bonds.
- Distinguish between different kinds of bonds.
- Estimate the value of a bond and compute a bondholder's expected rate of return.
- Identify the basic characteristics and features of preferred stock.
- Value preferred stock.
- Identify the basic characteristics and features of common stock.
- Value common stock.
- Calculate a stock's expected rate of return.

From *Lectures in Corporate Finance*, 6th Edition by Jayant R. Kale and Richard J. Fendler. Copyright © 2013 by Kendall Hunt Publishing Company. Reprinted by permission.

7.1 Chapter Introduction and Overview

Kumar woke on Tuesday morning with a harsh cough and a raw throat. Fortunately he had banked some sick days, so he called in and went back to bed. Around 11:00 AM, Kumar woke and decided to watch some TV. Since he was usually at work during the day, he had no idea what he might find on the tube. He really wanted to watch a cricket match, but he hadn't found one of these on TV since he moved to the United States to attend college. Although he loved America, and the job he got out of college was a dream compared to the limited opportunities that existed in his home country, he still missed hearing sportscasters talking about bowlers, wicket keepers, overs, bails, ducks, and, of course, yorkers.

Hoping against hope, he surfed the channels on his TV looking for a cricket match. As luck would have it, the batteries in his remote ran out just as he clicked on a financial news channel. Kumar knew absolutely nothing about the world of finance and most of what he saw and heard was completely foreign to him. Still, he didn't feel well enough to walk over to the TV and besides, he had no idea how to change the channel without the remote. So, Kumar decided to see if he could figure out how this subject could possibly be so important that it required a dedicated 24-hour station.

The newscaster seemed very excited about some recent wild fluctuations in the stock price of a particular, publicly traded company named DottsPam Imports, Inc. From the best Kumar could make out, DP Imp (as the newscaster kept saying) imported distilled spirits (mainly vodka, tequila, and rum) from manufacturers around the world for sale in the United States. Although the company was licensed to sell its products throughout the entire United States and Canada, the relatively young company currently only had contracts with distributors on the east coast.

There seemed to be a great deal of excitement about the company's flagship product, a Russian vodka named "Snowy Birch" to which DP Imp had exclusive import rights for the U.S. and Canadian markets. Apparently, last night Snowy Birch had received a rating of 96 (highest of any brand of vodka on the market) and a recommendation of "Excellent, A Truly Complex, yet Smooth and Refreshing Vodka" in the 2013 Ultimate Spirits Challenge competition. Related to winning that award, at 9:30 AM today, DP Imp signed a multimillion-dollar contract with the largest beverage distribution company in the world. Additionally, around 10:30 AM, two major music entertainers, athletes from several different sports teams, a few world dignitaries, and a former U.S. president all released statements saying that Snowy Birch was their vodka of choice.

The stock price chart displayed on the TV showed that DP Imp stock had moved from $12.34 per share at the start of the day to $27.48 by 10:45 AM. Within the last 20 minutes, however, the stock price had completely reversed directions, yet no one seemed to know why. Currently, the stock was selling for $18.80 per share. Kumar was mesmerized with all that was happening. Special reporters were speaking with financial market experts, someone who had the designation of a "forensic" accountant, and most recently a former FBI agent. New information seemed to be occurring by the minute and each new event pushed the stock price down further. Then a special bulletin notice appeared on the screen:

DottsPam Imports, Inc. CEO abruptly walks out of top-level meeting. Seen speeding away from company headquarters in car. CFO and Director of Sales investigating several recent curious transactions involving company CEO (a former lawyer), millions of dollars, and what appear to be several offshore bank accounts.

Within 10 minutes of this bulletin, the price of DP Imp stock fell below $1 per share, the beverage contract was cancelled and all endorsements were revoked. The company that was valued at over $100 million at 10:45 AM was essentially worthless less than 30 minutes later. Kumar was stunned. How could this possibly happen?

The blast of the horn from the car behind him snapped Kumar back to the present. That event, which happened just over 8 years ago, had completely changed Kumar's life and career. Wanting to know more about what happened that day to DottsPam Imports, Inc. stock and, more importantly, how security prices were determined in general, Kumar had returned to school to earn his MBA in finance. He then earned his CFA designation[1] and, after working for the past four years as a hedge fund research analyst, Kumar had been promoted this morning to top manager of a $750-million hedge fund.

A second longer blast of the horn made Kumar aware that the light had turned green. He punched the accelerator on his 2014 Jerez Black Metallic BMW M3 convertible, hitting 60 mph in just over 4 seconds. As he sped off, Kumar gazed into his rear view mirror at the anxious person behind him. He could barely make out a very melancholy-looking guy sitting behind the wheel of a burnt orange Chevrolet Sonic, or perhaps it was a Ford Fiesta. Probably the kind of car I would be driving too if I hadn't discovered the wonderful and amazing world of finance, thought Kumar . . . .

In this chapter, we will focus on applying the valuation techniques learned in Chapters 4 and 5 to the cash flows from many of the securities described in Chapter 6. You will learn how security prices are fundamentally determined and the key factors that impact their values. In addition to valuing securities, we shall also introduce the concept of the cost of capital, which is essential to capital budgeting decisions made by firms (the main topic of Chapters 9 and 10). We believe that you will enjoy this chapter, and we hope that perhaps you too will catch the same bug that Kumar caught (and of course, receive similar rewards).

7.2 The Cost of Capital

Recall the concept of the required rate of return from the earlier chapter on time value of money. We described an investor's required rate of return as the minimum return that investors would require for giving up the use of their money. How do investors determine this rate?

The most logical answer is that investors look at the market to determine required rates of return. After all, the market is the place where millions of investors agree to buy and sell securities at specific prices. And the price paid for a security represents an expected return. For example, if you pay $100 today for a security that is expected to return $110 exactly one year from today, your expected return on this security is 10%. How did the price of $100 today get determined? For any financial market transaction to occur, both the buyer and the seller must agree to a price. And because financial markets are dynamic, the price at any moment in time is an equilibrium value indicating the amount a new investor would pay to buy a security as well as the price at which a seller would sell a security.

---

[1] The Chartered Financial Analyst (CFA) designation is considered to be the gold standard of the investments finance field. Those who earn this certification possess an in-depth knowledge of financial asset valuation and the operations of the investment industry. Most portfolio managers and nearly all research analysts at hedge funds and private equity firms hold the CFA designation.

Referring back to the opening story, the reason DottsPam Imports stock rose in the early morning was because the number of buyers who wanted the stock based on the positive news about the future prospects of the company exceeded the number of sellers. And the only way to get more people to sell their stock was for the price to increase. After news that the CEO had embezzled large amounts of money from the company before boarding a plane for a country in South America (this is "the rest of the story") became public, sellers wanted to get rid of their stock as quickly as possible. The only way to get buyers to buy what was rapidly becoming a very bad situation investment was to dramatically lower the price. Eventually, the prospects of bankruptcy became so large that the stock completely quit trading because no one would buy the stock at any price, and thus DP Imp stock became worthless.

Note that there are many, many, many financial securities in the multitrillion-dollar financial markets and thus every single security has numerous comparable securities (we will define what we mean by comparable later, but for now, consider a security that has similar cash flow risk characteristics to be similar). The most fundamental principle of equilibrium financial markets is that **the price and expected return relationship of all comparable securities must be the same**.

For example, assume that there are 100 securities in the market with the same cash flow risk characteristics. For simplicity, we will define risk with an index that goes from 1 to 10, with 1 being low risk and 10 being high risk. Assume all 100 of these securities have a risk index value of 6.

As in the example above, for a simple one year security:

Expected return = (expected future cash flow/price) − 1.

Thus, if the cash flow expected one year from today is $110 and the current price is $100, then the expected return is 110/100 = 1.10 − 1 = .10 = 10%. Or, if the cash flow expected one year from today is $195 and the current price is $177.27, then the expected return is 195.00/177.27 − 1 = 1.10 − 1 = .10 = 10%.

Now assume that the prices of 99 of these securities relative to their individual expected future cash flows are such that the expected return on each of these 99 securities is 10%. If the risk of the 100th security is also 6, what must be the expected return on this 100th security? It **has to be** 10%? Why? Suppose the expected future cash flow on this 100th security was $230 and the current price of this security was $200. Then, the expected return would be 230/200 − 1 = 1.15 − 1 = .15 = 15%. So, the "world" of these securities would look as follows:

	100th Security	99 Other Securities
Expected return	15%	10%
Risk	6	6

In such a world, all rational investors would want to buy as much of the 100th security as possible. Similar to DP Imp stock in the early morning, this would increase the price of the 100th security. But suppose the price increased to $213.95. Now the return would be 230/213.05 − 1 = 1.075 − 1 = .075 = 7.5%. And the "world" of these securities would be:

	100th Security	99 Other Securities
Expected return	7.5%	10%
Risk	6	6

At this price/expected future cash flow relationship, no rational investors would want to buy the 100th security, and if no one wants the security, its price will decrease.

When will equilibrium occur? Obviously, when the price of the 100th security is such that its expected return is comparable to the other 99 securities. This will occur at a price of $209.09. At this price, the expected return on the 100th security is $230/209.09 - 1 = 1.10 - 1 = .10 = 10\%$, which is the same as the other similar cash flow risk characteristics securities on the market.

How fast does this price adjustment process work in the real world? About as close to instantaneous as you can imagine. When new information occurs that alters the risk-return relationship of one security relative to others, investors immediately begin placing buy or sell orders. As orders enter the market, disequilibrium happens and prices begin changing. Disequilibrium (i.e., more buy orders than sell, or more sell orders than buy, at the existing price) continues and the price keeps moving until a new equilibrium is achieved. Because huge amounts of money can be made or lost following new information, the sooner investors act, the more they can gain or less they will lose.

In fact, information in the financial markets is so important that we have laws especially designed to ensure that no single investor is allowed to use information before it becomes publicly available. These are called *insider trading* laws. To illustrate the potential value of inside information, consider another illegal activity perpetrated by the DottsPam Imports CEO. At the open of trading on that momentous day, the DP Imp CEO purchased 100,000 shares of the company stock at $12.34 per share. He purchased the stock because he knew, before anyone else, about the positive news concerning the award and about the contract with the national distribution company that was about to be signed. Then, after the price soared to $27.48, he sold all of these shares because he knew that his crime was about to be uncovered. By buying, and then selling, before the good, then bad, news was known by others, he banked a profit of over $1.5 million.

To prevent unfair profit taking such as this, insider trading laws severely punish those who are caught trading on inside information. The fines are often twice what the trader earns in profit and many inside traders end up serving federal prison sentences of many years. In case you are wondering, justice was served with regards to the DP Imp CEO. The FBI nabbed him just before his plane headed for South America took off, he was tried and convicted in federal court of embezzlement and insider trading, he paid millions of dollars in fines that caused him to file personal bankruptcy, and he was sent to jail for seven years. In fact, he currently shares a cell with Bennie Feldhaus, who you may remember from Chapter 1.

Now consider a firm that needs to raise money in the financial markets (mainly by selling bonds and/or stock) to expand its business. To determine the terms to require for the capital provided, investors will locate other securities in the market that are comparable to the firm that is seeking their funds. The return on these comparable investments will be the *minimum* that investors will require to give the firm the capital it seeks (that is, to buy the firm's newly issued bonds and/or stock). In other words, investors' required rate of return is determined as the *opportunity cost* of their funds. Recall also the fact that this required rate of return for investors was used as the discount rate in determining the value that investors place on an asset.

Suppose that for a particular investment, investors determine that the required rate of return is 15%. One can think of this 15% as the minimum "price" that investors are charging for their capital. Anyone who wants these investors' capital must pay a "price" of at least 15%. Now consider the situation from the point of view of the firm that wants the investors' capital.

To obtain these investors' capital, the firm will have to pay the investors a "price." The price that the firm pays to the investors is the "cost" of the capital to the firm. What is the relationship then between the investors' "price" for their capital (investors' required rate of return) and the "cost" of these investors' capital to the firm (firm's cost of capital)? The answer is very simple. Lending capital to the firm is similar to "selling" the capital and when the firm takes the investors' capital, it is akin to "buying;" thus, the investor is the "seller" and the firm is the "buyer."

Because, as we showed above, in a competitive financial market, security prices reflect required rates of return, *the firm's cost of capital is equal to the investor's required rate of return.* Splitting the cost of capital into its most common components, the investor's required rate of a return from a firm's debt (or, credit) securities would be the firm's *cost of debt* and the investor's required rate of return from the firm's equity would be the firm's *cost of equity.* In the rest of this chapter, we will describe how debt security (i.e., bond) prices are determined and once we understand how the bond price mechanism works, we show how firms can extract the cost of debt (what is called the bond's *yield to maturity*) from observed bond prices. Then we will describe how stock prices are determined, and once we understand the stock price mechanism, we show how firms can extract the cost of equity from observed stock prices.

7.3 Bond Valuation

We will now discuss the valuation of different types of debt securities. Additionally, having now seen the conceptual relation between the required rate of return and the cost of capital, we will also present methods for determining the cost of each of these debt securities.

7.3.1 Valuation of Consols

A consol or perpetual debt is a bond that pays coupon every period forever. Thus, an investor who buys a consol is buying the perpetuity of the fixed coupon. If the coupon is C dollars, the price of the consol is simply the present value of the perpetuity. In other words,

$$P_{consol} = \frac{C}{r_d^{consol}}$$

where r_d^{consol} is the cost of capital, d denotes the fact that a consol is a debt security, and the superscript tells us the type of the security.

Rearranging the above equation, we obtain the equation for the cost of a consol or perpetual debt as follows:

$$r_d^{consol} = \frac{C}{P_{consol}}$$

Suppose that in 2013, a firm issued consols that promised a coupon of $100 per year paid annually. If the investor's required rate of return is 10%, what is the price of the consol? The answer is pretty straightforward to compute.

$$P_{consol} = \frac{100}{0.10} = \$1,000$$

Now two years have passed since the issuing of these consols. The market price of these consols is now $960. What is the investor's required rate of return from such consols today? If the firm wanted to issue debt in the form of consols today, what would be its cost of capital? We compute the investor's required rate of return as follows:

$$r_d^{consol} = \frac{100}{960} = 0.1042 \text{ or } 10.42\%$$

Additionally, if the firm wanted to issue such consols today, it would have to ensure that investors received their required rate of return of 10.42%. Thus the firm's cost of debt capital would be 10.42%.

How would the firm go about doing this? It would have two obvious choices. One, it could promise a coupon of $100 per year and receive a price of $960 per consol. Or, it could promise a coupon of $104.20 per year and obtain a price of $1,000 per bond. Usually, firms like to sell bonds at their *par value* (sometimes also called the bond's *face value*), which is generally $1,000. Therefore, we suspect that the firm would be more likely to choose the second alternative.

Problem 7.1: A firm's perpetual debt promises a coupon of $80 per year forever. If the investor's required rate of return (i.e., yield to maturity) is 12%, what is the price of this bond?

Problem 7.2: ABC Corp. wants to issue perpetual debt to raise capital. It plans to pay a coupon of $90 per year on each bond with par value of $1,000. Consols of a comparable firm with a coupon of $100 per year are selling at $1,050. What is the cost of debt capital (i.e., yield to maturity) for ABC? What will be the price at which it will issue its consols?

Problem 7.3: If ABC (from the previous problem) wanted to raise $100 million dollars in debt, how many such consols would it have to issue?

Problem 7.4: If ABC wanted to issue its consols at par, that is, at a price of $1,000, what coupon must it pay?

Problem 7.5: What would be the price of a *comparable* consol that has a par value of $1,000 and a coupon rate of 8%?

7.3.2 Valuation of Zero-Coupon Bonds

Recall that a zero-coupon bond (ZCB), as the name implies, pays no periodic coupon. The only cash flow that investors receive is the par value (usually $1,000) at maturity. Then, it is easy to see that the price of a ZCB will be the present value of the par value of the bond. In other words,

$$P_{ZCB} = \frac{F}{\left(1 + r_d^{ZCB}\right)^{N'}}$$

where F is the par value of the bond, r_d^{ZCB} is the cost of ZCB debt capital, and N is the number of years to maturity.

Suppose that ABC Corp. wanted to issue a ZCB with a maturity period of 20 years. If the investor's required rate of return is 8%, the price that ABC will receive for this bond is $214.55. This is obtained with the help of the financial calculator (N = 20, I/YR = 8, FV = 1000, PMT = 0, PV = ?). Given the price of a ZCB and the maturity period, it is also possible to determine r_d^{ZCB}, the cost of debt capital. Suppose that a ZCB with 15 years to maturity is trading at a price of $400. To compute the r_d^{ZCB}, we enter into the financial calculator PV = – 400, FV = 1000, N = 15, PMT = 0, I/YR = ? to obtain 6.30% as the cost of capital for this ZCB.

Problem 7.6: Find the price of a ZCB with 25 years to maturity and r_d^{ZCB} of 14%.

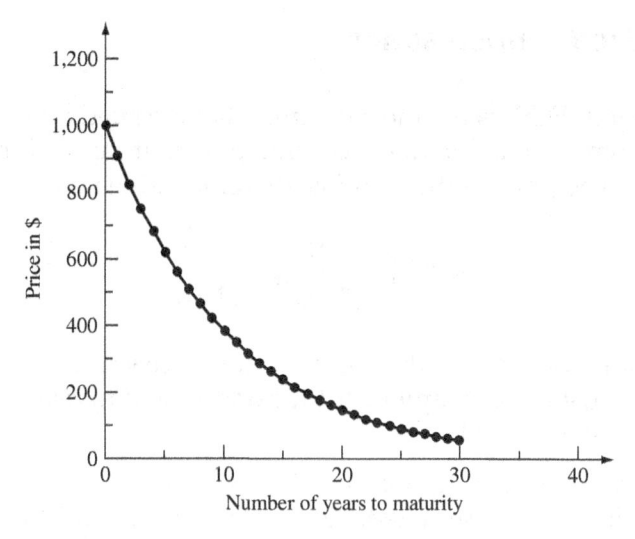

Figure 7.1 The Price of a Zero-Coupon Bond and the Time to Maturity (FV = 1,000 and r = 10%)

Problem 7.7: The ZCB of XCorp. is trading in the market at a price of $332. The bond has 17 years to maturity. What is XCorp's cost of ZCB's debt capital (i.e., yield to maturity)?

Can the price of a ZCB ever be greater than the par value? The answer is no, as long as the discount rate is positive. The reason for this is pretty straightforward. A ZCB gives you a single cash flow (the par value) in the future. For all positive discount rates, the present value of this cash flow must be less than the cash flow itself.

To illustrate this property, consider the graph in Figure 7.1. In this graph, we have plotted the price of a ZCB using a discount rate of 10% for periods to maturity varying from 30 to zero years. Or, you can interpret this graph as the price path over time of a ZCB that is issued with a maturity of 30 years.

Note from the graph below that as the ZCB approaches maturity (read graph from right to left), that is, zero years, the price becomes closer and closer to the par value. That is the way it should be. Consider how much you would pay now for receiving $1,000 next second. An amount extremely close to $1,000, we are sure.

7.3.3 Valuation of Fixed-Coupon Bonds

The fixed-coupon bond (FCB) is the most common bond issued by U.S. corporations. As you may recall, this bond promises fixed periodic coupon payments and a lump sum payment equal to par value at maturity. The price of this bond is, therefore, given by:

$$P_{FCB} = \sum_{t=1}^{N} \frac{C}{(1+r_d)^t} + \frac{F}{(1+r_d)^N}$$

where C is the periodic coupon, F is the par value (or, Face value), N is the number of periods to maturity, and r_d is the cost of debt capital, or the bond's yield to maturity (what we will sometimes also refer to as the bond's YTM).

For example, a typical bond description may be "8% coupon paid annually and 20 years to maturity." As before, unless otherwise stated, the par value is $1,000. Thus, this bond will provide an annuity (because coupon is paid annually) of $80 (8% of the par value) for twenty years and will pay the par value of $1,000 at the end of 20 years. The cash flows for this bond will look as follows:

Year	Expected Cash Flow
1	$80
2	$80
.	.
.	.
.	.
19	$90
20	$1080

If the investor's required rate of return is 10%, the price of this bond can be computed as follows: I/YR = 10, FV = 1,000, PMT = 80, N = 20, PV = ? to obtain $829.73. This would be the current equilibrium price of this bond.

Why do we call a bond's required rate of return the bond's *yield to maturity*? Because, if an investor buys the bond at today's price, the payments the investor expects to receive over the life of the bond (i.e., from now until the bond matures), represents an average annual return on the investor's initial investment (i.e., the price paid) of 10%. To see that this is the case, consider the amortization table where beginning balance is the price of the bond today, interest earned is the bond's yield to maturity times the beginning balance, and cash flow is the coupon payment in years 1 – 19 and the coupon payment plus the par value in year 20.

Year	Beginning Balance	Interest Earned	Cash Flow	Ending Balance
1	829.73	82.97	80.00	832.70
2	832.70	83.27	80.00	835.97
.	.	.	.	.
.	.	.	.	.

.	.	.	.	.
19	965.29	96.53	80.00	981.82
20	981.82	98.18	1080.00	0.00

Thus, the cash flows of $80 per year for 20 years plus a lump sum payment of $1000 in year 20 equals an average annual return of 10% (i.e., the bond's yield to maturity) on the initial investment of $829.73 to buy the bond today.

On the other hand, why do we call the bond's required rate of return the company's cost of capital? Because if the company issued 100,000 of these bonds today, the company would raise (100,000 bonds sold) x (829.73 per bond) = $82,973,000. That is, the company would be "borrowing" this amount of money from the bondholders. The annual payment of $80 per year for 19 years and then a final payment of $1,080 in the 20th year, represents an annual average cost of 10%. Of course, this MUST be the case. If investors are receiving a 10% annual return, and the "receipt" of this annual return is coming from the company, then the company must be paying the 10% that the investors are receiving.

Example Problem: Suppose that a firm has some FCBs outstanding that pay a coupon of 6% annually, have 12 years left to maturity, and have a market price of $830. What is this firm's cost of capital? What is the yield to maturity that an investor will receive if the investor buys this bond today?

Solution: FV = 1,000, PV = – 830, N = 12, PMT = 60, I/YR = ? to obtain 8.29%. This is the firm's cost of debt capital. It is also the bond's yield-to-maturity (YTM).

Let us suppose that the Qco. is considering issuing debt (FCB). The firm has estimated that its cost of debt capital is 8%. It has decided to issue 30-year FCBs. However, it is deciding on the coupon rate. The choices for the coupon rate are (a) 5%, (b) 8%, and (c) 11%. If the coupons are paid annually, the price of the bonds under the three alternatives would be:

a. *Coupon of 5%:* I/YR = 8, FV = 1,000, PMT = 50, N = 30, PV = ? to obtain $662.27 as the price.
b. *Coupon of 8%:* I/YR = 8, FV = 1,000, PMT = 80, N = 30, PV = ? to obtain $1,000.00 as the price.
c. *Coupon of 11%:* I/YR = 8, FV = 1,000, PMT = 110, N = 30, PV = ? to obtain $1,337.73 as the price.

Notice that the higher the coupon, the higher is the price. That should not be surprising; the higher the cash flow that investors receive, the higher will be the price that they will be willing to pay.

The above numbers illustrate another interesting property of FCBs. Note that:

- When the coupon rate is 5%, that is, lower than the yield to maturity (or discount rate), the price of the bond is lower than the par value ($1,000).
- When the coupon rate is 8%, that is, equal to the yield to maturity (or discount rate), the price of the bond is equal to par value.
- When the coupon rate is 11%, that is greater than the yield to maturity (or discount rate), the price of the bond is greater than the par value.

In fact, this will always be true. When the price of the bond is less than the par value, the bond is said to be *selling at a discount.* When the bond sells at a price that equals the par value, the bond is said to *sell at par.* Finally, when the price of the bond is greater than the par value, the bond is said to *selling at a premium*. As a general rule, corporations like to issue debt at par, that is, the coupon rate is set equal to the prevailing rate on comparable debt securities.

Important Bond Relationships (assuming all else constant)	
If YTM > Coupon rate	Price < Par Value
If YTM = Coupon rate	Price = Par Value
If YTM < Coupon rate	Price > Par Value
If YTM increases	Price will decrease
If YTM decreases	Price will increase

Finally, the coupon on the bond is not always paid once a year or annually. It is common to see firms paying coupons semi-annually or quarterly. In fact, most corporate bonds in the United States pay interest semi-annually.

Suppose that you want to find the price of a 10-year bond with a coupon of 8%, paid semi-annually, and a yield to maturity (YTM) of 10%. This bond gives you a cash flow of $40 (half of 8% of 1,000) every six months. That is, in 10 years it will give you 10 × 2 = 20 such cash flows. Additionally, at the end of these 20 six-month periods, you will receive $1,000. Thus, the price of this bond is given by

$$P = \sum_{t=1}^{20} \frac{40}{(1.05)^t} + \frac{1000}{(1.05)^{20}}$$

The first term of the above pricing equation is the present value of the 20 periodic (once every six months) payments of $40 discounted, as we did in the past with semi-annual compounding, at half the discount rate, that is, 0.5 × 10 = 5%. The second term is the present value of the $1,000 that is to be received at maturity. Notice that we have discounted this future cash flow also for 20 periods at a discount rate of 5%. You might wonder why we should use semi-annual compounding for this cash flow because it is received as a lump sum at the end of 10 years. The reason is consistency. You receive two cash flows at the end of 10 years. One is the (last) coupon payment of $40 and the other is the par value of the bond of $1,000. At what rate are you discounting the $40 cash flow? At a rate of 5% for 20 periods. Then the other cash flow of $1,000 from the same bond at the same time should also be discounted at the same rate, that is, at 5% for 20 periods.

The calculator solution for this bond is now straightforward. Enter: FV = 1,000, PMT = 40, I/YR = 5, N = 20, PV = ? to get $875.38. Note that all the calculator did was make the solution of the above equation quick and simple, yet it still merely solved the equation above.

If the coupon had been paid quarterly, the price could be obtained by entering FV = 1,000, PMT = 20, I/YR = 2.5, N = 40, PV = ? in your calculator to yield $874.49. In this case the bond makes 40 (the number of quarters in 10 years) payments of $20 (quarter of 8% of 1,000) and a final payment of $1,000. The discount rate is 0.25 × 10 = 2.5%.

If a bond pays coupon semi-annually or quarterly, you must remember the following in computing the cost of debt = the bond's yield to maturity. You must multiply the value you obtain for I/YR by two if the coupon is semi-annual and by four if it is quarterly. For example, suppose that a 10% coupon bond with 14 years to maturity pays coupon semi-annually and is trading at

$1,050 in the market. To compute the cost of capital or yield to maturity, you would enter the following in your calculator: FV = 1,000, PMT = 50, PV = −1,050, N = 28, I/Y = ? and obtain I/YR to be 4.676%. The cost of debt capital is therefore 4.676 × 2 = 9.352%.

Now try the following problems.

Problem 7.8: A firm is planning to issue $50 million of fixed-coupon debt. Each bond will have a par value of $1,000, a coupon of 9% paid annually, and maturity period of 25 years. If the market rate for such debt is 12%, what will be the market price of such a bond and how many bonds will the firm have to issue?

Problem 7.9: A firm is trying to determine its cost of debt capital. It has some bonds outstanding. These bonds pay a coupon of 7% annually and have 11 years to maturity. The market price of these bonds is $821.50. What is the firm's cost of debt?

Problem 7.10: The market interest rate is 12%. What is the price of a 15-year, 9% coupon bond that pays coupon semi-annually?

Problem 7.11: Suppose that the coupon of the bond in the previous problem is paid quarterly. What would be the price of the bond?

Problem 7.12: Find the firm's cost of capital for the following two bonds that it has outstanding. (a) 8% coupon bond with 13 years to maturity, semi-annual coupon, and market price of $980. (b) 12% coupon bond with six years to maturity, quarterly coupon, market price $1,180.

Problem 7.13: Suppose that a bond is trading at a price of $940. This bond has 20 years to maturity and pays coupon interest annually. The market rate of interest for such a bond is 11%. What is the coupon rate for this bond?

Problem 7.14: A bond has coupon rate of 10% and the coupon is paid quarterly. The price of this bond is $1,075 and the market rate is 9%. How many years does this bond have until it matures?

7.4 Preferred Stock Valuation

As we noted in the previous chapter, preferred stock is a hybrid security that pays a fixed dividend every year forever. Thus, it is perpetuity. Therefore, the price of preferred stock is simply the present value of a perpetuity. In other words,

$$P_{ps} = \frac{D}{r_p},$$

where D is the periodic dividend on the preferred stock and r_p is the firm's cost of capital for preferred stock or, equivalently, the investor's required rate of return. Rearranging the above relation yields the following simple relation for the cost of preferred stock:

$$r_p = \frac{D}{P_{ps}},$$

Applying the above relations to numbers is simple. The price of a preferred stock that pays a dividend of $3 per year when the cost of capital is 12% is:

$$\frac{3}{.12} = \$25.$$

Similarly, if a preferred stock with a dividend of $2.80 is selling at a price of $22, the cost of capital is:

$$\frac{2.80}{22} .1273 \text{ or } 12.73\%$$

Problem 7.15: Miced Corporation issued preferred stock with a par value of $700. The stock promised to pay an annual dividend equal to 19.0% of the par value. If the investor's required rate of return for this stock is 10.0%, what is the price this stock?

Problem 7.16: Sign Research, Inc.'s preferred stock has a par value of $1,000 and a dividend equal to 13.0% of the par value. The stock is currently selling for $907.00. What is Sign Research, Inc.'s cost of capital for preferred stock?

Problem 7.17: Tell Corporation plans a new issue of preferred stock. Similar risk stock currently offers an annual return to investors of 17.0%. If the company wants the stock to sell for $569.00 per share, what annual dividend must the company's preferred stock offer?

7.5 Valuation of Common Stock

Besides fixed-coupon debt, equity is the preferred mode of financing for most U.S. corporations. Unfortunately, valuation of equity is significantly more difficult than the pricing of bonds. In the case of bonds, the future cash flows are generally known—a stream of coupon payments and the par value at maturity. In the case of common stock, because equity is a residual claim, the future cash flows (dividends or selling price) are not fixed. In addition, equity does not have a maturity date. Thus, the cash flows from equity last forever.

Accordingly, it is necessary to make several assumptions to derive frameworks for valuing equity. In what follows, we begin with very strong (unrealistic) assumptions and obtain fairly simple formulae. As we progress, the assumptions will become more realistic but the valuation technique will become more complex.

7.5.1 Assuming a Constant Dividend Stream

The easiest scenario is when we assume that the dividends to the stock are constant. Under this assumption, the pricing technique for equity will be identical to that for preferred stock. In other words,

$$P_e = \frac{D}{r_e},$$

where D is the constant dividend per period and r_f is the cost of equity capital. In this case, the cost of equity can be computed as follows:

$$r_e = \frac{D}{P_e}.$$

As you can see, when we make the unrealistic assumption that the dividends from a stock will remain constant forever, we obtain a simple valuation formula.

Problem 7.18: You are considering buying common stock in Caeration, Inc. The firm is expected to pay a constant divided of $5.20 per share every year forever. If you require an annual return of 20.0% on your investment, what is the most you should pay for the stock today?

7.5.2 Assuming That Dividends Grow at a Constant Growth Rate

Let us add a small dose of realism to the previous scenario. Instead of assuming that dividends will be constant forever into the future, let us assume that dividends will grow at a constant rate of g per period. Let D_t denote the dividend in time t and let D_0 be the dividend that the firm has just paid, that is, at t = 0. Then:

$$D_1 = D_0(1+g),$$
$$D_2 = D_1(1+g) = D_0(1+g) \times (1+g) = D_0(1+g)^2,$$
$$D_3 = D_2(1+g) = D_0(1+g)^2 \times (1+g) = D_0(1+g)^3,$$
$$\text{and } D_t = D_{t-1}(1+g) = D_0(1+g)^{t-1} \times (1+g) = D_0(1+g)^t.$$

Then the price of the stock, that is, the PV of future cash flows is:

$$P_e = \sum_{t=1}^{\infty} \frac{D_t}{(1+r_e)^t} = \sum_{t=1}^{\infty} \frac{D_0(1+g)^t}{(1+r_e)^t}$$

The expression seems impossible to solve. However, as in the past, our friends in the mathematics field have proved that the above summation is exactly equal to:

$$P_e = \sum_{t=1}^{\infty} \frac{D_0(1+g)^t}{(1+r_e)^t} = \frac{D_0(1+g)}{r_e - g} = \frac{D_1}{r_e - g}.$$

Example Problem: You are considering buying common stock in Corpor Technology, Inc. Yesterday, the firm paid a dividend of $2.00 per share (that is, $D_0 = 2.00$). You have projected that dividends will grow at a rate of 8.0% per year indefinitely. If you require an annual return of 16.0% on this investment, what is the most you should pay for the stock today?

Solution: First note that $D_1 = D_0(1+g) = 2.00(1.08) = 2.16$. Then:

$$P_0 = \frac{D_1}{(r-g)} = \frac{2.16}{(.16-.08)} = \frac{2.16}{.08} = 27.00$$

Thus, when dividends are assumed to grow at a constant rate of g, the price of a share of common stock can be found by the above (fairly easy) formula. Rearranging the above yields the following relation for the cost of equity capital:

$$r_e = \frac{D_1}{P_e} + g.$$

In the above relation, the first term, $\frac{D_1}{P_e}$, is also known as the *dividend yield* or the dividends per share and the second term, g, is the *capital gains yield.* The required rate of return from a stock *re* is, therefore, *the sum of the dividend yield and the capital gains yield.*

Suppose that a stock is expected to pay a dividend of $2 (that is, $D_1 = 2.00$).[2] This dividend is expected to grow at the rate of 5% forever. The investor's required rate of return is 15%. The price of this stock should then be:

$$P_0 = \frac{2.00}{.15-.05} = 20.00.$$

---

[2] It is very important to learn the terminology for stock prices. The equation is based on D_1, which is the dividend that is expected to be paid one year from today. D_0 is the dividend paid yesterday, or sometime described as the dividend just paid. If you are given the dividend just paid, you must first compute $D_1 = D_0(1+g)$.

Notice that when the firm is *expected* to pay the dividend, that value becomes D_1. Suppose we change this problem by assuming that a firm has just paid a dividend of $2.00 and everything else is the same as before. In this case, $2.00 is D_0 and $D_1 = \$2.00 \times (1 + 0.05) = \$2.10$, and the price of the stock is:

$$P_0 = \frac{2.10}{.15 - .05} = 21.00.$$

Take a look at the pricing formula, $\frac{D_1}{r_e - g}$, again. In this formula, if g is greater than r_e, the denominator re will be negative and the price will be negative too. We know that prices cannot be negative. Thus, for this formula to work, the growth rate, in addition to being constant, must be less than r_e, the investor's required rate of return. Can the growth rate be greater than r_e? Sure it can. However, it can never be greater than r_e forever. Suppose that r_e for a particular stock is 15%. Can this stock's dividend grow at, say, 20% forever? If it did, the investors would be strange people. Even though the cash flow grows at a rate of 20%, they require a return of only 15%. It doesn't make sense. Thus, the growth rate can be greater than r_e for some periods but in the long run, it has to be the case that either g decreases or re increases so that g is less than r_e.

We have computed the price of a stock whose dividends grow at a constant rate forever. If you look at the expression with which we began the derivation of the formula, you will notice that the price of the stock is the present value of all future dividends. In that case, what happens if you sell the stock after a few years? Does it affect our ability to use the formula? The answer is that it does not. Intuitively you can see why it does not. Suppose that there are two investors, one of whom plans to hold a stock forever and the other for only five years. Will the market price be different for these two persons? Clearly not! We can see why with some numbers equally easily.

Consider a stock that pays a constant dividend of $2.00 per year forever. Assuming a discount rate of 10%, we know that the price of this stock should be:

$$P_0 = \frac{2.00}{.10} = 20.00$$

Now suppose that you plan to buy this stock today and then sell it after five years. What will be the cash flows to you? For the first five years (t = 1 through t = 5) you will receive the yearly dividend of $2.00. At the end of five years, that is, at t = 5, you will sell the stock and receive the selling price. How much will you obtain for this stock? Well, the person who buys it from you will pay a price, which is the present value of all the future cash flows that the buyer will receive from this stock. What are they? Again, $2.00 per year forever. Therefore, the price that you receive at t = 5 will be the present value of the dividends from t = 6 onward forever. In other words, whether you hold the stock or sell it after five years, the present value of all the flows that you receive are the same. Therefore, the price does not depend upon whether you sell the stock.

Problem 7.19: What is the price of a stock that is expected to pay a dividend of $3.50 next year (i.e., $D_1 = 3.50$) and this dividend is expected to grow at a rate of 6% per year forever? The appropriate discount rate is 12%.

Problem 7.20: The price of a stock in the market is $40. You know that the firm has just paid a dividend of $4.00. The dividend growth rate is expected to be 7%. What is the investor's required rate of return from this stock?

Problem 7.21: A firm is expected to pay a dividend of $3.25 on its stock next year. The price of this stock is $45 and the investor's required rate of return is 15%. What is the growth rate expected by the market in the dividend stream?

Did you obtain the answer for the above question? Note that you have to compute g, the growth rate. You can rearrange the formula $r_e = \dfrac{D_1}{P_e} + g$ as follows:

$$g = r_e - \dfrac{D_1}{P_e} = 0.15 - \dfrac{3.25}{45} = 0.778 = 7.78\%$$

7.5.3 Non-Constant Dividend Growth

Now suppose that you had to value a stock in the real world. To do so, you would have to forecast the future dividend stream from the stock. It is natural that you will be able to forecast dividends in the near future (say the next three years) more confidently than the later stream of dividends.

One possibility is to forecast specific values for the dividends expected in the first three or so years and then assume a constant growth rate for subsequent dividends. For example, in valuing the stock of ABC Corp., suppose that you forecast that dividends will be $2.00, $3.00, and $3.50 in the next three years, respectively. After that you expect dividends to grow at a constant rate of 5% per year forever. Let us suppose that the appropriate discount rate for ABC's stock is 15%.

So, the projected future dividends are: $D_1 = \$2.00$, $D_2 = \$3.00$, $D_3 = \$3.50$, $D_4 = \$3.50 \times (1.05) = \$3.675$, and so on. Displayed in a cash flow chart, we would have:

Year	Cash Flow
1	$2.00
2	$3.00
3	$3.50
4	$3.675
.	Grow at 5% per year every year to infinity
.	
.	
.	

Consider the dividend stream from t = 4 onwards. It is a stream with constant growth. Therefore, if one were at t = 3, the future dividend stream from this stock would be as follows: $3.675 the next year (t = 4) and a constant growth thereafter of 5% per year. Thus, the price of this stock at t = 3, denoted by P_3, can be determined with the constant growth formula as follows:

$$P_3 = \frac{D_4}{(r_e - g)} = \frac{3.675}{(0.15 - 0.05)} = \$36.75$$

Note that the price at t = 3, P_3, is the present value of all dividends after t = 3 (that is, the dividends in years 4, 5, 6, 7, . . ., infinity). To determine the price of the stock today (i.e., at t = 0, we can therefore, display the future cash flows to the stock as follows:

Year	Cash Flow
1	$2.00
2	$3.00
3	$3.50
4	$3.675 + $36.75

You can think of the above as keeping the stock for three years and selling it for $36.75. Recall from our earlier discussion that, in valuing a stock, it does not matter whether you sell the stock. Therefore, the price of the stock at t = 0, denoted by P_0, is:

$$P_0 = \frac{2}{1.15} + \frac{3}{(1.15)^2} + \frac{40.25}{(1.15)^3} = \$30.47.$$

Another possible scenario in stock valuation is as follows. Suppose firm A has just paid a dividend of $1. You expect the dividend to grow by 20% per year for the first two years, by 15% per year in years three and four, and then settle down to a constant growth rate of 6% per year in years 5 to infinity. If the appropriate discount rate is 12%, what is the current price of the stock?

First, compute the dividends you expect to receive up to and including the first year of constant growth (note that the first year of constant growth is year 5):

$$D_0 = \$1.00,$$
$$D_1 = D_0 \times (1 + g_1) = 1 \times (1.20) = \$1.20,$$
$$D_2 = D_1 \times (1 + g_2) = 1.20 \times (1.20) = \$1.44,$$
$$D_3 = D_2 \times (1 + g_3) = 1.44 \times (1.15) = \$1.656,$$
$$D_4 = D_3 \times (1 + g_4) = 1.656 \times (1.15) = \$1.9044,$$
$$D_5 = D_4 \times (1 + g_5) = 1.9044 \times (1.06) = \$2.0187$$

Note that from $t = 5$ *onward*, the stock dividend has a constant growth rate. Therefore, the *price of the stock at $t = 4$* can be computed by the formula as follows:

$$P_4 = \frac{D_5}{r_e - g} = \frac{2.0187}{0.12 - 0.06} = \$33.645.$$

To find P_0, the price at $t = 0$, we then have the cash flow chart:

Year	Cash Flow
1	$1.20
2	$1.44
3	$1.656
4	$1.9044 + 33.645

The price of the stock at $t = 0$ is then computed as follows:

$$P_0 = \frac{1.20}{1.12} + \frac{1.44}{(1.12)^2} + \frac{1.656}{(1.12)^3} + \frac{35.5494}{(1.12)^4} = \$25.99.$$

Now attempt the following problems. In solving these problems, drawing a cash flow time line or creating a cash flow table may prove to be extremely useful.

Problem 7.22: ABC Corp. is expected to pay the following dividends in the future. In the first year, $1.50, $2.00 in the second year, and after that the dividend is expected to grow at a constant rate of 4%. Assuming a discount rate of 10%, compute the current price of ABC stock.

Problem 7.23: XYZ Corp. is expected to have dividend growth rates of 25% in the first two years and after that the dividend is expected to remain constant forever. The company just paid a dividend of $1.00 (that is, $D_0 = 1.00$). Assuming a discount rate of 11%, compute the current price of XYZ stock.

Problem 7.24: PQR Co. is not expected to pay any dividend for the next three years. At $t = 4$, it will pay a dividend of $3.00, and the dividend is expected to grow at a constant rate of 5% forever after that. If the appropriate discount rate is 10% for this stock, what is the current stock price?

Problem 7.25: You expect EXRON Corp. to pay no dividends for the next two years. In years 3 and 4, the dividend will be $4 per year. After that, the dividend will grow at a constant rate of 7% per year. If the appropriate discount rate is 10%, what is the price of EXRON stock today?

In this chapter, we applied the "discounted cash flow" valuation concept to the pricing of common securities such as bonds, preferred stocks, and equity. As you must have noticed, the important thing is to be able to determine the stream of future cash flows and the appropriate discount rate. Having done that, the pricing of a security is a fairly simple matter of computing present values.

Of course, if security valuation in practice were so simple, the stock market and other financial markets would not hold such mystique. Note that everywhere in this chapter, the future cash flows and the discount rates were always assumed to be known. Determining these two variables is a matter of great skill, and the ability to estimate them separates the winners from the losers in the financial markets. Also, factors are constantly changing as new information is constantly being discovered. And because new information is by definition unknown and therefore random, security prices are random. This is what makes investing as much fun to dedicated investors as going to Las Vegas is to dedicated gamblers. You will learn more about this topic if you decide to take another finance class in either the theory of asset valuation or investments.

The principles we developed in this chapter demonstrate the fundamental valuation process for bonds, preferred stock, and common stock. These principles are important for corporations because a corporation's main interest is in determining the fundamental cost of capital, not the price of some security five minutes from now so they can make an instant profit. Both bond yields and investors' required rate of return on stock form the basis of the cost of capital for a company. This cost in turn is the benchmark against which projects the company can invest in are compared. How companies evaluate capital budgeting (i.e., long term) projects and how they estimate relevant cash flows for these projects are the topics covered in the final, two chapters of this book.

Assignment 7.1

1. Using a discount rate of 8%, value the following bonds: (a) a consol that pays a coupon of $82.50 per year, (b) a zero-coupon bond with 15 years to maturity, and (c) a 7% coupon bond that has 20 years to maturity with coupon paid annually.

2. Value the following bonds assuming a discount rate of 9%: (a) a 7% coupon bond that pays coupon semi-annually and has 30 years to maturity, (b) a 10% coupon bond that pays coupon quarterly and has 20 years to maturity.

3. ABC Co. has 9% coupon bonds outstanding (coupon is paid annually) that have 14 years to maturity. These bonds are currently trading at $978 per bond. What is ABC's cost of debt?

4. STU Co. has 8% bonds outstanding (coupon paid quarterly) that have 17 years to maturity. These bonds are trading at $1,020 per bond. What is STU's cost of debt?

Assignment 7.2

1. QWE Co. plans to issue preferred stock that pays a dividend of $2.25 per year. The company has estimated that the investors' required rate of return is 11%. What is the price that QWE expects to receive for this preferred stock? Suppose that after issuing the preferred stock, QWE finds that the preferred stock is trading at $24 per share. What can you say about QWE's estimate of the investors' required rate of return? What is the actual required rate of return?

2. The common stock of WER Co. is expected to pay a dividend of $1.50 per share forever. If the appropriate discount rate is 9%, what should be the price of the stock?

3. The common stock of ERT Co. is expected to pay a dividend of $2.50 per share next year. The dividend is expected to grow at the rate of 3% per year for ever. If the appropriate discount rate is 10%, what should be the price of the stock?

4. The common stock of RTY Co. is expected to pay a dividend of $1.00 per share for the next five years. After that, the dividend will grow at a rate of 5% per year forever. If the appropriate discount rate is 12%, what should be the price of the stock?

Assignment 7.3

1. The stock of TYU Co. is trading at $38 per share. The company just paid a dividend of $2 per share. The growth rate in dividends is projected to be 4% per year forever. What is TYU's cost of equity capital?

2. YUI Co. will pay dividends of $2, $1, and $3 in the next three years, respectively. Then the dividend is expected to grow at a constant rate of 6% per year. If the cost of equity is 14%, what is the current price of the stock?

3. UIO Co. just paid a dividend of 1.75. The company is expected to experience abnormally high growth in the next five years: 50% in the first two years, 30% in the next two years, and 20% in year 5. After that, the growth is expected to settle down to 7% per year forever. Assuming a discount rate of 15%, compute the current price of the stock.

4. IOP Co. just paid a dividend of $1.00. For the next three years, its growth rate is expected to be 35%. In the three years after that, the growth rate in dividends is expected to be 20%. After that the dividends will remain constant. Assuming a discount rate of 15%, compute the current price of the stock.

Additional Questions and Problems

1. You are considering buying bonds in Aphoolog, Inc. The bonds have a par value of $1,000 and mature in 28 years. The coupon rate is 10.0% and the coupon payments are annual. If you believe that the appropriate discount rate for the bonds is 8.5%, what is the current equilibrium price of these bonds?

2. You are considering buying bonds in Aphoolog, Inc. The bonds have a par value of $1,000 and mature in 28 years. The coupon rate is 10.0% and the coupon payments are semiannual. If you believe that the appropriate discount rate for the bonds is 8.5%, what is the current equilibrium price of these bonds?

3. You are considering buying bonds in Aphoolog, Inc. The bonds have a par value of $1,000 and mature in 28 years. The coupon rate is 10.0% and the coupon payments are quarterly. If you believe that the appropriate discount rate for the bonds is 8.5%, what is the current equilibrium price of these bonds?

4. Does the pattern in the prices that you computed for problems 1, 2, and 3 (note the price changes you observe are due to changes in the frequency of the coupon payments only) make sense? Why or why not?

5. Econall, Inc. currently has an issue of bonds outstanding that will mature in 20 years. The bonds have a par value of $1,000 and a coupon rate of 6.5% with annual coupon payments. If these bonds are currently selling for $890, what is the current yield to maturity?

6. Econall, Inc. currently has an issue of bonds outstanding that will mature in 20 years. The bonds have a par value of $1,000 and a coupon rate of 6.5% with semiannual coupon payments. If these bonds are currently selling for $890, what is the current yield to maturity?

7. Econall, Inc. currently has an issue of bonds outstanding that will mature in 20 years. The bonds have a par value of $1,000 and a coupon rate of 6.5% with quarterly coupon payments. If these bonds are currently selling for $890, what is the current yield to maturity?

8. Does the pattern in the yields to maturity that you computed for problems 5, 6, and 7 (note the YTM changes you observe are due to changes in the frequency of the coupon payments only) make sense? Why or why not?

9. Inetward Devices, Inc. has bonds outstanding with a $1,000 par value and a maturity of 30 years. The bonds have an annual coupon rate of 7.0%, with semi-annual coupon payments. If the yield to maturity on the bonds is 9.75%, what is the current price of these bonds?

10. Inetward Devices, Inc. has bonds outstanding with a $1,000 par value and a maturity of 20 years. The bonds have an annual coupon rate of 7.0%, with semi-annual coupon payments. If the yield to maturity on the bonds is 9.75%, what is the current price of these bonds?

11. Inetward Devices, Inc. has bonds outstanding with a $1,000 par value and a maturity of 10 years. The bonds have an annual coupon rate of 7.0%, with semi-annual coupon payments. If the yield to maturity on the bonds is 9.75%, what is the current price of these bonds?

12. Does the pattern in the prices that you computed for problems 9, 10, and 11 (note the price changes you observe are due to changes in the number of years remaining to maturity only) make sense? Why or why not?

13. You are considering buying bonds in Attpach Partners, Inc. The bonds have a par value of $5,000 and mature in 18 years. The annual coupon rate is 11.0% and the coupon payments are semiannual. If the bonds have a yield to maturity of 10.25%, what is the current price of these bonds?

14. You are considering buying bonds in Ximagas, Inc. The bonds have a par value of $10,000 and mature in 15 years. The annual coupon rate is 5.75% and the coupon payments are semi-annual. If the bonds currently sell for $12,245, what is the yield to maturity on these bonds?

15. You are considering buying bonds in Semics PLC. The bonds have a par value of $250 and mature in 8 years. The annual coupon rate is 6.8% and the coupon payments are semiannual. If the bonds have a yield to maturity of 7.5%, what is the current price of these bonds?

16. You are considering buying bonds in Genere PLC. The bonds have a par value of $100 and mature in 15 years. The annual coupon rate is 8.0% and the coupon payments are semiannual. If the bonds currently sell for $91.25, what is the yield to maturity on these bonds?

17. You are considering buying bonds in Corpor Technology Partners. The bonds have a par value of $1000 and mature in 36 years. The annual coupon rate is 8.3% and the coupon payments are annual. The bonds are currently selling for $1,336.28 based on a yield-to-maturity of 6.0%. What is the bond's expected capital gain/loss if the bonds are held until maturity?

18. On January 15, 2012, TEX Consulting, Inc. issued some $1000 par value bonds. These bonds have a coupon rate of 8.25% and the coupon payments are quarterly. On the original issue date, the bonds had 30 years to maturity and the original YTM on these bonds was 8.75%.

Exactly one year after issue (i.e., on January 15, 2013), these bond traded at a price that resulted in a YTM of 6.25%. If you had bought one of these bonds on the issue date and sold the bond exactly one year later, what was your percentage capital gain or loss?

19. ASD Co. issued an 8% coupon (paid annually) 20-year bond 20 years ago (t = 0). The company originally issued the bond at par. For the first five years after the issue, the interest rate remained the same as that at the issue date. For the next five years, the appropriate interest rate was 7%. In the subsequent five years the interest rate rose to 11%, and in the last five years of the bond, the interest rates were at 9%. Compute the price of the bond at (a) t = 4, (b) t = 6, (c) t = 14, (d) t = 17, and (e) t = 19.

20. Zeta Corporation has a $1,000 par value zero-coupon bond outstanding. What is the current price of this bond if the appropriate discount rate is 4% and the bond matures in eight years?

21. The Johnson Company needs to raise $100,000,000 for an expansion project. The CFO is debating whether to issue zero-coupon bonds or semi-annual coupon bonds. In either case the bonds would have the same nominal required rate of return (i.e., YTM), a 30-year maturity and a par value of $1,000. If he issues the zero-coupon bonds, they would sell for $99.38. If he issues the semi-annual coupon bonds, they would sell for $886.88. What coupon rate is the Johnson Company planning to offer on the coupon bonds?

22. SDF Co. wants to raise $20,000,000 through issuing preferred stock. The cost of preferred stock is estimated to be 11%. If the company wants to issue 1,000,000 shares of the preferred stock, how much should be the promised dividend per stock?

23. Fifteen years ago, Alpinces Investments issued preferred stock with a par value of $80. The stock promised to pay an annual dividend equal to 12% of the par value. If the investor's required rate of return for this stock is 9.5%, what is the price this stock?

24. Sign Research, Inc.'s preferred stock has a par value of $75 and a dividend equal to 8% of the par value. The stock is currently selling for $82.50. What is Sign Research, Inc.'s cost of capital for preferred stock?

25. Bellution Partners plans a new issue of preferred stock. Similar risk stock currently offers an annual return to investors of 7.8%. If the company wants the stock to sell for $50.00 per share, what annual dividend must the company's preferred stock offer?

26. The common stock of Hyperion Inc. just paid an annual dividend of $1.50 (that is, $D_0 = 1.50$). Its dividends are expected to grow at a constant rate of 4% per year forever. If the required rate of return for this stock is 12%, what is the price of the stock?

27. FGH Co. is in a declining industry. It has just paid a dividend of $4.00 per share. The dividend is expected to *decline* at a rate of 5% in the future. Assuming a discount rate of 20%, what is the current stock price?

28. The common stock of TED, Inc. is expected to pay a dividend of $2.50 per share exactly one year from today (that is, $D_1 = 2.50$). The dividend is expected to grow at a constant rate forever. The required rate of return for this stock is 20%. If the current price of the stock is $17.86, what is the expected growth rate of the dividends?

29. The common stock of Darkover Inc. just paid an annual dividend of $1.00 (that is, $D_0 = 1.00$). The dividend is expected to grow at a constant rate forever. The required rate of return for this stock is 12%. If the current price of the stock is $15.00, what is the expected growth rate of the dividends?

30. The stock of Wabbit, Incorporated is trading at $72.25 per share. The company just paid a dividend of $5.12 per share. The growth rate in dividends is projected to be 6% per year forever. What is Wabbit's cost of equity capital?

31. A firm expects to pay dividends at the end of each of the next four years of $2.00, $1.50, $2.50, and $3.50. If growth is then expected to level off at 8%, and if you require a 14% rate of return, how much should you be willing to pay for this stock?

32. The common stock DFG Co. is trading at $24 per share. In the past the company has paid a constant dividend of $3 per share. However, the company has just announced new investments that the market did not know about. The market expects that with these new investments, the dividends should grow at 3% per year forever. Assuming that the discount rate remains the same, what will be the price of the stock after the announcement?

33. Baxter Company just paid a dividend of $2.00 per share and is expected to pay a dividend one year from today of $2.14 per share. The future growth rate in dividends is expected to remain equal to the growth rate in Year 1 forever. Baxter stock has a required rate of return of 26%. Baxter's dividend payout ratio is 40% and the company's debt ratio is 62%. Given the information above, compute the current market price of Baxter Company stock.

34. The stock of Takone, Inc. currently sells for $15.00 per share. The company just paid a dividend of $2.10 per share and the current market price per share (that is, $15.00) is based on investor belief that the dividends of the company will remain constant forever. The market, does not know, however, that Takone is about to announce the introduction of a modified product line that will cause the future earnings and therefore dividends of the company to grow at a rate of 4% per year forever, starting today. This new growth rate will begin with the dividend to be paid one year from today. The modified product line will not in any way affect the required rate of return for the stock of Takone, Incorporated. Assuming that the market reacts rationally, what will be the new stock price of Takone, Incorporated after the announcement?

35. The Frenall Company just paid a common stock dividend of $4.00 per share. The required rate of return on Frenall stock is 18.4%. Due to a major restructuring of the company's production process, Frenall's dividends are expected to decline by 25% in year 1, 14% in year 2, and 6% in year 3. From that point on, the company's dividends are expected to grow at a rate of 4.4% per year forever. Given these expectations, compute the current equilibrium market price of Frenall's stock.

Chapter 8

Risk and Return and the Capital Asset Pricing Model

8.1 A Review of Investment Returns
8.2 Definitions Relating to Returns and Risk
8.3 Simple Average Returns versus Compound Average Returns
8.4 Historic Returns and Risk by Asset Class
8.5 The Capital Asset Pricing Model
8.6 The Risk and Return Trade-off
8.7 Using CAPM to Evaluate Investment Performance
8.8 Summary
    List of Terms
    Questions
    Assignment

The objectives of the chapter are to:

- Demonstrate the risk/return relationship;
- Show that historic returns are consistent with that risk/return relationship;
- Define and explain the capital asset pricing model;
- Define systematic and nonsystematic risk and how CAPM deals with them;
- Show the benefits associated with diversification; and
- Use the risk/return relationship to evaluate investment performance.

From *Basic Principles of Finance: An Introductory Text*, 1st Edition by Joseph Woolridge and Gary Gray. Copyright © 2011 by Kendall Hunt Publishing Company. Reprinted by permission.

This chapter addresses what determines the required and expected rates of return associated with an investment. The principle relating to return versus risk, the first principle—**Higher Returns Require Taking More Risk,** shows the direct trade-off between the expected rate of return on an asset and its risk. We represent that trade-off by the diagonal line in Exhibit 8-1.

Finance theory assumes that a rational investor prefers to receive a higher percentage return on an investment to a lower return, and would rather accept less risk than more risk in earning that return. However, the proverbial free lunch does not exist in the investment world. A trade-off occurs between a higher expected return and greater risk of an investment. Safe investments have low returns. High returns require investors to take big risks.

It's important that we all start on the same page when discussing expected returns and risk. In this section, we define some terms that relate to the calculation of returns on an asset. We then tackle the thorny issue of understanding risk.

8.1 A Review of Investment Returns

Suppose you buy a share of IBM for $155 on December 31st and sell that share on December 31st of the following year for $180. During the year, you receive $20 in cash dividends. What is the annual return on your investment in IBM stock?

$$\text{Return} = (\text{Change in Price} + \text{Cash Payment}) / \text{Purchase Price}$$
$$\text{Return} = (\$25 + \$20) / \$155 = 0.29 \text{ or } 29\%$$

(Eq. 8-1)

The returns that you receive on a *stock* consist of *dividends*, if dividends are paid by the company, plus the appreciation (*capital gain*) or minus the depreciation (*capital loss*) in the price of the stock. The returns that you receive on a *bond* consist of periodic (usually every six months) *interest* payments and the repayment of *principal*. Additionally, you may have capital gains or losses associated with a bond if you sell it prior to its maturity.

In the United States, dividends paid on stocks and interest paid on bonds are typically classified as *ordinary income* and are added to the taxpayer's salary to get total ordinary income for the year.

In the United States, a *capital gain* is defined as a positive change in price of a stock, bond or other asset. In the IBM example, the capital gain was $25. Since the stock was sold during the tax

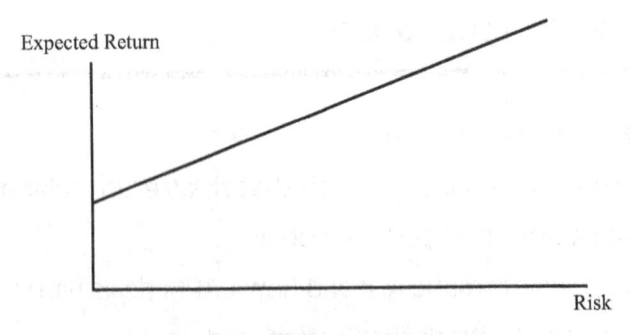

Exhibit 8-1 Risk/Return Graph

year, we say the capital gain was *realized* and a payment of a tax on the capital gain may be due. If the stock price had gone to $180 but you did not sell the stock, the capital gain is *unrealized*. Generally, only realized gains are taxed in the United States.

> *Capital gain* is a positive change in price of a stock, bond or other asset.

To encourage longer-term investment, U.S. tax laws sometimes differentiate among the length of time an asset is held. For example, if an asset is held for one year or longer, it may be categorized as a *long-term capital gain*. If an asset is held for less than a year (or some other period), it may be categorized as a *short-term capital gain*. Long-term capital gains are usually taxed at a lower rate than short-term capital gains and ordinary income. Tax rates may be revised frequently—usually with a change of administration in the White House. In some years, ordinary income, short-term capital gains, and long-term capital gains may all be taxed at the same rate.

Suppose you buy a bond for $980 and sell that bond one year later for $920. You receive an interest payment on the bond of $35. What is your return?

$$\text{Return} = (-\$60 + \$35) / \$980 = -.0255 \text{ or } -2.55\%$$

In this example, the change in price is negative and you incur a *capital loss*. Capital losses can offset capital gains and portions of ordinary income, and capital losses may reduce the federal and state income taxes that you pay.

> *Capital loss* is a negative change in the price of a stock, bond or other asset.

8.2 Definitions Relating to Returns and Risk

8.2.1 Definitions Relating to Returns

Expected Return on a Risky Asset—$E(R_i)$ is the rate of return an investor expects to receive on a risky asset over a period of time. The expected return consists of interim cash flow payments, such as dividends on a stock or interest on a bond, plus or minus any changes in the price of the asset over time. When we discuss the Capital Asset Pricing Model later in this chapter, we describe how to calculate the expected return on a risky asset by using a very simple equation.

Expected Return on a Portfolio of Risky Assets is the sum of the expected rate of return on each risky asset in a portfolio, multiplied by its portfolio weight. The portfolio weight is the percentage of the total portfolio's value that is invested in each risky asset. We discuss this calculation later in this chapter

Expected Return on the Market—$E(R_m)$ is the rate of return an investor expects to receive on the market portfolio which consists of all assets available to investors. The expected return on the market is usually measured by the recent average return on the stock market or a return associated with a stock market index. Many investors use the rate of return on the S&P 500 Index or on the Wilshire 5000 Index as a measure of market performance for stocks in the United States.

Return on the Risk-Free Asset—R_f is the rate of return that an investor receives on a safe asset—free from credit risk. Obligations of the U.S. Treasury are assumed to be risk-free because it is believed that the U.S. Government will always meet its financial obligations. To meet those obligations, the government has powers that companies and individuals do not have—it can borrow money, increase taxes, or print more money.

8.2.2 Definitions Relating to Risk

Risk reflects the *uncertainty* associated with the possible future returns of an asset. Buying Treasury Bills is a low-risk investment. You are assured of receiving your original principal plus interest when the T-bill matures. On the other hand, the risk of investing in a high-flying biotech stock is high. The return that you receive depends upon the future price of the company's stock. Often the stock price may depend on the company receiving FDA approval on a new drug, or on a set of other uncertain events occurring. Many things could go wrong and torpedo the stock's price. Or everything can go right and the stock price could multiply. ***Risk is the part of an asset's price movement that is caused by a surprise or an unexpected event***. Risk is measured by the standard deviation of the return on the asset as discussed below.

The risk of a stock is subdivided into two categories: *unsystematic risk* and *systematic risk*.

- *Unsystematic risk* or *firm specific risk (FSR)* is the risk caused by a surprise event that affects one company, such as an accounting irregularity, new drug discovery, or a patent expiration. Unsystematic risk is unique to a stock on an industry sector. The effects of unsystematic risks for an investor are greatly reduced by proper diversification of the assets in a portfolio. The stock market does not reward investors for unsystematic risk because that risk can be minimized or eliminated through proper diversification.

- *Systematic risk* is the risk caused by a surprise event that affects the entire economy and all assets to some degree, such as an increase in interest rates, a terrorist attack, or the declaration of war. The level of systematic risk for an asset can not be reduced by diversification. In the stock valuation approach that we use, ***the expected return on an asset depends only on an asset's systematic risk.***

Beta—(β_i) is a measure of the systematic risk of an asset. The market has a beta of 1.0. The beta of a stock with the price movement similar to the market also has a beta of 1.0. A stock that generally has a price movement that is greater than the price movement of the S&P 500 Index, such as a technology or internet stock, has a beta greater than 1.0. A stock with an average price movement that is less volatile than the market, such as the stock of a public utility, has a beta less than 1.0. We discuss beta in greater depth below.

Market Risk Premium—$[E(R_m) - R_f]$: is equal to the expected return on the stock market (e.g., the expected return on the S&P 500 Index—$E(R_m)$) minus the rate of return on the risk-free asset (R_f). It is the additional return that investors expect to receive if they buy a stock of average risk (beta = 1.0), as opposed to a Treasury bond. Assume McDonald's stock has a beta of 1.0. If investors require an 8% return on McDonald's stock, and 10-year Treasury yields are 5%, the market risk premium is: (8% − 5%) = 3%. Market risk premiums increase when investors become more risk-averse, and decrease when investors become less risk-averse.

Table 8-1 Standard Deviation of ABC's Stock Return

Year	Observed Return	Average Return	Deviation of Return	Squared Deviation
1	9.00%	10.50%	−1.50%	0.000225
2	15.00%	10.50%	4.50%	0.002025
3	−3.00%	10.50%	−13.50%	0.018225
4	21.00%	10.50%	10.50%	0.011025
Totals	42.00%		0.00%	0.0315

Standard Deviation of Return—(σ): Overall risk on an asset is usually measured by the variability of returns. The standard deviation is the statistic that is normally used to measure how wildly or tightly the observed stock returns cluster around the average stock return. A higher standard deviation means wilder fluctuations and greater risk.

It is not difficult to calculate a stock's standard deviation. Here's how to do it for a distribution of stock returns:

1. Take the simple average return of the distribution of returns;
2. Take each individual observed return and subtract the average of the returns;
3. Square the resulting difference and add the squares to get the sum of the squares;
4. Divide the sum of the squares by (the total number of observations minus 1)—the result is the variance of the distribution;
5. Finally, take the square root of the variance to get the standard deviation of the returns.

While this may seem complicated to read and explain, it is easy to compute using any standard spreadsheet program like Excel, or a hand held calculator. Furthermore, the interpretation of the standard deviation is much simpler than its calculation.

An example may be helpful. Assume that we observe that ABC stock over a four-year period has the following annual returns: 9%, 15%, −3%, and 21%, as shown in Table 8-1.

The distribution of returns for the four-year period is shown in column 2 of Table 8-1. The average annual return over the four years is 10.5% as shown in column 3. The sum of the deviations around an average is always equal to zero, as shown at the bottom of column 4. The sum of the squares of the deviations divided by (n − 1) yields the *variance* of the returns—in this case it is equal to [.0315/(4 − 1)] = **0.0105**. The square root of the variance is the *standard deviation* of the distribution, in this case (0.0105)^(1/2) = **10.25%**.

A high standard deviation means a big spread of possible returns and a high risk that the actual return will not equal the expected return. In finance and economics, risk has both positive and negative implications.

8.3 Simple Average Returns versus Compound Average Returns

Let's assume that Martha the portfolio manager tells you that she has achieved good investment performance over the past two years. Two years ago her portfolio skyrocketed 100%.

Table 8-2 Martha's Investment Performance
Simple & Compound Average Returns

Year	Beginning Value	Ending Value	Annual Return
1	$10	$20	100%
2	20	4	−80%
			20%
Simple Average Return			**10%**
Compound Average Return			**−36.75%**

This year hasn't been as good, with her stocks losing 80%. She says that her average yearly return over the past two years is 10%—a pretty respectable showing in a tough stock market. Is Martha correct, or is she a pathological liar?

Let's closely examine her claim of a two-year average return of 10%.

First, let's figure the average of her returns. Her average yearly return over the past two years is: [+ 100% (year 1 return) + (−80%) (year 2 return)] / 2 = *(100%−80%)/2* = **10%**, as she alleges.

For fun let's verify her claim by injecting some real numbers into the equation. We keep this example simple. Let's assume her portfolio consists of one stock, Stock A, which she bought two years ago for $10 per share. Her timing and analysis were impeccable and Stock A went up 100% to $20 at the end of the first year. The next year was a bad year for the stock market and Stock A, because Stock A tanked and dropped 80% to $4 per share.

When we look at real dollars as opposed to averages, it's apparent that her actual 2-year return is negative. A $10 portfolio went up to $20 and then down to $4, a 2-year loss of 60%—a $10 portfolio was reduced to $4. This is a far more dire result than one would suspect from the positive 10% *average performance* that Martha is touting. How can there be two such different results?

The problem is embedded in the calculation of simple averages. In fact, if there is a negative percentage return in the distribution of returns, the calculation of a simple average percentage return is **biased upward**.

Table 8-2 shows how Martha's investments performed over the past two years. The simple average annual return, or arithmetic mean, is easy to calculate and is equal to the sum of the annual returns (20%) divided by the number of returns (2) equal to **10%**. The total percentage return over the two-year period is also easy to calculate. Martha's investment started at $10 and fell to $4, a loss of 60% over the two-year period. Below, we show how to calculate the compound average return.

The compound average return is calculated by:

- Dividing the most recent value—(A) ($4 at the end of Year 2) by the beginning value— (B) ($10 at the beginning of Year 1);
- Taking the resulting ratio to the (1/T) power, where T is the number of years in the compounding period; and

- Subtracting 1.0 to bring it into percentage terms. In math terms, the previous sentence looks like this: $[(A/B)^{\wedge}(1/T) - 1.0]$. The calculation of the compound annual return above is:

$$[(\$4/\$10)^{\wedge}(1/2) - 1.0] = [(.4)^{\wedge}(1/2) - 1.0] = [0.6325 - 1.0] = -\underline{\mathbf{36.75\%}}$$

Many investment managers and advisors use simple averages to portray their historic performance. Often times simple averages are a misleading way to assess investment returns—compound or geometric averages are far more representative of actual investment performance. Be careful when you read sometimes advertising material that bases performance records upon simple average returns.

With simple averages, a larger percentage gain is required to offset a given percentage loss. Let's take a real life example of the investment performance of a highly focused mutual fund that specialized in investing in Internet stocks. The Pro-Funds Ultra OTC Mutual Fund incurred a drop of 94.71% between the NASDAQ high in March 2000 and April 4, 2001. Let's assume that you invested $1,000 in the Ultra OTC Fund in March 2000. Thirteen months later it would have dropped to $52.90. A market rally occurred between April 4, 2001, and May 2, 2001, and the Ultra OTC Fund rose an enormous 95.6% in less than a month. Jim's $52.90 investment increased by 95.6% to $103.50—a very nice increase. However, you still find yourself down 89.65% below the March 2000 high—the point at which you invested in the mutual fund. The average return for these two unequal time periods is: (–94.71% + 95.6%) / 2 = 0.45%. The true return for your fifteen-month holding period is negative (–89.65%).

The following equation (Equation 8-2) yields the percentage gain required to make an investment whole again after suffering a loss:

Percentage Gain to Break Even = 1 / (100% – % drop)   (Eq. 8-2)

In the example above, the equation looks like this:

$$1 / (100\% - 94.71\%) = 1 / (.0529) = 1{,}890\%.$$

So your investment would need to increase by almost nineteen hundred percent for you just to break even. The likelihood that you will ever break even on this investment appears to be somewhat remote.

8.4 Historic Returns and Risk by Asset Class

To get a sense of the types of returns that we should expect in the future from an investment, let's look at historic average returns on different classes of financial assets. We want to observe if lower risk investments generally have offered lower returns and higher risk investments have offered higher returns. Let's again look at the results of the Ibbotson and Sinquefield study shown in Table 8-3. Their compound and simple average returns by asset class over the past 76 years are shown below:

Do the average returns rank in the same order that you would rank the risk of the investments? Most of us would answer yes. Treasury bills are virtually risk-free. Long-term government bonds have price risk and interest rate risk but no default risk. Corporate bonds have price risk and interest rate risk and they also carry the risk that the corporation could default on its interest and principal payments. Interestingly, the standard deviation of corporate bonds is slightly lower than

Table 8-3 Ibbotson & Sinquefield Study

Asset Class	Compound Average Annual Return	Simple Average Annual Return	Std. Dev. of Return
U.S. Treasury Bills	3.70%	3.80%	3.10%
U.S. Treasury Bonds	5.40%	5.80%	9.40%
Corporate Bonds	5.90%	6.20%	8.60%
Large Company Stocks	10.40%	12.40%	20.40%
Small Company Stocks	12.70%	17.50%	33.30%

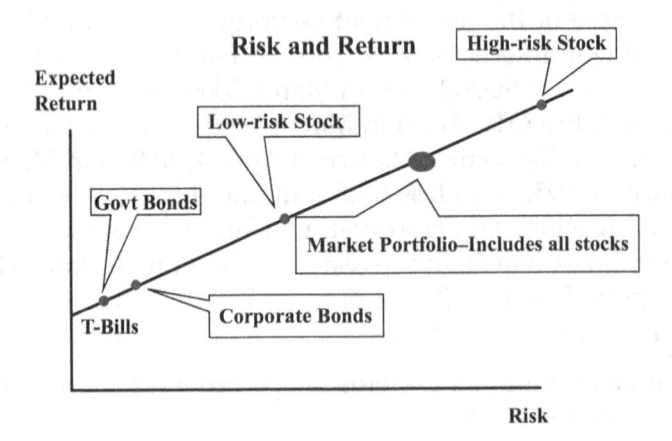

Exhibit 8-3 Risk of Return

government bonds. Common stocks are by far the most risky of the five investment classes, with small company stocks exceeding the returns and risks of large company stocks. The standard deviation of return is how we measure price volatility and risk, associated with the five asset categories.

The results of the I&S study are important and show the direct relationship between the expected return of an asset and the risk associated with receiving that return. An investment in a Treasury bill with no default risk and little price volatility has a lower expected average return (3.8%) than a large cap stock (10.7%). The Treasury bill also has a lower risk measure of 3.2% relative to a portfolio of large company stocks with a standard deviation of 20.2%. A graphical representation of the expected returns and risks associated with these asset classes is shown in Exhibit 8-3.

Returns on individual stocks can swing even more wildly than the returns that were calculated on the portfolios of large stocks and small stocks. However, on average, investing in common stocks and accepting risk have increased returns significantly.

8.5 The Capital Asset Pricing Model

8.5.1 CAPM—an Explanation

The *capital asset pricing model* (CAPM) is a theory about the pricing of risky assets and the tradeoff between the risk of the asset and the expected returns associated with the asset. In our earlier discussion two types of risk are associated with a stock: firm-specific risk or *unsystematic risk*; and market or *systematic risk*, measured by a firm's *beta*. CAPM or the *market model* is an expression of how expectations of stock returns are generated. The CAPM model consists of the following components:

- $E(R_i)$ represents the *expected rate of return on risky asset i*;
- $E(R_m)$ represents the rate of return an investor would expect to earn by placing her money in a *well diversified portfolio of stocks*. Frequently, the return associated with the S&P 500 Index is called the market return, although the S&P 500 ignores many U.S. firms and most foreign firms;
- (R_f) represents the *rate of return on the risk-free asset*;
- $[E(R_m) - (R_f)]$ represents the *expected market risk premium*—the excess return that you expect to receive above the risk-free rate for investing in a diversified portfolio of risky stocks;
- Beta—(β_i) is a measure of the market related *systematic risk of an asset*;

We explain CAPM with an example for IBM. We've talked about the trade-off between risk and return. As a *base rate of return*, the expected return on every risky asset should be at least that of the risk-free rate of return. How much higher the stock's expected return should be above the risk-free rate is a function of the risk associated with the asset. Below, $E(R_{ibm})$ is the expected annual rate of return for the stock of IBM. We won't know the actual rate of return until the end of the year but the market model says this about $E(R_{ibm})$:

$$E(R_{ibm}) = (R_f) + \beta_{ibm} * [E(R_m) - (R_f)] \qquad \text{(Eq. 8-3)}$$

According to CAPM, if we multiply the market risk premium, $[E(R_m) - (R_f)]$, by IBM's beta, β_{ibm}, and add in the risk-free rate and the extra return for any firm-specific risk, we get IBM's expected return for the year.

Firm specific return represents the *extra return* received by a firm due to some event affecting only that firm. For example, if IBM announced the award of a new and important patent, or that its revenue would be much higher than expected, or that it discovered a way to reduce its manufacturing costs by 30%, then IBM's stock price would jump. The FSR of IBM might be 5%, 10%, or even 20% to reflect the good news, but the news should not significantly affect the rest of the stock market. Of course, if IBM announced that profits will fall or that they are being sued for billions of dollars or that their costs will rise, then the share price will fall and FSR will be negative. The key to firm specific returns is this—the FSR for any company is just as likely to be positive as it is to be negative, and *averages 0%* for all firms in the market.

Let's pop some numbers into the IBM equation shown above. Let's assume that the risk-free rate is 5%, that the expected return on the market is 10%, that the beta for IBM is 1.25, and that the expectation of FSR for IBM is 0. Here is our expected return for IBM stock:

$$E(R_{ibm}) = 5\% + 1.25 * [10\% - 5\%]$$

$$E(R_{ibm}) = 5\% + 1.25 * [5\%] = 12.5\%$$

That wasn't so tough!

8.5.2 What Is Beta?

In Equation 8-3 above, what does it mean that the estimate of IBM's beta is 1.25?

Beta indicates how responsive IBM's return is to changes in the excess market return. Excess market returns are *magnified* by IBM's beta of 1.25. If IBM's beta is 1.25, it means that on average when the excess market return is up 10%, IBM is up 12.5% (1.25 * 10%), (before adding FSR). When the excess market return is down 20%, IBM, on average, is down by (1.25 * 20%) 25%.

Suppose some other company had a beta of 3 (they seldom are this large). This company's returns would triple the excess market returns before the FSR is included. If the excess market return is 10%, this firm's excess market return would be 30% on average (since FSR is zero on average) and if the excess market return is –5%, this firm would be down 15% on average. The larger a firm's beta, the more responsive is that firm's return to excess market returns. Conversely, if a company had a beta of only 0.50, then that firm would not see such wild swings in its return over time as the market goes up or down.

How do we measure a firm's beta? To estimate beta in the real world, investment professionals will use 60 or more pairs of monthly or weekly returns for the performance of a stock versus the performance of a stock market index (e.g. S&P 500 Index). They will have the stock market index return on the horizontal axis and the firm's returns on the vertical axis. They plot these 60 or more points and use regression analysis to fit the line through them. *The slope of this line is the estimate of beta.*

Below is a graph (Exhibit 8-4) that may help you to understand the concepts of calculating beta. For both IBM and the overall market, ten months (the 10 dots shown on the graph) of returns were observed and plotted. Then a regression line was fitted to those points. If IBM did not have any firm specific risk, each point would be on the regression line. For each point, the vertical distance from the point to the line measures IBM's firm specific return for that particular month. If the point is above the line, IBM experienced a good firm specific return, and if the point is below the line, IBM experienced a bad firm specific return. The slope of the regression line is IBM's beta. A steeper line means IBM's return is more sensitive to the return on the overall market. For example, if IBM has a greater beta it has more market risk. A less steep line indicates a lower beta and less market risk.

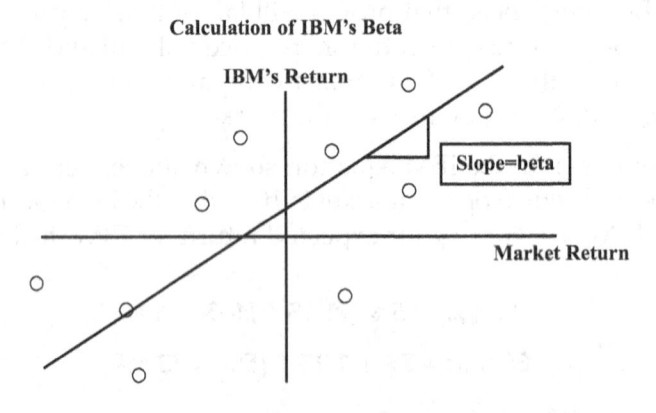

Exhibit 8-4   Calculation of IBM's Beta

8.5.3 CAPM and Portfolios

The term *portfolio* refers to a group of specific securities (stocks, bonds, mutual funds) owned by an investor. Just as each stock has a beta and a firm-specific component to its return, so each portfolio has a beta and what is called a portfolio specific return component.

Suppose you invest 40% of your money in IBM and 60% of your money in AT&T. The return on your portfolio can be written as:

$$R_{portfolio} = 0.40 * R_{ibm} + 0.60 * R_{att}$$

We say the portfolio return is a weighted average of the returns on IBM and AT&T. The weights are the fractions invested in each security. Since IBM and AT&T each have a beta and an FSR component to their returns, we could work out that the portfolio with 40% invested in IBM and 60% invested in AT&T, which also has a beta and an FSR, so that:

$$E(R_{portfolio}) = (R_f) + [(.4 * \beta_{ibm}) + (.6 * \beta_{att})] * [E(R_m) - (R_f)]$$

The expression above is simpler than it looks. It just tells us that the portfolio's beta is a weighted average of the betas for IBM and AT&T.

Suppose we change our portfolio by adding General Motors (GM) stock. We invest 40% of our money in IBM, 30% in AT&T, and 30% in GM. Then

$$E(R_{portfolio}) = (R_f) + [(.4 * \beta_{ibm}) + (.3 * \beta_{att}) + (.3 * \beta_{ge})] * [E(R_m) - (R_f)]$$

Even with three securities, the portfolio's beta is a weighted average of the individual betas for IBM, AT&T, and GM, and the portfolio's FSR is a weighted average of FSR(IBM), FSR(AT&T), and FSR(GM). Mutual funds, retirement funds, and other large portfolios may invest in the shares of several hundred companies. No matter how many companies are involved, each of these large portfolios has a beta and an FSR that are just weighted averages of the betas and FSR for the individual companies.

Our portfolio containing IBM, AT&T, and GM has *four* sources of uncertainty affecting the return for this portfolio. First, there is the market return, (R_m). The market return affects the return of every stock in the portfolio, and the effect of the market return for each stock depends on that stock's beta. Additionally, there are the three FSRs. Each FSR is caused by independent events that are specific to the individual firm, so the FSRs are not connected to one another in any way.

8.5.4 Beta, Firm Specific Returns, and Diversification

Suppose half of your money is in General Electric (GE) and half is in General motors (GM). Then your portfolio FSR is:

$$FSR_{portfolio} = 0.50 * FSR_{ge} + 0.50 * FSR_{gm}$$

Remember that the FSR of GE is just as likely to be positive as negative—the firm-specific news for GE is as likely to be good as it is to be bad no matter what the market return might be. The same is true for the FSR of GM. It's like tossing a coin twice to determine the FSR for the portfolio. There is some chance that one of the FSRs is positive and the other is negative so that they come close to canceling each other out. This is the essence of *diversification*. A portfolio's firm specific return component can be made small by investing in a large number of companies.

Suppose you had the shares of 100 different firms in your portfolio. The FSR component of your portfolio will be practically insignificant. Think of 100 tosses of the coin to get the 100 FSRs that are in the portfolio. Your money is spread evenly among them, each of which is multiplied by 0.01. The number of FSRs that are positive will very likely be near 50, as will the number of FSRs that are negative. The small return that remains after the positives and negatives cancel one another is multiplied by 0.01. This leads to the following belief that underlies modern portfolio theory:

> *Investors who hold large portfolios are NOT concerned about firm-specific return or risks. The process of **diversification** involves investing in enough firms that the FSRs of the individual companies tend to cancel out one another.*

A *well-diversified portfolio* is one whose FSR component is so small as to be insignificant. Suppose you select companies at random and spread your money equally across companies. How many companies do you need before your portfolio becomes well diversified? In the principle relating to diversification we found that **Asset Diversification Will Reduce Risk**. Academic studies have found that twenty unrelated stocks seem to be sufficient for a fairly well-diversified portfolio.

8.5.5 CAPM and Well-diversified Portfolios

Are well-diversified portfolios free of risk? Absolutely not! Diversified portfolios have reduced their unsystematic risk to close to zero, but still have market or systematic risk. CAPM and modern portfolio theory assume that Rational Investors Are Risk Averse and assumes that all investors own a well-diversified portfolio. The CAPM equation looks as follows for a well-diversified portfolio:

$$E(R_{portfolio}) = (R_f) + \beta_{portfolio} * [E(R_m) - (R_f)] \qquad \text{(Eq. 8-4)}$$

What happened to the FSRs? By definition, a well-diversified portfolio has enough firms in it that the aggregate of the FSRs is virtually zero, so they drop out of the equation. There is only one source of uncertainty for a well-diversified portfolio, and that is *uncertainty over the performance of the market in general.*

Portfolios that are composed of high-risk stocks have a high beta and portfolios composed generally of low-risk stocks have a low beta. A high-risk portfolio has mostly high-beta companies, like the biotechnology stocks, while a low-risk portfolio might be composed of mostly low-beta companies such as a utility fund. Well-diversified portfolios are identical to one another except for their betas. They have no firm-specific risk. They simply follow the market, magnifying the market return if the portfolio beta is greater than one, and dampening the swings of the market if the portfolio beta is less than one.

Most money is invested in well-diversified portfolios, such as pension funds, mutual funds, and funds managed by financial institutions. When an individual investor considers a single stock such as IBM for her portfolio, the key question is how much additional risk that stock will contribute to the portfolio. We already saw that firm-specific risk disappears through the inclusion of a large number of companies in the portfolio. However, if IBM is added to the portfolio, IBM affects the portfolio's beta—which is a weighted average of all of the stocks in the portfolio. The sole contribution that one company makes to the risk of a well-diversified portfolio is through its beta. High beta companies make well-diversified portfolios more risky while low-beta companies lower the risk of a portfolio.

8.6 The Risk and Return Trade-off

The standard example of a risk-free asset is the short-term Treasury bill. If you expect to own a T-bill to its maturity, the return on the T-bill is known with certainty at the time it is purchased and its return in no way depends on the market return. Therefore, T-Bills have a beta of zero.

Suppose you invested in the entire stock market. You could do this by putting a little of your money in the stock of each and every company. An easier way to do this is to invest in a stock index fund—a mutual fund that invests in all companies that make up a particular index. Some mutual funds invest in the stocks that make up the Wilshire 5000, a stock index that tracks the performance of all United States stocks, or invest in the stocks in the S&P 500. Your index fund investment should give the return (neglecting fees) close to the average return of the market, so its beta is close to 1.0.

Suppose you want an investment with a beta of 0.75. One way to do this is to put 75% of your money in the overall stock market, and put the remaining 25% of your money in T-Bills. The beta of this portfolio is just a weighted average of the two individual investments or

$$B_{portfolio} = (0.25 * 0.00) + (0.75 * 1.00) = 0.75$$

You can have a portfolio with a beta equal to just about any number you prefer by allocating your money between T-Bills and the overall market in the proper proportions.

Suppose the T-Bill rate is 4% (approximately the average for the 20th century) and the expected return on the overall market is 12% (approximately the average for the 20th century). Then you can have a portfolio with a beta equal to any number you want just by investing some money in T-Bills and some in the overall market as shown in Table 8-4 below:

Note the following about Table 8-4:

- The portfolio beta is just a weighted average of the beta for T-Bills (that's 0) and the beta for the overall market (that's 1.0);
- The expected return is just a weighted average of the return for T-Bills and the expected return for the overall market;
- As the risk of the portfolio increases (remember that beta measures risk), the expected return increases.

What does it mean to invest (–25%) of your money in T-bills, as shown in Table 8-4? It means you borrow some money at 4% (actually shorting T-bills) and combining the borrowed money with your own to invest in the overall stock market. Hedge funds do this all the time. They borrow money, or take on leverage, and invest that money in risky assets. As a simple example, suppose you had $100 to invest in stocks. Let's assume that you borrow $25 at 4%, add it to the $100 that you have, and invest the entire $125 in the overall market. If the overall market returns 20% for the year, you have $150. However, you must pay back $25 plus $1—representing the interest on $25 @ 4%, so the $150 falls to $124. The return on your own $100 is 24%. The overall market returned 20% but through borrowing, you levered your return to 24%. Of course, borrowing to invest in the stock market won't look so good if the market falls.

The betas and expected returns can be used to construct a risk-return line. Beta is on the horizontal axis and expected return in on the vertical axis. Since beta is the only measure of risk, any and all investments should lie somewhere on this risk-return line.

The graph representing the CAPM is shown in Exhibit 8-5:

Table 8-4 Expected Portfolio Returns

Beta	% in T-Bills	% in Market	Exp. Ret. Portfolio
0.00	100%	0%	4%
0.25	75%	25%	6%
0.50	50%	50%	8%
0.75	25%	75%	10%
1.00	0%	100%	12%
1.25	–25%	125%	14%

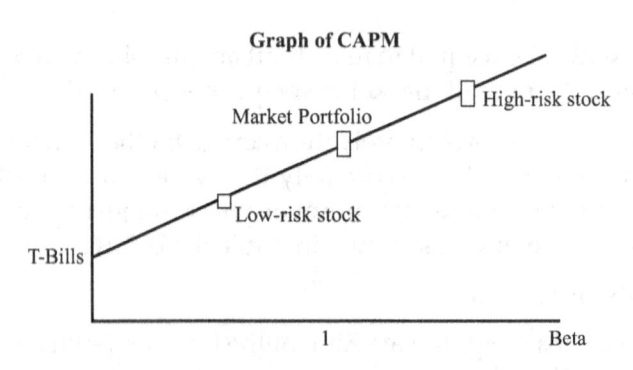

Exhibit 8-5 Graph of CAPM

214 Chapter Eight

8.7 Using CAPM to Evaluate Investment Performance

Suppose that you want to evaluate the performance of a mutual fund or of an investment advisor that manages pension fund money. One way might be to compare their average annual returns. However, some managers invest primarily in bonds and others in stock. Just because the managers picking stocks have higher average returns than those picking bonds doesn't mean they are better investment managers. Fund managers who invest in higher risk securities should be expected to earn higher average returns because of the increased risk. To properly evaluate investment performance, we must adjust for the risk associated with a portfolio.

As an example, let's suppose that during the past five years, a portfolio manager held a portfolio with an average beta of 0.50. This manager could easily hold a portfolio of this risk level by investing half of her money in T-Bills and the other half in the overall market without even making an attempt to decide which stocks are good investments and which stocks are bad investments. Did the manager do better picking stocks than she could have done by pursuing the no-brainer alternative strategy of holding a portfolio consisting of ½ T-Bills and ½ of an overall stock index fund?

Let's assume that Meredith managed a $2 billion portfolio over the past five years. The portfolio's beta was 0.50 and its average annual return was 15%. Over this same period of time, T-Bills averaged a 6% per year return and the overall market averaged a return of 18% a year. How did Meredith's performance compare with the markets?

Any investor could have split her money equally between T-Bills and a stock index fund and have earned an average portfolio return of:

$$\text{Average return} = (0.50 * 6\%) + (0.50 * 18\%) = 12\%$$

Another way to get that 12%, assuming that the expected return on the market was also equal to the observed return of 12%, is to use the CAPM form of the equation to get:

$$E(R_{portfolio}) = (R_f) + \beta_{portfolio} * [E(R_m) - (R_f)]$$
$$E(R_{portfolio}) = 6\% + 0.5 * [18\% - 6\%] = 12\%$$

(Eq. 8-5)

Meredith, for the same level of risk, earned an average return of 15%—so she outperformed our benchmark no-brainer strategy by 3%. This 3% is called the *alpha* of her performance. A positive alpha means an investor outperformed the returns expected under the CAPM benchmark, while a negative alpha means the investor performed worse than the returns expected under CAPM.

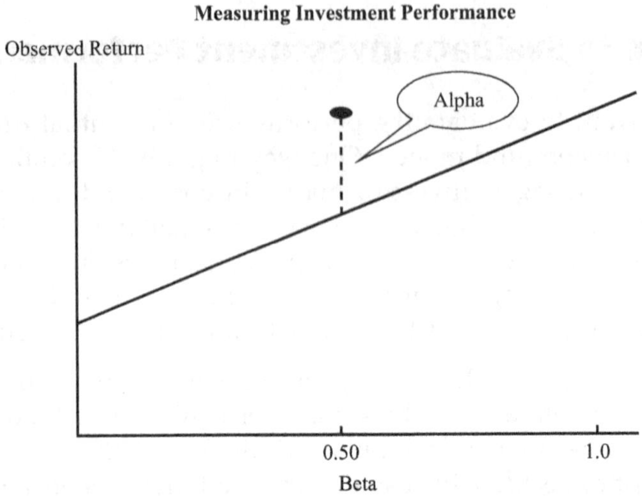

Exhibit 8-6 Measuring Investment Performance

$$Alpha = Observed\ Return - Expected\ Return \quad \text{(Eq. 8-6)}$$

A positive alpha is the vertical distance above the risk-return line. For this problem, Meredith's $2 billion portfolio had a beta of 0.50 and an average return of 15%. Her return was 3% higher than the 12% return that was expected for a beta of 0.5 using the CAPM. Meredith had a positive alpha of 3%—a very strong performance. An investor who performs below the CAPM risk/return line has a negative alpha.

8.8 Summary

This chapter addresses the issues relating to what determines the required and expected rates of return associated with a risky asset or investment. There is a direct trade-off between the expected rate of return on an asset and its risk. It's important that we all start on the same page when discussing expected returns and risk. We defined terms that relate to the calculation of returns on an asset and we tackled the thorny issue of understanding risk.

This chapter:

- Demonstrated the risk/return relationship;
- Showed that historic returns are consistent with that risk/return relationship;
- Defined and explained the capital asset pricing model;
- Defined the systematic and nonsystematic risk and how CAPM deals with them;
- Showed the benefits associated with diversification; and
- Used the risk/return relationship to calculate alpha and evaluate investment performance.

List of Terms

1. **Ordinary income** – Income derived from regular business activities.

2. **Realized capital gain** – When a stock is sold at an increase in price and the investor realizes that gain and a payment of tax may be due.

3. **Unrealized capital gain** – If the stock price increase but the investor does not sell the stock, the gain is unrealized and is not taxed.

4. **Long-Term capital gain** – An asset held for one year or more.

5. **Sort-Term capital gain** – An asset held for less than one year, usually subject to taxes.

6. **Expected return on a risky asset – E(Ri)** – The rate of return an investor expects to receive on a risky asset over a period of time.

7. **Expected return on a portfolio of risky assets** – The expected rate of return on each risky asset in a portfolio, multiplied by its portfolio weight.

8. **Expected return on the market – E(Rm)** – The rate of return an investor expects to receive on a diversified portfolio of common stock.

9. **Return on the risk-free asset – Rf** – The rate of return that an investor receives on a safe assets, one that is free from credit risk.

10. **Market Risk Premium – {E(Rm) – Rf}** – The additional return that investors expect to receive if they buy a stock of average risk as opposed to a Treasury bond.

11. **Risk** – The chance that an investment's actual return will be different than expected. This includes the possibility of losing some or all of the original investment. It is usually measured by calculating the standard deviation of the historical returns or average returns of a specific investment.

12. **Unsystematic risk or firm specific risk** – Risk that affects a very small number of assets. Sometimes referred to as specific risk.

13. **Systematic risk** – The risk inherent to the entire market or entire market segment. Defined by beta.

14. **Beta** – A measure of the volatility, or systematic risk, of a security or a portfolio in comparison to the market as a whole. Also known as "beta coefficient."

15. **Market risk** – Also known as unsystematic risk, the risk inherent in the market from economic forces, etc.

16. **Standard deviation of return** – A measure of the dispersion of a set of data from its mean. The more spread apart the data is, the higher the deviation. In finance, standard deviation is applied to the annual rate of return of an investment to measure the investment's volatility (risk).

17. **CAPM** – A model that describes the relationship between risk and expected return and that is used in the pricing of risky securities.

    $$\bar{r}_a = r_f + \beta_a(\bar{r}_m - r_f)$$

    Where:

    r_f = Risk free rate
    β_a = Beta of the security
    $\bar{r}_m$ = Expected market return

    The general idea behind CAPM is that investors need to be compensated in two ways: time value of money and risk. The time value of money is represented by the risk-free (rf) rate in the formula and compensates the investors for placing money in any investment over a period of time. The other half of the formula represents risk and calculates the amount of compensation the investor needs for taking on additional risk. This is calculated by taking a risk measure (beta) which compares the returns of the asset to the market over a period of time and compares it to the market premium (Rm-rf).

18. **Portfolio** – The group of assets—such as stocks, bonds and mutual funds—held by an investor.

19. **Well-diversified portfolio** – A portfolio including a number of securities. Investing in more than one security leads to diversification and hence lower risk.

20. **Performance evaluation** – Evaluating the performance of stocks, bonds or portfolios of securities. To properly evaluate investment performance, we must adjust for the risk associated with a security or portfolio.

21. **Positive alpha** – An investor who performs above the CAPM line. The investor outperformed the returns expected under the CAPM benchmark.

22. **Negative alpha** – An investor who performs below the CAPM line. The investor underperformed the returns expected under the CAPM benchmark.

Questions

1. **What is the risk/return relationship?**
   The more risk an investor is willing to take on, the higher then return she expects to compensate her for this increased risk taking.

2. **How do you calculate annual return on your investment in a stock or in a bond?**
   The formula for calculating this return is Return = (Change in price + cash payment or interest or dividend) / Purchase price

3. **Do you pay interest on the dividends earned for the stock or the interest received for the bonds that you are holding?**
   Dividends paid on stocks and the interest earned on bonds are taxed as ordinary income.

4. **How do you define expected return on a risky assets and expected return on a portfolio of risky assets?**
   The Expected return on a risky asset – $E(R_i)$ – is the rate of return an investor expects to receive on a risky asset over a period of time. The Expected return on a portfolio of risky assets is the expected rate of return on each risky asset in a portfolio, multiplied by its portfolio weight.

5. **What do we mean by expected return on the market and return on the risk-free asset?**
   The Expected return on the market – $E(R_m)$ – is the rate of return an investor expects to receive on a diversified portfolio of common stock. The Return on the risk-free asset – R_f – is the rate of return that an investor receives on a safe assets, one that is free from credit risk.

6. **What are the two types of risk associated with a stock? How do you differentiate them?**
   There is unsystematic or firm specific risk, and systematic or market risk. Unsystematic risk can be diversified away and systematic risk cannot be. It is also measured by the beta coefficient.

7. **How do you calculate market risk premium and the standard deviation of return?**
   The market risk premium is calculated by $\{E(R_m) - R_f\}$. The standard deviation of returns is calculated by taking the square root of the variance of stock returns.

8. **What is the reason that small company stock have an average annual return of 12.5% compared to just 3.8% for Treasury bills?**
   Small cap stocks have a larger standard deviation, meaning that they have greater risk, therefore investors should expect to be rewarded with a higher return for taking on this added risk. T-Bills have no risk of defaulting, hence they are riskless. And investors do not need a greater return to hold this security in exchange for the peace of mind associated with a low risk investment.

9. **What is the formula for CAPM and how does it take care of systematic and unsystematic risk of a stock?**

$$\bar{r}_a = r_f + \beta_a(\bar{r}_m - r_f)$$

Where:

r_f = Risk free rate
β_a = Beta of the security
$\bar{r}_m$ = Expected market return

Systematic risk is shown through the beta coefficient. Firm specific risk, FSR, can be added to this formula to show unsystematic risk, however, diversification through a portfolio causes unsystematic risk to have no effect on the return, hence FSR is absent from the formula.

10. **What is a beta of a firm and that of a portfolio?**
The beta is a measure of the stock or portfolio's movement in response to a movement in the market.

11. **How does a well-diversified portfolio reduce the unsystematic risk to near zero?**
In a diversified portfolio, the FSR, or firm specific risk, is basically non-existent because different companies may have positive or negative FSR values which will cancel each other out of the equation.

12. **How does the investment performance of a mutual fund or of an investment advisor evaluated? What is positive alpha and what is negative alpha?**
The performance of mutual funds and investment advisors are measured through compound average returns and a simple, although biased, average return. Alpha may be used to measure the performance of mutual funds. Positive alpha is when an investor performs above the CAPM line. The investor outperformed the returns expected under the CAPM benchmark. The Negative alpha is when an investor performs below the CAPM line. The investor underperformed the returns expected under the CAPM benchmark.

Assignment 8.1

1. Ted Turner bought Bank of America stock on 1st January at a price of $63 and sold it at $70 exactly after a year. In between he earned a dividend of $0.60 each quarter. What is his return on investment?

   (a) 11.11%

   (b) 14.67%

   (c) 13.20%

   (d) 3.80%

2. In the example above, did he make a capital gain or capital loss?

3. Jack Welch bought a bond at $980 and sold it at $950 after a year. He earned an interest of $30 in that year. How much profits or loss did he make?

   (a) 3.0%

   (b) 5.0%

   (c) −2.4%

   (d) 0.0%

4. Find the market risk premium for a stock which is expected to give a return on market of 10%. The beta of the stock is 1.0. [Hint: Use www.marketguide.com to find out the return on T-Bills]

5. Find out the Standard Deviation of Returns for a stock with annual returns of 3%, 5%, 9% and −7% over the last four years.

6. Consider a utility company stock with an annual return of 8% and a standard deviation of 10%. Assuming a normal distribution and two standard deviations, what can we expect as the maximum and minimum return on the stock?

   (a) 18% and 2%

   (b) 18% and −6%

   (c) 26% and −6%

   (d) 26% and 2%

7. Use CAPM model to find out expected return on the stock of Apple for an expected return on market of 12%. [Hint: Get the value of beta for Apple and the value of Risk free rate of return for T-bills from www.marketguide.com or from www.finance.yahoo.com]

8. If a company has a beta of 1.5 and the expected return on market is 10%, what is the firm's expected return with firm specific risk equal to zero?

    (a) 15%

    (b) 11.5%

    (c) 5%

    (d) 25%

9. Use 3 yrs monthly data for IBM and the market return to plot a graph of market return versus that of IBM. Find the slope of the regression line to get beta of IBM.

10. You want to maintain a portfolio of stocks with IBM as 40%, Apple 40% and rest Microsoft. Use return on market as 12% and the firm specific rates of return as zero for all three firms and find out the rate of return of the portfolio.

11. You want to have a portfolio with a beta of 0.85. You have decided to invest partly in the S&P 500 index and the rest in T-bills. How much will you invest in Index and how much in T-Bills?

    (a) 85% and 15%

    (b) 15% and 85%

    (c) 50% and 50%

    (d) 70% and 30%

12. A top investment manager at Goldman Sachs managed a portfolio of over $5 billion and earned annual return of 15% (with a beta of 0.5 over last 3-year period). During that period, T-bills averaged 4.5% and the market averaged 16%. How did he perform compared to the market? Did he have a positive Alpha or negative Alpha?

    (a) Positive Alpha of 5.25%

    (b) Negative Alpha of 5.25%

    (c) Positive Alpha of 4.75%

    (d) Negative Alpha of 4.75%

Chapter 9
Basics of Capital Budgeting

9.1 Chapter Introduction and Overview
9.2 Capital Budgeting Techniques
9.3 Using the Financial Calculator for NPV and IRR
9.4 Some Warnings on the Use of the IRR Criterion
9.5 Independent versus Mutually Exclusive Projects
9.6 The Payback Period Criterion
9.7 Estimating the Weighted Average Cost of Capital
9.8 Recap
   Assignments
   Additional Questions and Problems

After studying Chapter 9, you should be able to:

- Explain the purpose and importance of capital budgeting.
- Determine whether a new project should be accepted using the net present value.
- Determine whether a new project should be accepted using the profitability index.
- Determine whether a new project should be accepted using the internal rate of return.
- Determine whether a new project should be accepted using the payback period.
- Explain which decision criterion should be used to maximize shareholder wealth.
- Compute the cost of capital for a company and project.

From *Lectures in Corporate Finance*, 6th Edition by Jayant R. Kale and Richard J. Fendler. Copyright © 2013 by Kendall Hunt Publishing Company. Reprinted by permission.

9.1 Chapter Introduction and Overview

While in graduate school, Nika discovered a way to clone a lemon and an apple tree. She called the resulting product a Lemple tree. Thinking the concept had some potential financial value, her dad and some of his lawyer friends patented the name, process, and product.

The tree produces a fruit, called a lemple. Unfortunately, lemples have a very tough, inedible skin and the inside of the fruit is quite mealy. On the other hand, Lemple juice is delicious. Lemple juice resembles naturally sweetened lemonade and is extremely high in vitamins A, C, and D. Additionally, it is completely calorie and caffeine free, yet it gives adult drinkers a long-lasting jolt similar to many energy drinks now on the market. Given a choice, kids choose Lemple juice over sugar-laced carbonated beverages, to the delight of their parents, and adults choose Lemple juice because it is calorie- and sugar-free and it provides a natural boost in energy.

To date, Lemple, Inc. has produced and sold Lemple juice to stores throughout the southeastern United States. Although sales are booming and profits are through the roof, Nika is very concerned about the short shelf life of her product. Approximately one week after being squeezed out of the fruit, Lemple juice becomes cloudy and sour. Nika refuses to add preservatives to the product, so the short shelf life is dramatically restricting the company's potential market. By the time products can be shipped to the west coast, they are almost at the expiration date.

At a recent lunch meeting with Mei, Lemple's chief engineer, and Blair, Lemple's CFO, the group brainstormed the idea of creating and selling a home Lemple machine similar to a Keurig coffee maker. Homeowners would merely drop a lemple into a reservoir in the machine and close the lid. The machine would then extract the juice from the lemple, instantly chill the beverage to a perfect drinking temperature and dispense the product into a glass. The idea was brilliant and Mei was confident that she could produce the product. Nika and Blair had to decide if production and manufacturing costs could be justified by the expected future cash flows the Lemple juice maker could produce for the company.

After several long weeks of discussions and numerical estimates, Blair and Nika had developed the following cash flow characteristics of the new product.

Year	Expected Cash Flow
0	($12,500,000)
1	$1,000,000
2	$3,000,000
3	$5,000,000
4	$6,000,000
5	$5,000,000
6	$4,000,000
7	$2,000,000

Mei provided the initial cost figures, and she was confident that these were highly accurate. Blair and Nika believed that the new product would take several years to catch on, so cash flows started small and grew through year 4. At that time, they estimated that other companies would figure out a way to produce a competing product. Also, Lemple's patents expired in about six years. Therefore, they decided to end the estimated cash flow stream from the Lemple maker in year 7.

Should they spend the $12,500,000 today that is necessary to produce and sell the machine? Are the cash flows worth the cost? What techniques do companies typically use to make these types of decisions, and if there is more than one technique used, which is the best technique?

In the previous chapter, we used the concept of discounted cash flows to value debt and equity securities. The purpose of this chapter is to use similar valuation techniques for evaluating the investment by a firm in real assets. These investments in real assets, which we will call projects, can be of several types, the common ones being investments in new plant and machinery, cost-saving technologies, research and development, new products, new markets for existing products, store renovations, and such. A project, as far as we are concerned, is any company decision that involves cash outflows (costs) made to receive expected future cash inflows (benefits). The decision that we will consider here is a pretty straightforward one. Given the cash flow stream (outflows and inflows), is the project a worthwhile investment? Decisions of this sort are commonly termed as capital budgeting decisions. In this chapter, we shall consider several capital budgeting techniques and evaluate the validity of each of them.

9.2 Capital Budgeting Techniques

Consider a typical decision that you may have to make in your day-to-day life. Suppose that you are deciding whether to replace your existing automobile. What is the standard framework for your decision making? You will first determine the costs of replacing your car and also the benefits of owning the new car. You will then compare the two and if the benefits outweigh the costs, you will replace the car. If not, you will keep the old car. You, and most other individuals, probably follow this rule in making decisions of an economic nature. Calling such a decision a project, we can state the rule as follows: *Accept the project if the benefits from the project are greater than the cost of the project.*

Well, why shouldn't firm managers follow the same rule? In fact, for making capital budgeting decisions, that is, investments in projects, you will see that the same rule applies. It turns out that this rule takes on different forms. Instead of describing these seemingly different methods first, let us begin with the rule that we stipulated as the logically most suitable rule.

Let C denote the cost associated with the project and let B denote the benefits, and let us, for the time being, not worry about how B and C are calculated. According to our rule, then, we should *accept the project if benefits are greater than cost.* That is B > C. This rule can be restated a few different ways. *Accept the project if the difference between benefits and costs is positive.* Or, *accept the project if the ratio of benefits to cost is greater than one.* In other words, we can rewrite the basic rule above in the following equivalent ways:

a. Accept if $B - C > 0$, or

b. Accept if $\dfrac{B}{C} > 1$.

According to (a) above, accept the project if the benefits net of costs are positive. This rule is one of the most famous finance rules and is called the ***net present value (NPV)*** rule. It states that, *accept the project if the NPV is positive* where NPV is defined as B − C. The second rule (b) is called the *profitability index (PI) rule*. It states that, *accept the project if the profitability index is greater than one*, where PI is defined as the ratio $\frac{B}{C}$.

An important thing to note is that whenever the NPV of a project is positive (B − C > 0), the PI for the project must also be greater than one ($\frac{B}{C} > 1$). In other words, *when the decision is about accepting or rejecting a project, the NPV and the PI rule give the same answer.* If the NPV rule says accept, so will the PI rule, and if the NPV rule says reject, so will the PI rule.

So far, we have not said anything about how B, the benefits, and C, the costs of the project, are to be determined. We are sure that you have a pretty good idea about how to do this already. Recall that a project is nothing but a stream of cash flows that occur over a period of time. From our earlier discussions, we know that money has time value and we know how to compare cash flows that occur at different points in time. Applying these concepts to capital budgeting, we have the following. *The benefit (B) of a project is the present value of all future cash inflows and project cost (C) is the present value of all future cash outflows.*

We can now restate our NPV and PI relations more precisely as follows:

$$\text{Net present Value(NPV)} = B - C = \sum_{t=0}^{N} \frac{CIF_t}{(1+r)^t} - \sum_{t=0}^{N} \frac{COF_t}{(1+r)^t}, \text{ and}$$

$$PI = \frac{B}{C} = \frac{\sum_{t=0}^{N} \frac{CIF_t}{(1+r)^t}}{\sum_{t=0}^{N} \frac{COF_t}{(1+r)^t}},$$

where

- CIF_t = the cash inflow at the end of period t,
- COF_t = the cash outflow at the end of period t,
- r = the appropriate discount rate for the project's cash flows,
- N = the number of years in a project's economic life.

By *appropriate discount rate* we mean that it is the rate of return that investors require from the project or, equivalently, the firm's *cost of capital* for the project.

The above relations are the most general ones for NPV and PI. In most projects, the costs occur at the beginning, that is, at t = 0 and the cash inflows occur in the future. Following is an example of a typical project cash flow stream.

```
   ($5,000)      $3000        $3000        $3000
   |─────────────|────────────|────────────|
   t = 0         t = 1        t = 2        t = 3
```

The project depicted above costs (or requires an investment of) $5,000 in the beginning (t = 0) and then generates cash flows of $3,000 per year for three years. Assuming a discount rate of 10 percent, the NPV of this project is:

$$NPV = \frac{3,000}{1.1} + \frac{3,000}{(1.1)^2} + \frac{3,000}{(1.1)^3} - 5,000$$
$$= 7,460.56 - 5,000$$
$$= 2,460.56.$$

And the PI is:

$$PI = \frac{7,460.56}{5,000} = 1.4921.$$

According to our rules, because NPV > 0 and PI > 1, the project should be accepted.

In the above example, we used a discount rate of 10%. Suppose we use a higher discount rate. What will happen to the NPV and the PI? Both will decrease. In fact, if we increase the discount rate sufficiently, the NPV will become negative and the PI will become less than one. For example, when the discount rate is 30%, the NPV is barely positive at $448.39 and if a discount rate of 40% is used, the NPV of the project becomes −$233.24. Thus, at 30%, the NPV is positive and at 40%, the NPV is negative. Then, it must be the case that at some rate between 30 and 40%, the NPV must be zero. It turns out that this rate is 36.31%. At this rate, the NPV of the project is zero. That is,

$$\frac{3,000}{1.3631} + \frac{3,000}{(1.3631)^2} + \frac{3,000}{(1.3631)^3} - 5,000 = 0.$$

In other words, at the discount rate of 36.31% B = C, or the present value of future cash inflows equals the cost of the project. The discount rate at which the NPV of the project is zero is called the *internal rate of return (IRR)* of the project.

Recall that in the relationship between the discount rate and NPV, lowering the discount rate increases the NPV and increasing the discount rate lowers the NPV. The IRR is the discount rate at which NPV is zero. Then, if we used a discount rate that is less than the IRR, what will be the NPV? Positive. On the other hand, if we use the discount rate greater than the IRR, the NPV will be negative. In computing the NPV, recall that we have to use the firm's cost of capital (investor's required rate of return) as the discount rate. Then, if IRR is greater than the cost of capital (r), the project has a positive NPV, implying that benefits are greater than costs and, therefore that the project is acceptable. On the other hand, if the project's IRR is less than the cost of capital, the benefits are less than the cost, or, equivalently, the NPV is negative, implying that the project should be rejected. We, thus, have a third capital budgeting technique, the IRR. The decision rule is to accept the project if IRR is greater than the cost of capital.

Intuitively, one can think of the IRR as the return from the project. Then the project should be accepted if the return is greater than the required rate of return.

Let us state again the three capital budgeting decision criteria:

1. NPV > 0, accept the project; NPV < 0, reject.
2. PI > 1, accept the project; PI < 1, reject.
3. IRR > r, accept the project; IRR < r, reject.

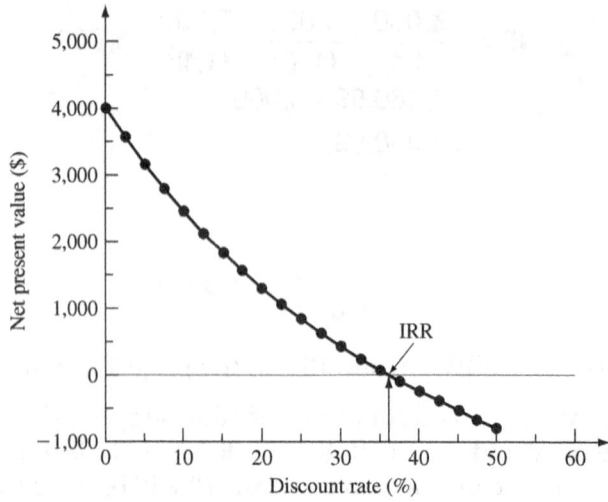

Figure 9.1 Project NPVProfile, –$5,000 at t = 0 and Three Future Cash Flows of $3,000

NPV and IRR are the two most important capital budgeting techniques. The relation between them may become clearer with the following graph (Figure 9.1).

The graph in Figure 9.1 plots the NPV of the project on the vertical axis for different discount rates. When the discount rate is zero, the NPV is 4000. As the discount rate increases, the NPV decreases. The graph showing the NPV values for different discount rates is called the project's NPV profile. The discount rate at which the NPV profile intersects the horizontal axis, that is, when the NPV is zero, is the IRR.

9.3 Using the Financial Calculator for NPV and IRR

For the project in the problem in the previous section, we could have computed NPV and IRR with the calculator the following way.

9.3.1 Net Present Value (NPV)

First, compute the present value of a three-year annuity of $3,000 using a discount rate of 10 percent. That is, in the financial calculator enter, N = 3, I/YR = 10, PMT = 3,000, PV = ? to obtain a present value of PV = $7,460.56. Then, subtract the cost of the project, $5,000, from this value to obtain the NPV as follows:

$$NPV = \$7,460.56 - \$5,000 = \$2,460.56.$$

The NPV is positive; therefore the project should be accepted.

9.3.2 Internal Rate of Return (IRR)

To compute the IRR, we must find the discount rate that make NPV equal to zero, that is B − C = 0. In other words, we need to find a discount rate such that B = C. That is, we need to find a discount rate that will make the present value of the three-year $3,000 annuity equal the cost of $5,000. To do this, enter in the calculator:

N = 3, PV = −5000, PMT = 3,000, I/YR = ? to obtain 36.31% as the IRR.

Or, we could also use the CF register. Enter,

CF0 = −5000; CF1 = 3000, CF2 = 3000, CF3 = 3000, CF4 = 3000, IRR = ? IRR = 36.31 %.

IRR is greater than the cost of capital (i.e., 10%), so the project should be accepted.

In general, you will find using the CF register and directly computing NPV or IRR to be the most efficient way to complete capital budgeting technique problems.

Example Problem: A firm is considering investment in a project that costs $1,200 and yields cash flows of $500 in the first year, $600 in the second year, and $700 in the third year. Compute the NPV and IRR of this project. The appropriate discount rate for this project is 10%.

Solution: Let us first create a cash flow table for this project.

Year	Cash Flow
0	(1,200)
1	500
2	600
3	700

9.3.3 Compute Project NPV

Enter CF0 = − 1200, CF1 = 500, CF2 = 600, CF3 = 700, I/Yr = 10, then press NPV button, you will get NPV = $276.33. Because NPV > 0, this project should be accepted. Note that all you have done is computed the present value of each cash flow and summed the present values as per below:

Year	Cash Flow	Present Value (at 10%)
0	(1,200)	(1,200)
1	500	454.54
2	600	495.87
3	700	525.92
Sum of present values		276.33

9.3.4 Compute Project IRR

Since the cash flows are already entered into the CF register, merely press the IRR button, you will get IRR = 21.92%. Note that if you discount each of the cash flows at this rate, you will find that the sum of the present values = 0 as below:

Year	Cash Flow	Present Value (at 21.92%)
0	(1,200)	(1,200)
1	500	410.10
2	600	403.64
3	700	386.26
Sum of present values		0.00

And because the NPV > 0 and IRR > 10 percent, the project should be accepted.

Example Problem: Without any other time value calculations, compute the profitability index (PI) for the project above.

The NPV is $276.33, so we know that

$$B - C = \$276.33.$$

Because the cost is $1,200, we know C. Substituting this value for C, we obtain

$$B - 1,200 = 276.33, \quad \text{or}$$
$$B = 276.33 + 1,200 = 1,476.33.$$

Therefore,

$$PI = \frac{B}{C} = \frac{1,476.33}{1,200} = 1.2303.$$

Note that for a *normal project* (a project where the year 0 cash flow is negative and all future cash flows are positive—these are the only type of projects we will consider in this class) a simple way to find PI is to use the following equation:

$$PI = \frac{\text{NPV} + \text{Absolute Value of CFO}}{\text{Absolute Value of CFO}}$$

For the project above, we found that NPV = 276.33 and the absolute value of CF0 = 1200. Thus, using our simple equation, we have:

$$PI = \frac{276.33 + 1200}{1200} = \frac{1476.33}{1200} = 1.2303.$$

And, of course, since PI > 1, the project should be accepted. Note that using the simple PI equation, it become immediately obvious that is NPV > 0, PI must be greater than 1 and if NPV < 0, PI must be less than 1. Thus, NPV and PI will ALWAYS give the same accept/reject answer.

Problem 9.1: Compute the NPV, IRR, and PI of the following project that a firm is considering. The firm's cost of capital for this project is 12%. The project will require an initial investment of $6 million and it will generate cash flows $750,000 per year forever.

Problem 9.2: Assuming a discount rate of 14%, compute the NPV, IRR, and PI of a project that costs $8 million and generates cash flows of $1 million per year for 10 years.

Problem 9.3: The cost of capital for a firm is 15%. Should it invest in the following project? Use all the three methods: NPV, IRR, and PI.

Year	Cash flow
0	−$2,300,000
1	$ 700,000
2	$ 850,000
3	$1,200,000
4	$ 650,000
5	$ 300,000

Problem 9.4: If the IRR of the project defined by the cash flows below is 12%, what is the NPV of the project at a discount rate of 10%? (Note that you first must determine the initial cash flow for the project. Hint: The IRR is the discount rate that makes the NPV of the project equal to 0).

Year	Cash flow
0	$X
1	$5,000
2	$6,000
3	$8,000
4	$3,000

Basics of Capital Budgeting   231

9.4 Some Warnings on the Use of the IRR Criterion

You must have noticed that in all the examples that we did above, in determining whether a project is acceptable, all the three capital budgeting criteria, NPV, IRR, and PI, gave the same accept or reject answer. However, this not always the case, particularly for NPV and IRR. We will discuss some situations where either NPV and IRR yield different accept/reject decisions or IRR yields peculiar answers. In either case, you will notice that *the NPV criterion always leads to the correct decision.*

In the projects we have considered so far, the cost of the project occurred in the beginning and the cash inflows occurred later. Is it possible to have a project where the cash inflows occur first and the outflow occurs later? The answer is yes. (Can you think of an example?)

Consider the project that yields a cash flow of $120 at t = 0 and requires a cost of $100 to be paid at t = 1. Let us first calculate the NPV of this project with r = 10%.

$$NPV = 120 - \frac{100}{1.1} = \$29.09$$

Because NPV is positive, the project is acceptable. Now let us compute the IRR. Enter N = 1, PV = 120, FV = –100, I/Y = ? in the calculator. We obtain an IRR of –16.667%. Does this seem strange? Let us see if using this discount rate yields a zero NPV.

$$120 - \frac{100}{1+IRR} = 120 - \frac{100}{1-0.16667}$$
$$= 120 - \frac{100}{0.03333} = 0$$

Thus, the IRR is indeed negative. According to our decision rule, we accept the project if the IRR is greater than the cost of capital. In this case the IRR is less than the r of 10%. Thus, according to the IRR rule, the project should be rejected.

Would you reject this project, a project that gives you $120 today and requires you to pay $100 one year later? Certainly not! What is happening here? Let us draw an NPV profile of this project. This is given in Figure 9.2.

Do you see a difference between this NPV profile and the one in Figure 9.1 for the normal project? The previous one was declining and this one is increasing in the discount rate. Think about it. If you have a project that requires the cash outflow later, the higher the discount rate, the better off you are. Why? Think of it like this. Suppose you wanted to guarantee that you had the $100 that is required to be paid at t = 1. What would you do? You would deposit the present value of $100 in a bank account. Note, however, that the higher the interest rate that the bank pays you, the less that you would need to deposit. In other words, the higher the discount rate the less the amount that you have to put aside. Or, the higher the discount rate the lower the present value of the cost of the project. Thus the higher the NPV.

For projects of this type, the IRR method does not fit. The NPV method, however, does give the correct accept/reject decision. We had asked you to think of a project of this type. Did you? A project that involves borrowing money for later repayment fits the description.

There is another scenario in which NPV and IRR give different answers. Think of a project that yields a cash inflow of $100 at t = 0 and a cash outflow of $121 at t = 1. The NPV of this project at r = 10% is −10, which implies that the project should be rejected. The IRR of this project is, however, 21%, which implies that the project should be accepted. You can see that it is not a particularly desirable project. The reason that IRR gives the peculiar answer is similar to the one given earlier. Note that NPV is again appropriate.

Finally, consider the following project cash flows: at t = 0, −$400, at t = 1, $2,500, and t = 2, −$3,000. Suppose that the discount rate is 70%. Then,

$$\text{NPV} = -400 + \frac{2{,}500}{1.7} - \frac{3{,}000}{(1.7)^2} = \$32.53.$$

The project is, therefore, acceptable. Let us now draw the NPV profile of this project. This is shown in Figure 9.3.

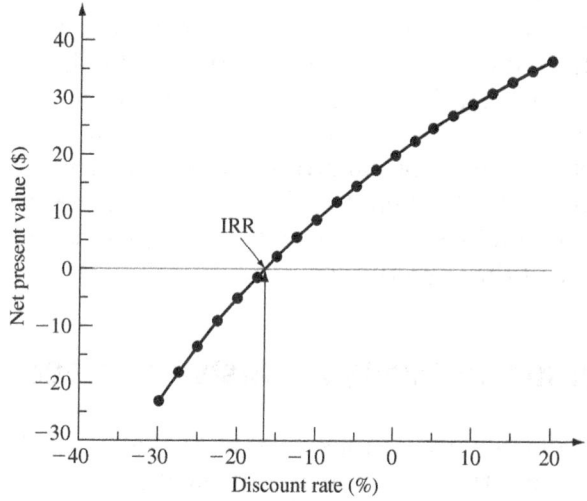

Figure 9.2 Project NPV Profile, CF at t = 0 is 120 and at t = 1, is −100

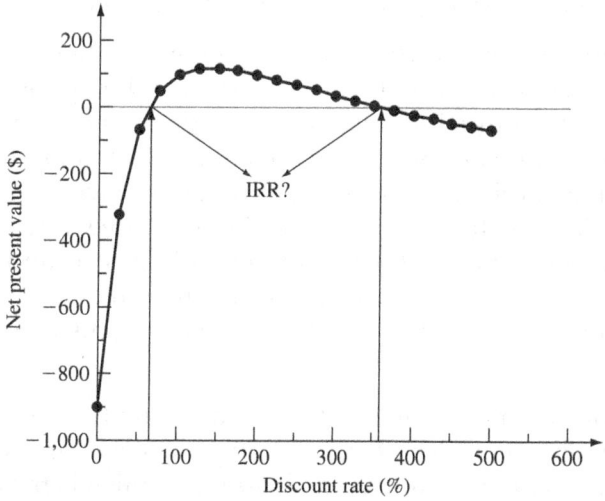

Figure 9.3 Project NPV Profile, Cash Flows At t = 0, 1, and 2 Are −$400, $2,500, −$3,000

Basics of Capital Budgeting 233

What is the IRR for this project? If you enter the cash flows into the calculator and compute the IRR using the IRR function, you will obtain an IRR of 61.98%. However, from the NPV profile in Figure 9.3, you know that this IRR is the first discount rate at which NPV is zero. You see that the NPV is zero also when the discount rate is approximately 363%. So what is the IRR for this project? Well it has two, approximately 62% and 363%. Is one more correct than the other? No. Both give zero NPV and hence are IRRs. Is the project acceptable? On the basis of the IRR criterion, it is difficult to say because the discount rate is greater than one IRR and less than the other. In such cases, when there are *multiple IRRs*, the IRR method loses meaning. Note, however, that the NPV method is still valid.

The question then arises, when do we have multiple IRRs? It turns out that this is pretty easy to figure out. Count the number of sign changes in the cash flow stream of the project. If there is just one sign change, there is just one IRR. On the other hand, if there are more than one sign changes, the number of IRRs may be more than one. For example, in the project above, there are two sign changes and there are two IRRs.

In view of the above, you must be wondering about which capital budgeting criterion to use. For normal projects (recall that a normal project is a project that has a cash outflow at time 0 followed by cash inflows thereafter), it does not matter, because all the three methods give you the same answer. In fact, when the NPV profile is smoothly declining in the discount rate, both NPV and IRR give identical answers. However, in some cases the IRR criterion causes confusion, specifically for non-normal projects. For non-normal projects, the NPV profile is not smoothly declining. If it is increasing in the discount rate, then the IRR criterion will reject acceptable projects. If the NPV profile crosses the horizontal zero-axis more than once, we have multiple IRRs and it is better to stay away from the use of the IRR criterion.

9.5 Independent versus Mutually Exclusive Projects

Thus far, we have the rules that a normal project that has a positive NPV, IRR > cost of capital or PI > 1, should be accepted. These rules are true as long as any and all projects that the firm is considering are *independent*. Independent projects have nothing to do with one another; they are completely separate, and not at all related. Thus, they are "independent" from each other. A firm should ALWAYS accept all independent projects for which NPV > 0.

There are, however, many situations where one might have to choose between one of several different projects, all of which may be acceptable! This occurs when projects are *mutually exclusive*. Two projects are said to be mutually exclusive if accepting one necessarily implies that the other will have to be forgone. For example, if you have a piece of land on which you can either build a house or a store, but not both, then the house and the store will be two mutually exclusive projects. Or, if a company is looking to buy a new machine and three different machines are available that all perform the same function but have different initial costs and/or different potential expected future cash flows, choosing one machine means the others are not needed. The three machines are mutually exclusive and in this case, the company wants to make sure it chooses the BEST project.

The interesting aspect of this analysis is that with two mutually exclusive projects, you have to rank the projects. It is possible that each of the mutually exclusive projects has a positive NPV, but because you can choose only one, you have to determine which is the best. It is this determination of the ranking of mutually exclusive projects that we shall spend some time on now.

Consider the following two mutually exclusive projects and assume that the discount rate for each is 10%.

Cash Flow and Criteria	Project A	Project B
C0	−10,000	−10,000
C1	5,000	4,800
C2	5,000	4,800
C3	5,000	4,800
Project NPV	2,434.26	1,936.89
Project IRR	23.38%	20.71%
Project PI	1.24	1.19

Which of the two projects would you choose? Irrespective of whether you use the NPV, IRR, or PI method, project A is better.

But of course, this problem was too simple. Consider instead the following two mutually exclusive projects and assume that the discount rate for each is 10%.

Cash Flow and Criteria	Project X	Project Y
C0	−10,000	−1,000
C1	4,000	500
C2	5,000	520
C3	6,000	540
Project NPV	2,276.48	290.01
Project IRR	21.65%	25.62%
Project PI	1.23	1.29

Now which project would you select? Project X has a higher IRR and a higher PI, but Project Y has the higher NPV. The correct choice would be project Y—the project with the largest NPV. The conflict in ranking here occurs because the two projects have a different initial cost. These projects are called projects of *different scale*.

Because they have a different initial cost, in comparing the two projects, you must take into account what you would do with the $9,000 left over if you invest in project X. The implicit assumption is that you would earn your required rate of return (remember opportunity cost) of 10%. Thus, investment in Project Y actually means that you invest $1,000 in Project Y and $9,000 at 10%.

Let us call this project Y*. Project Y* costs $1,000 + $9,000 = $10,000 and yields t = 1 cash flow of $500 (from Project Y) + $900 (from investing $9,000 at 10%) = $11,400 in year 1. In year 2 it yields $520 from Project Y + $900 = 1,420. Finally, in year 3 it yields $540 + $900 + $9,000 (the original principle deposit) = $10,440.

Basics of Capital Budgeting 235

Cash Flow and Criteria	Project X	Project Y*
C0	−10,000	−10,000
C1	4,000	1,400
C2	5,000	1,420
C3	6,000	10,440
Project NPV	2,276.48	290.01
Project IRR	21.65%	11.20%
Project PI	1.23	1.03

The NPV of this properly defined project Y* is $290.01 and the IRR is 11.20%. Now project X is better with the NPV, IRR, and PI criteria.

Can you figure out why the NPVs of Y and Y* are the same? They have to be. Project Y* is nothing but the combination (or portfolio) of project Y and another project that has a return exactly equal to the discount rate and thus an NPV of zero. Accordingly, by value additivity (remember that) the NPV of Y* is the sum of the NPVs of the two projects, that is, $290.01 + $0 = $290.01. This also illustrates the fact that when two mutually exclusive projects have different scales, choosing the project with the higher NPV is always correct.

Consider yet one last problem of two mutually exclusive projects. The discount rate is 10%.

Cash Flow and Criteria	Project P	Project Q
C0	−3,000	−3,000
C1	1,000	1,900
C2	2,000	1,900
C3	3,000	1,900
Project NPV	1,815.93	1,725.02
Project IRR	36.19%	40.50%

Here the NPV is higher for Project P and IRR is higher for Project Q. This conflict in ranking cannot be explained with scale differences because both projects cost the same. In this case, the conflict occurs because of the differences in the implicit reinvestment rate assumptions in the NPV and IRR frameworks. In the IRR framework, the assumption is that all intermediate cash flows are reinvested at the IRR. In the case of the NPV method, the assumption is that all intermediate cash flows are reinvested at the discount rate used in calculating the NPV.

The above explanation probably does not make much sense. Think about the reinvestment assumption in the following sense. Let us consider the Project Q again. Under the IRR scenario, you would have to put $3,000 in a bank account that pays 40.50% (the IRR of Project Q) interest to obtain the $1,900 per year for three years as you would in Project Q. On the other hand, what is the value of Project Q? It is the present value of future cash flows, that is, $4,725.02. If you invested this amount at 10% (the discount rate), you would obtain $1,900 per year for three years. Now, which of the two investment scenarios seems more reasonable? Clearly the latter! Remember that the discount rate is the investor's required rate of return and is, by definition, the return that one could earn on similar investments in the market. Thus, the discount rate is a much better estimate of the reinvestment rate than the IRR of a project.

Because the reinvestment rate assumption in the NPV method is more reasonable, the NPV method gives the more appropriate ranking in the above two projects. Project P is preferable because it has the higher NPV. Note that the reinvestment rate assumption matters in this case because the two projects differ in the manner in which they generate cash flows. Project P generates the higher cash flows later, whereas Project Q gives constant cash flows. Irrespective of the explanations, it is true that choosing between two mutually exclusive projects on the basis of their NPVs is *always* correct. The exception to this rule is when the two mutually exclusive projects have unequal lives. We will consider this in the next chapter.

Problem 9.5: Consider the following projects, for a firm using a discount rate of 10%:

Project	NPV	IRR	PI
A	$200,000	12.2%	1.04
B	$201,000	11.0%	1.01
C	$60,000	10.1%	1.61
D	($235,000)	9.0%	0.95

If the projects are *independent*, which, if any, project(s) should the firm accept? Why?

Problem 9.6: Consider the following projects, for a firm using a discount rate of 10%:

Project	NPV	IRR	PI
A	$200,000	12.2%	1.04
B	$201,000	11.0%	1.01
C	$60,000	10.1%	1.61
D	($235,000)	9.0%	0.95

If the projects are *mutually exclusive*, which, if any, project(s) should the firm accept? Why?

9.6 The Payback Period Criterion

As we saw in the previous section, the NPV, IRR, and PI techniques for capital budgeting utilize the concept of discounted cash flows. Therefore, the use of these methods, the NPV method in particular, is consistent with the concept of the time value of money. There is another project selection criteria that does not use these concepts. This criterion is known as the *payback period* criterion.

Simply stated, the payback period is the number of periods it takes the cash inflows from a project to recover the original cost of the project. For example, suppose that a project costs $10,000 and generates cash flows of $2,000 per year for 10 years. How long will it take for this project to recover the original investment of $10,000. The answer is pretty easy—five years. Then five years is the payback period of this project. On the basis of the payback period of five years, should this project be accepted? The answer here is not clear.

Recall that the NPV, IRR, and PI criteria had very clearly defined rules for accepting or rejecting projects. The payback period criterion, however, does not. A firm chooses an arbitrary number of years as the critical number. If the payback period is less than this number, the project is accepted, else it is rejected. Thus, the project with a payback period of five years will be accepted if the critical number is greater than five years and rejected if it is less than five years. Thus, the accept/reject rule for the payback period method is arbitrary.

Example Problem: Compute the payback periods for the following two projects.

Project	C_0	C_1	C_2	C_3	C_4	C_5
A	−9,000	2,000	3,000	4,000	5,000	6,000
B	−11,000	2,000	3,000	4,000	5,000	6,000

Answers: Payback period for A = 3 years, B = 3.4 years.

In the above problem, computing the payback period for project A is straightforward. However, for B, we need to make an assumption. Note that at the end of three years, 9,000 of the cost of the project (11,000) is recovered, leaving 2,000 to be recovered. In the fourth year, the cash inflow is 5,000. Thus it would take the first $\frac{2000}{5000} = 0.4$ fraction of the year to recover the remaining cost of the project. The payback period is, therefore, 3.4 years. The assumption is that cash flows are received evenly throughout the year. Suppose that, on the other hand, cash flows from the project were received only at the end of each year. In this case, the payback period for project B would not be 3.4 years but 4 years. Unless otherwise stated, in payback period calculations, assume that cash flows are received evenly throughout the year.

Problem 9.7: Compute the payback periods for the following two projects.

Project	C_0	C_1	C_2	C_3	C_4
A	–50,000	25,000	20,000	15,000	10,000
B	–85,000	50,000	30,000	30,000	5,000

It is easy to see the shortcomings of using the payback period criterion for project selection. First, it is an arbitrary decision rule because the critical number is arbitrarily chosen. Second, it ignores the time value of money. Third, it ignores the cash flows that occur after the critical number. Let us illustrate the third shortcoming as follows. A firm uses two years as the critical number for the payback period. This firm is faced with two projects whose cash flows are as follows:

Project	C_0	C_1	C_2	C_3
A	–1,000	500	510	10
B	–1,000	0	0	99,000,000

According to the payback rule, given the critical number of two years, project A will be accepted and B will be rejected.

The second shortcoming of the payback period criterion, that it ignores the time value of money, can be rectified by using discounted values of the cash flows. Thus, one can compute the *discounted payback period*. However, the other two shortcomings are inherent in the rule and cannot be rectified.

Despite the obvious shortcomings that the payback period rule has, corporations use it quite widely. It is, however, used primarily as a secondary project selection criterion and then usually only for small, minor decisions. For example, a firm may require a project to have positive NPV first and also satisfy some payback criterion. The primary reason for its popularity is that it could serve as a control on errant managerial behavior. In your later finance courses, you will spend enough time on this aspect of finance.

9.7 Estimating the Weighted Average Cost of Capital

The cost of capital is integral to each of the capital budgeting evaluation techniques discussed in this chapter that use the concept of time value of money. To compute an NPV, we discount all cash flows by the cost of capital. To determine whether a project's IRR is sufficient, we compare it to the cost of capital. To derive a profitability index, cash inflows and outflows must first be discounted by the cost of capital.

In the previous chapter, we mentioned that the cost of capital is the price that a company must pay to investors for the funds that the investors provide. That is, the cost of capital is the return that the project must generate to adequately compensate all investors for the money given to the firm to fund the project. In this chapter, we show that companies use money provided by investors to fund capital budgeting projects. More specifically, companies use money provided by investors to buy new plant and equipment, to pay for research and development, to finance the development of new products or markets, and so on.

Investors provide funds to a company in two basic forms: debt and equity. For long-term capital budgeting projects, the main sources of funds provided are through corporate bonds and common stock. If 40% of a project is financed with debt and 60% of a project is financed with equity, then the *weighted average cost of capital* (WACC) is just the weighted average of the cost of debt and the cost of equity, or:

$$\text{WACC} = (.40)(\text{Cost of debt}^*) + (.60)(\text{Cost of equity}).$$

This overall return will provide all investors with their individual requirements. For example, assume that debt investors require an after-tax return of 10% and equity investors require a return of 20%. Assume that a company raises $10,000,000 to finance a one-year project. The funds come from debt and equity investors, with $4,000,000 coming from the issuance of new corporate bonds and $6,000,000 coming from either the new issuance of common stock or from retained earnings (the equity cost of both of these are the same, although proving this fact is well beyond the scope of this book—just trust us on this one for now). To give these investors their required returns, the overall return on the project must be:

$$\text{WACC} = (.40)(10\%) + (.60)(20\%) = 16\%.$$

A 16% project return will mean that the project will generate a return of $1,600,000. Thus, the $10,000,000 will generate a cash flow in one year of $11,600,000. Of this return, $4,400,000 will be returned to the bondholders (representing their required return of 10% on their initial $4,000,000 investment) and the remaining $7,200,000 will go to stockholders (representing their required return of 20% on their initial $6,000,000 investment).

Thus, in general, for any percentages of debt and equity (commonly referred to as the weight of debt and the weight of equity, where the sum of the weights must equal 1),

$$\text{Cost of Capital} = (\text{Weight of Debt}) \times (\text{Cost of Debt}^*) + (\text{Weight of Equity}) \times (\text{Cost of Equity}).$$

Entire courses are devoted to the estimation of the cost of capital, and there are many theoretical and estimation nuances and refinements to consider to properly estimate a firm or project's cost of capital. One particular nuance is that the cost of debt should be the "after tax" cost of debt. Because interest on debt is deductible for a firm (but returns to equity are not), as long as the project returns:

$$(1 - T) \times (\text{Required Return to Bondholders}),$$

where T is the company's tax rate, then the company will earn enough to pay bondholders what they require. This is the reason for the "*" after Cost of Debt in the equation above. Specifically,

$$\text{Cost of Debt}^* = (1 - T) \times (\text{Required Return to Bondholders}).$$

So, to estimate the cost of capital for a firm, we need to know the following: the weight of debt, the weight of equity, the required return to bondholders, the company tax rate, and the cost of equity. Estimating the first two measures involves issues concerning a firm's "optimal capital structure." For simplicity, we will just assume that we know the appropriate weights for debt and equity for problems that we will consider in this book. The company's tax rate is easy to find from tax laws. The average corporate tax rate in the United States is about 30%, so we will use this rate for most of the problems we consider. Finally, the required return to debt and the cost of equity are items that we discussed in the previous chapter. Specifically, we showed in the previous chapter that the *cost of debt is just the yield to maturity on a company's currently outstanding bonds* and that the *cost of equity is the discount rate in the constant growth stock formula* or *the cost of equity as determined by CAPM with the company's beta.*

To see how to compute the cost of capital for a firm, consider the following example. Fillips, Inc. is trying to estimate its current cost of capital. Fillips believes that the appropriate weight of debt is 35% and the appropriate weight of equity is 65%. Fillips has a tax rate of 30%. Fillips' bonds currently trade in the market for a price of $835. These $1,000 par value bonds have a coupon rate of 10% (annual coupon payments), and they mature in 28 years. Fillips' common stock trades for $22 per share. The dividend just paid by Fillips was $3.15 (that is, $D_0 = 3.15$) and future dividends are expected to grow at a rate of 4% per year forever.

- First, we compute the yield to maturity for Fillips' debt. FV = 1,000, PMT = 100, PV = –835, N = 28, CPT I/Y = 12.1%

- Second, find the after tax cost of debt as:

Cost of Debt* = (1 – .30) × (YTM) = (.70)(12.1%)

$$= 8.47\%$$

- Next, we compute the cost of equity using the constant growth stock price equation, solving for r_e,

$$r_e = \frac{D_1}{P_e} + g,$$

where, as shown in Chapter 9, D_1 is the dividend expected to be paid in year 1, P_e is the current market price of the firm's stock, and g is the growth rate, that is, the expected perpetual growth rate in dividends. Thus, we have:

r_e = (3.15)(1.04)/22 + .04

$$= .189$$

$$= 18.9\%$$

- Finally, solve the equation for cost of capital:

WACC = (Weight of Debt) × (Cost of Debt*) + (Weight of Equity) × (Cost of Equity)

$$= (.35)(8.47\%) + (.65)(18.9\%) = 15.25\%$$

Thus, the cost of capital that Fillips should use to compute the NPV or PI of a project is 15.25% and the rate that IRR should be compared to is 15.25%.

Problem 9.8: KimKups, Inc. is trying to estimate its current cost of capital. KimKups believes that the appropriate weight of debt is 55% and the appropriate weight of equity is 45%. KimKups has a tax rate of 30%. KimKups' bonds currently trade in the market for a price of $1,210. These $1,000 par value bonds have a coupon rate of 8.5% (semi-annual coupon payments) and they mature in 26 years. KimKups' common stock trades for $52 per share. The dividend just paid by KimKups was $5.00 (that is, $D_0 = 5.00$), and future dividends are expected to grow at a rate of 6% per year forever. Compute KimKups' cost of capital.

Problem 9.9: Blair, Lemple's CFO, estimates that the company's optimal capital structure is 30% debt and 70% equity. Lemple currently had $1000 par value bonds outstanding with a coupon rate of 7.25% (semi-annual payments), a maturity date of 26 years from today and a current market price of $945.50. Blair believes that the cost of any new debt would be the same as the YTM on this existing debt. Lemple's beta is 1.45, the risk-free rate is 3%, and the expected rate of return on the market portfolio is 12%. (Use the CAPM, $R_e = R_f + (R_m - R_f)$, to determine Lemple's cost of equity capital). Finally, Lemple's tax rate is 35%.

a. What is Lemple's weighted average cost of capital?

b. Using this cost of capital as the appropriate discount rate for the Lemple juice machine project, and the projected cash flow estimates below, what is the project's NPV, IRR and PI?

Year	Expected Cash Flow
0	($12,500,000)
1	$1,000,000
2	$3,000,000
3	$5,000,000
4	$6,000,000
5	$5,000,000
6	$4,000,000
7	$2,000,000

c. Should Lemple, Inc. invest in this project? Why or why not?

9.8 Recap

We discussed four capital budgeting techniques in this chapter. They are the net present value (NPV), internal rate of return (IRR), profitability index (PI), and payback period criteria. The first three use the concept of the time value of money and have clear-cut decision rules for accepting or rejecting a project. The payback period requires an arbitrary decision rule.

The decision rules for the three discounted cash flow methods are:

1. **NPV > 0, accept the project; NPV < 0, reject.**
2. **PI > 1, accept the project; PI < 1, reject.**
3. **IRR > r, accept the project; IRR < r, reject.**

For independent projects that are normal, all of the discounted cash flow techniques will provide the same accept/reject decision. For mutually exclusive projects, however, only NPV always gives the correct answer. In this case, the project with the largest NPV is ALWAYS the best. Therefore, since NPV always gives the correct answer for independent projects and always gives the correct answer for mutually exclusive projects, NPV is the BEST technique to use in all circumstances when evaluating a capital budget project or projects.

Assignment 9.1

1. Compute the NPV, IRR, PI, the payback periods, and the discounted payback periods for the following projects. Assume a discount rate of 9%.

Project	C_0	C_1	C_2	C_3	C_4	C_5
A	−9,000	2,200	3,300	4,400	5,100	1,000
B	−11,000	2,500	3,500	4,500	5,500	3,500
C	−23,000	11,000	6,800	3,600	14,100	0
D	−13,000	0	6,100	0	0	8,200

2. MNB Corp. is considering the purchase of another company called NBV Corp. The owners of NBV are asking for $200 million in cash. The managers of MNB estimate that the assets of NBV will generate cash flows of $26 million per year for 10 years and can then be resold as scrap for $20 million. The appropriate discount rate is 12%. Compute the NPV, IRR, and PI for this investment.

3. BVC Co. is considering the purchase of VCX Co. The managers of BVC estimate that the assets of VCX will generate $10 million in cash flows next year and that these cash flows will grow forever at a rate of 5% per year. The appropriate discount rate is 14% and the purchase price is $100 million. Compute the NPV, IRR, and PI for this investment.

Assignment 9.2

1. Compute the NPV of the following project using discount rates of 0, 10, 20, 30, 40, 50, 60, 70, and 80%.

Project	C_0	C_1	C_2
A	−7,500	19,800	−12,600

2. Draw the NPV profile of Project A and estimate the IRRs from the graph.

Assignment 9.3

1. You are contemplating the purchase of a rental property. The property consists of 12 apartment units, each of which rents for $600 per month. The cost of maintaining the entire property is $1,800 per month. The appropriate discount rate is 1% per month. If the property has an economic life of 10 years and can be sold for $500,000 at the end of its economic life, what is the maximum that you would pay for this property?

2. You own a rental property. This property consists of 20 dwelling units, each of which is rented out for $6,000 per year. The maintenance cost is $33,000 per year. The economic life of the property is 12 years, at the end of which it can be sold for $400,000. The appropriate discount rate is 12%. For this property, you have just received an offer from a potential buyer of $675,000 to be paid now. How will you determine whether you should sell?

3. Gargets, Inc. is trying to estimate its current cost of capital. Gargets believes that the appropriate weight of debt is 25% and the appropriate weight of equity is 75%. Gargets has a tax rate of 30%. Gargets' bonds currently trade in the market for a price of $1,000. These $1,000 par value bonds have a coupon rate of 8.5% (annual coupon payments), and they mature in 26 years. Gargets' common stock trades for $20 per share. The dividend just paid by Gargets was $1.50 (that is, $D_0 = 1.50$) and future dividends are expected to grow at a rate of 5% per year forever. Compute Gargets' weighted average cost of capital (WACC).

4. Melvyn, Inc. is trying to estimate its current cost of capital. Melvyn believes that the appropriate weight of debt is 60% and the appropriate weight of equity is 40%. Melvyn has a tax rate of 30%. Melvyn's bonds currently trade in the market for a price of $695. These $1,000 par value bonds have a coupon rate of 5.5% (semi-annual coupon payments), and they mature in 25 years. Melvyn's common stock trades for $26.50 per share. The dividend just paid by Melvyn was $2.10 (that is, $D_0 = 2.10$) and future dividends are expected to grow at a rate of 5.5% per year forever. Compute Melvyn's weighted average cost of capital (WACC).

Additional Questions and Problems

1. Compute the NPV, IRR, PI, the payback periods, and the discounted payback periods for the following projects. Assume a discount rate of 11%.

Project	C_0	C_1	C_2	C_3	C_4	C_5
A	−1,000	400	400	400	500	500
B	−6,000	1,500	1,500	1,500	1,500	1,500
C	−29,000	0	0	14,100	22,340	
D	−17,000	0	0	0	24,200	8,200

2. Consider a project that has the following cash flows: −1,010 at t = 0, 1,996 at t = 1, and −740 at t = 2. How many IRRs does this project have? Compute them. If the cost of capital is 20%, should this project be accepted?

3. Consider the project with the following expected cash flows:

Year	Cash flow
0	−$ 200,000
1	50,000
2	50,000
3	$ 200,000

   a. If the discount rate is 0%, what is the project's net present value?

   b. If the discount rate is 5%, what is the project's net present value?

   c. What is this project's internal rate of return?

4. A project has an NPV of $6,900. This project requires a cash outflow of $15,000 in the beginning and then from t = 1 onwards, it generates cash flows $4,500 per year for eight years. Compute the IRR, PI, and the cost of capital for this project.

5. A project requiring a $1 million investment has a profitability index of 0.96. What is its net present value?

Basics of Capital Budgeting 251

6. Which one of the following is true about the internal rate of return rule of capital budgeting:

   a. When it leads to an acceptance decision, NPV is always greater than one.

   b. When evaluating a single independent normal project, it leads the same decision as the decision based on profitability index

   c. It gives multiple answers if the cash flows don't change signs.

   d. It should be preferred over NPV when the two result in conflicting decisions. e. It ignores cash flows that are expected to occur in the far future.

7. Which statement is always correct? (Note: PI stands for Profitability Index.)

   a. If the NPV of the project is positive, then the IRR is smaller than 1.

   b. If the NPV of the project is positive, then the IRR is greater than 1.

   c. If the NPV of the project is negative, then the PI is greater than 1.

   d. If the NPV of the project is negative, then the PI is greater than discount rate.

   e. If the NPV of the project is positive, then the PI is greater than 1.

8. For a normal project (that is, a single negative cash (out)flow in year 0 followed by positive cash (in)flows in all future years), if you increase all cash inflows of any project by an inflation rate and do not change the discount rate, then the NPV of the project will

   a. increase.

   b. decrease.

   c. stay the same.

   d. decrease if the project has a single IRR and increase if the project has multiple IRRs.

   e. increase if the NPV of the project was originally positive and decrease if the NPV of the project was originally negative.

9. A five-year project—if taken—will require an initial investment of $80,000. The expected end-of-the-year cash inflows are as follows:

Year	Amount
Year 1	$10,000
Year 2	$42,000
Year 3	$42,000
Year 4	$18,000
Year 5	$22,000

   Given that the appropriate discount rate for this project is 15%, compute the NPV, IRR, and PI. Should this project be accepted or rejected? Why?

10. The following table lists the capital budgeting analysis of four different *mutually exclusive* projects with an equal life:

Project	NPV	IRR	Discount rate
A	$3,000	10.5% and 17%	11%
B	$5,050	13.4%	12%
C	$4,800	14.4%	13%
D	$3,100	21.5%	14%

Which project would you choose?

11. You have the following information on four *independent* projects with an equal life:

Project	IRR	NPV	Initial cost
A	10%	$3,500	$ 8,000
B	13%	$5,000	$20,000
C	15%	$4,000	$ 500
D	25%	$4,500	$ 1,000

Which project(s) would you choose?

12. Thompson Industries has a project with the following projected cash flows:

- Cash flow year 0: ($240,000)
- Cash flow year 1: $25,000
- Cash flow year 2: $75,000
- Cash flow year 3: $150,000
- Cash flow year 4: $150,000

a. What is the IRR of this project?

b. Using a 10% discount rate for this project, what is the NPV of this project? Should the project be accepted or rejected?

c. Using a 15% discount rate for this project, what is the NPV of this project? Should the project be accepted or rejected?

d. Using a 20% discount rate for this project, what is the NPV of this project? Should the project be accepted or rejected?

13. Your required rate of return is 8%. If you invest $150 today, you will receive the following cash flows:

At the end of Year 1	$70
At the end of Year 2	$80
At the end of Year 3	$90

What is the NPV of the project?

14. Given the cash flows of the four projects, A, B, C, and D, calculate the payback period for each project. Assume that the cash flows are equally distributed over the year for payback period calculations.

PROJECTS	A	B	C	D
Year 0 Cash Flow	($10,000)	($25,000)	($45,000)	($100,000)
Year 1 Cash Flow	$ 4,000	$ 2,000	$10,000	$ 40,000
Year 2 Cash Flow	$4,000	$8,000	$15,000	$30,000
Year 3 Cash Flow	$4,000	$14,000	$20,000	$20,000
Year 4 Cash Flow	$4,000	$20,000	$20,000	$10,000
Year 5 Cash Flow	$4,000	$26,000	$15,000	$0
Year 6 Cash Flow	$4,000	$32,000	$10,000	$0

a. If management sets the accept/reject cut-off period at two years, which project(s) would be accepted?

b. If management sets the accept/reject cut-off period at three years, which project(s) would be accepted?

c. If management sets the accept/reject cut-off period at four years, which project(s) would be accepted?

15. If the payback period of the following project is 2.5 years, what is the project's NPV assuming a discount rate of 16%? What is the project's IRR? What is the project's PI?

Year	NCF
0	???
1	$600
2	$800
3	$1,600
4	$1,400
5	$1,200
6	$1,000

16. Pickens, Inc. is trying to estimate its current cost of capital. Pickens believes that the appropriate weight of debt is 50% and the appropriate weight of equity is 50%. Pickens has a tax rate of 30%. Pickens' bonds currently trade in the market for a price of $1,095. These $1,000 par value bonds have a coupon rate of 11.6% (annual coupon payments), and they mature in 24 years. Pickens' common stock trades for $68.25 per share. The dividend just paid by Pickens was $5.25 (that is, $D_0 = 5.25$), and future dividends are expected to grow at a rate of 7% per year forever. Compute Pickens' weighted average cost of capital (WACC).

17. Zubee, Inc. is trying to estimate its current cost of capital. Zubee believes that the appropriate weight of debt is 80% and the appropriate weight of equity is 20%. Zubee has a tax rate of 30%. Zubee's bonds currently trade in the market for a price of $8785. These $10,000 par value bonds have a coupon rate of 7.8% (semi-annual coupon payments) and they mature in thirty years. Zubee's common stock trades for $33.75 per share. The dividend just paid by Zubee was $2.90 (that is, $D_0 = 2.90$) and future dividends are expected to grow at a rate of 3.75% per year forever. Compute Zubee's weighted average cost of capital (WACC).

Chapter 10

Advanced Topics in Capital Budgeting

10.1 Chapter Introduction and Overview
10.2 Project Discount Rates and Relevant Cash Flows
10.3 A Capital Budgeting Example
10.4 Equivalent Annual Series
10.5 Concluding Thoughts and Remarks
    Assignments
    Additional Questions and Problems

After studying Chapter 10, you should be able to:

- Understand the importance of good capital budgeting to financial management.
- Realize the importance and difficulty with estimating the appropriate discount rate for a project
- Identify the guidelines by which cash flows should be measured.
- Explain how a project's benefits and costs—that is, its incremental after-tax cash flows—are calculated.
- Describe the difference between independent and mutually exclusive projects.
- Compare projects with different lives using the equivalent annual series technique.

From *Lectures in Corporate Finance*, 6th Edition by Jayant R. Kale and Richard J. Fendler. Copyright © 2013 by Kendall Hunt Publishing Company. Reprinted by permission.

10.1 Chapter Introduction and Overview

Imo Sherman owns and operates a delivery business in Atlanta, Georgia. Sherman's company, Imo's Immediate Delivery (referred to by most clients as IID), delivers business packages and letters throughout a 50-mile radius of the center of the city. IID has an excellent reputation, few legitimate competitors, and is highly profitable. The company currently has a fleet of 20 delivery vehicles (trucks) and employs 32 drivers and support personnel. Imo Sherman is the sole owner/manager of the business.

IID guarantees pickup and delivery within two hours of placement of an order. Interestingly, this full money-back guarantee is easy to meet for pickups and deliveries outside of the main downtown area. Within the five-mile radius of the heart of the city, however, traffic and limited parking make it extremely difficult to fulfill the guarantee. In fact, nearly 30% of all orders in this area end up being fulfilled free of charge.

Accordingly, Imo is contemplating adding a fleet of bicycles to his business. He is thinking about purchasing 30 bicycles and hiring 20 riders (10 additional riders will double as vehicle drivers and bicycle riders as demand dictates). He will also need to purchase a piece of land adjacent to the main downtown area (about five miles from the heart of the city) and construct a garage to store the bicycles and to use as a hub to connect bicycles with vehicles for pickups and deliveries that span the downtown area and outside the downtown area.

Imo estimates that the bicycles and associated equipment will cost $25,000, the land will cost $75,000, and construction of the garage will cost $100,000. Should Imo spend $200,000 to expand this part of his business? This is a capital budgeting problem, and therefore answering this question requires application of the techniques that you learned in the previous chapter; specifically, computation of the project's NPV, IRR, or PI. As we are sure you realize, we are missing two items needed to compute and evaluate these values.

1. The project cash inflows
2. The appropriate discount rate

In the prior chapter, these items, specifically the project's cash flows and the discount rates applicable to the project, were provided. In this chapter we will investigate how companies estimate projected cash flows (both inflows and outflows) for a project. We will learn what items and relevant and what items are not relevant for capital budgeting projects. Identifying and estimating all relevant project cash flows, and determining the appropriate discount rate for those cash flows, is the single most important task that any successful business faces. For large projects, companies spend weeks, and even months, estimating these variables.

In fact, estimating the relevant cash flows and the appropriate discount rate for capital budgeting projects is one of the most difficult tasks of corporate financial management. However, the time is worth the effort. Studies consistently show that over the last 30 years, those companies that have created the greatest wealth for their owners are mainly those that have invested the greatest amount of time, energy, and money to doing good capital budgeting. Because maximizing shareholder wealth is the goal of financial management, it seems only natural that this topic must be given significant attention in the real world.

10.2 Project Discount Rates and Relevant Cash Flows

Estimating relevant cash flows actually involves many of the activities that were covered in the first half of this book. Pro forma income statements and corresponding balance sheets for each year of the life of the project must first be constructed. This also involves estimating all related working capital requirements and changes in these requirements associated with any forecasted annual changes in sales. These issues were covered in Chapters 4 and 5. Then, the pro forma statements must be converted into cash flow statements. This procedure was the basis of Chapter 3. Finally, relevant cash flows must be identified and separated from non-relevant cash flows.

In this chapter, we will discuss several important items and issues to remember when determining a firm's or a project's relevant cash flows. The procedures outlined in this chapter are purposely limited in scope. Complete details concerning cash flow estimation are left to advanced finance books and courses. Our goal here is to provide a basic understanding of, and appreciation for, the process of determining whether a capital project should be accepted or rejected.

1. Project Discount Rates

With regards to the appropriate project discount rate, we completely relegate determining and estimating this variable to a later course in finance. The primary reason for this is that to determine the appropriate discount rate, we must study the area of "risk" in much greater detail than was covered in Chapter 8. Additionally, it is necessary to cover the topics of optimal capital structure and the valuation of options, to determine appropriate individual project discount rates. These topics, although interesting, are beyond the scope of any introductory finance course.

We will note here, however, that consistent with all that you have learned in this class to date, appropriate project discount rates must reflect the riskiness of the specific project. A project that is merely an extension of the company's current business (for example, a major grocery store chain opening a new store in a new location), will have a level of risk that is essentially equivalent to the risk inherent in all of the firm's assets. In this case, the weighted average cost of capital (WACC) that we learned about in the prior chapter is usually the appropriate discount rate for the project.

If, however, the risk of the project is significantly different from the overall risk characteristics of the firm's main line of business, use of the company's WACC will lead to poor (and just plain wrong) decisions. For example, assume that a major grocery store chain is contemplating building and operating a nuclear power plant. The grocery store estimates that the cash flows for the project will be as follows:

Year	Net Cash Flow
0	($7.5 billion)
1	$1 billion
2	$1 billion
.	.
.	.
.	.
20	$1 billion

Because grocery stores are relatively low risk businesses (they generally have betas less than one), assume that the company's WACC is 8%. Should the grocery store accept this project? If you use a discount rate of 8%, you will find that this project has an NPV of $2.32 billion. So, yes, the grocery store should build and operate a nuclear power plant.

However, do you think that any rational investor would give this much money to a grocery store to run a nuclear plant? Who will the nuclear scientists be—the butchers from the meat department? Who will run daily operations—the people who restock the shelves? Obviously, a grocery store does not have the expertise to run such a plant and therefore no investor would give the company money *at this rate* to venture down this path. Investors will require the same return that they could earn on a comparable investment. The natural comparable investment would be the cost of capital to a nuclear power company.

Assume the average WACC for a nuclear power company is 20%. If the grocery store uses that discount rate for this project, it will find that the NPV is –$2.63 billion. And the grocery store will stay out of the nuclear power business, just like we hope that nuclear power companies will stay out of the grocery store business. Thus, discount rates must reflect the risk of the project. But, as we noted above, determining this rate for individual projects is left to more advanced finance courses. In this chapter, as we did in the previous chapter, we will either give you the project's appropriate discount rate or we will assume that the appropriate discount rate is the firm's existing WACC.

2. Relevant Cash Flows

As we learned in the prior chapter, once relevant cash flows and an appropriate discount rate have been estimated, computation of a project's NPV, IRR, and PI is a fairly simple task. Assume that Imo estimates that the annual net cash flows from adding the bicycle fleet will be as follows:

Year	Net Cash Flow
0	($200,000)
1	$ 50,000
2	$ 60,000
3	$ 75,000
4	$ 80,000
5	$ 90,000

For simplicity, we will assume that the project will only last five years and that Imo has included the salvage value in the fifth year estimated cash flow figure of $90,000. Imo also has estimated that the appropriate discount rate for this project (that is, the project's cost of capital) is 18%.

Problem 10.1: Compute the bicycle project's NPV, IRR, and PI.

Problem 10.2: Should IID accept or reject this project?

As a now "seasoned pro" in cash flow valuation (do you realize how much you have learned and how far you have progressed in this course?), we are certain that you realize that computing these evaluation metrics are easy. A much more interesting question is where did the cash flow estimates come from? And, more importantly, what if the cash flows are estimated incorrectly? For example, assume that Imo incorrectly computed the cash flows for the project. Assume that he included items that were not relevant and he excluded items that were relevant. Suppose that if he would have done the estimation correctly, he would have instead computed the following cash flows for the project:

Year	Net Cash Flow
0	($200,000)
1	$ 45,000
2	$ 50,000
3	$ 60,000
4	$ 75,000
5	$ 80,000

Now at a discount rate of 18%, the NPV of this project is actually –$15,784.43. If Imo would have accepted this project based on his incorrect cash flow estimates, this mistake would have resulted in a decrease in his wealth (remember, he is the sole owner of the company) of nearly $16,000 because the NPV of a project is the direct change in shareholder wealth that will occur if the company chooses to accept the project. If NPV is positive, shareholder wealth will increase—that is the ultimate reason why we consider NPV to be the BEST capital budgeting evaluation technique. If, however, NPV is negative, then shareholder wealth will decline. It would have been much better for Imo to have not considered this project at all than to have embarked on a project that actually had a negative NPV. Better yet, if he had properly estimated the cash flows initially, he would have avoided this potential mistake in the first place.

In the next several sections to this chapter, we note several items that must be considered when estimating project cash flows. As you will see, the main issue involves identifying and including all possible relevant net cash flows and identifying and excluding all possible non-relevant cash flows.

1. Cash Flows Must Be "Cash" Flows

The first, and the most important, thing to note about determining a project's cash flows is that *cash flows should be cash.* This statement may sound a little silly, but nonetheless it is extremely important. From your study of financial statements in the earlier part of this course, you undoubtedly recall the basic outline of a firm's income statement. Let us consider the following simple income statement for ASD Corp.

Income Statement
ASD Corp.
For the Year Ending December 31, 2013

Net sales	$125,000
Cost of goods sold	80,000
Depreciation	15,000
EBIT	**30,000**
Tax at 30%	9,000
Net income	**$21,000**

What is the cash flow to ASD in 2013? Is it equal to the net income of $21,000? The answer is no. To see this, let us suppose that there is a person Ms. X in ASD whose job it is to keep track of the cash. All the cash that comes in goes into Ms. X's pocket and all the cash that goes out is from Ms. X's pocket. Then, assuming that all sales are cash sales, $125,000 will go into Ms. X's pocket from sales. Again assuming that costs of goods sold are paid in cash, an amount of $80,000 will leave Ms. X's pocket leaving $125,000 − $80,000 = $45,000 in Ms. X's pocket.

Will the $15,000 for depreciation leave Ms. X's pocket? No, because depreciation, as we all know, is not a cash expense. How about the $9,000 for tax? Like it or not, this amount will certainly leave Ms. X's pocket, leaving $36,000 in it. There are no other inflows or outflows of cash from Ms. X's pocket. Therefore, in 2013, we know that ASD Corp. had a *net cash flow* of $36,000. This is *not* the same as the net income from the income statement. The cash flow is higher than the net income by $15,000, and this amount is the same as the depreciation expense.

The fact that the difference between the net income and the cash flow is exactly equal to the depreciation expense is not a coincidence. Depreciation is not a cash expense. The only reason that it enters an income statement is because it can be deducted for income tax purposes. Therefore, a common method for estimating the cash flow from the income statement is to add the depreciation back to the net income.

Net cash flow = net income + depreciation expense

As you might recall from the first section of the book, net income plus depreciation expense is commonly referred to as free cash flow.

Let us view this idea another way. Suppose that depreciation expense were not tax deductible. In this case, ASD's income statement would be as follows:

Income Statement
ASD Corp.
For the Year Ending December 31, 2003

Net sales	$125,000
Cost of goods sold	80,000
EBIT	**45,000**
Tax at 30%	13,500
Net income	**$31,500**

Here, the cash flow and the net income would be identical (assuming that all sales are cash sales and that all expenses are paid immediately in cash). The difference between the cash flows when depreciation is tax deductible and when it is not is $36,000 − $31,500 = $4,500. Note that this difference is equal to the depreciation expense multiplied by the tax rate. In other words, under the existing tax system, depreciation provides a tax shield. The depreciation non-cash expense of $15,000 reduces taxable income and therefore reduces taxes, which is a cash expense, by $15,000 × 0.30 = $4,500. Therefore, we have the following alternative way of writing the cash flow equation:

Net cash flow = (Revenue − Costs) × (1 − t_c) + (t_c × Depreciation).

where, t_c is the corporate tax rate and

(t_c × Depreciation) = Depreciation tax shield.

Depreciation is just one of the reasons why the net income from a firm's financial statement might not represent the cash flow. There are other reasons, too. The most common reason is the accrual method used in accounting. Sales are entered as such even if the cash from those sales is not received. Thus, the sales number from the income statement might not reflect the actual cash received by the firm. The same may be true for the expenses of the firm.

In fact, we covered this concept in Chapter 3. Recall that cash flow from operating activities is generally not the same as net income. To convert accrual accounting net income to cash flow from operations, we first added depreciation to net income and then added or subtracted changes in balance sheet accounts that were related to income statement variables (specifically, changes in accounts receivable, inventory, accounts payable, and accruals). This same procedure is required to find the cash flows associated with a given project. That is why it is necessary to construct pro forma income statements and balance sheets for each year of the projected life of the project. From these, we can determine cash flow from operating activities, which are essentially equal to total project cash flows. We are not done, however, because we must still separate relevant from non-relevant cash flows.

Creating pro forma income statements and balance sheets for all years of the life of a project, and the extracting net cash flow from operating activities from these statements, is tedious and time consuming. If we tried to solve problems like this in this chapter, it might take hours (or even longer) to solve a problem. To simplify our calculations in this introductory course, we will assume throughout the rest of this chapter that the balance sheet of the company will remain "frozen" through the life of the project. This means that there will be no changes in accounts receivable, inventory, accounts payable or accruals, and thus, net cash flow is always determined as:

Net cash flow = (Revenue − Costs) × (1 − t_c) + (t_c × Depreciation)

for all years of the life of the project.

2. *Ignore Interest Expenses*

Note that in the income statement of ASD Corp. there was no interest expense. Is it a cash expense? Most certainly! Do we take it into account when we determine a project's cash flow? The answer is no. The reason for this is somewhat complex and will require studying other topics in corporate finance such as capital structure. However, for the time being, let us simply state that in determining the NPV of a project, we must ignore how a project is financed. In other words, we do not consider whether the firm issued debt or equity to finance (pay for) the project.

Intuitively, the reason for this can be illustrated with the following examples. Suppose you are buying a car from a dealer. You also own a significant amount of equity in your home. You can borrow the money for the car either by taking a car loan from your bank or you can raise it by selling a part of your ownership in your house to another person. Will the dealer charge you a different price if the cash you gave him was from a loan from a bank or from your sale of a part of the house? The dealer doesn't care. In other words, the price of the car will not be affected by how you have raised the money to pay for it.

On the other hand, suppose that you have decided the model of the car that you are going to buy but have not yet agreed to the price. A respected consumer magazine gives a scathing report on the quality of this model. According to this report, the quality of this car is so poor that the resale value is expected to be a lot lower than what was earlier expected. Irrespective of how you finance the automobile purchase, will the price that you will pay be affected? Most certainly, you will now pay a lower price.

The point made by these examples is that, in a simple world, the value of a project is determined by the cash flows that the project's assets generate and not by how the project is financed. Note that in the above statement we included the phrase: "in a simple world." This phrase is actually much more important than it might appear. When the world is not simple or not perfect, additional items begin to matter and project evaluation becomes more complicated. But, as we stated in the beginning of this chapter, such intricate details are here relegated to more advanced courses in corporate finance.

3. All Project Cash Flows Must Be Incremental

Consider a soft drink company called Quoqua Quola. Currently this company manufactures and sells a soft drink called QuoquaQuola. It sells 10 million units of this drink per year and, to keep matters simple, suppose that from each unit it earns $10 in cash. Thus, currently, its cash flow is $100 million per year. This company is considering the project of introducing a diet drink, DietQuoque, to the market. The marketing people of the company estimate that this new product will have sales of five million units per year. Assume that this product will also generate $10 per unit and that it will require an investment of $400 million. What are the cash inflows for the DietQuoque project? Can you come up with a number? Is it $50 million per year?

Let us think about this for a minute. Look at the kind of product we are considering here. It is highly likely that a significant portion of the sales of DietQuoque will be to persons who are switching from the regular QuoquaQuola. Therefore, the introduction of this product will reduce the sales of the regular drink. Is that a relevant factor to consider for the diet drink project? It certainly is. Now suppose that of the five million units of the diet drink sales, one million are to those who have switched from the company's regular drink. Can you determine the appropriate per year cash inflow for the diet drink project? The answer is $40 million per year. Of the $50 million of the diet drink sales, $10 million are due to the reduction in the regular drink sales. Therefore, as far as the firm is concerned, the net cash inflow from the project is only $40 million. If you believe this, then you have understood the concept of incremental cash flows. In capital budgeting, only *incremental cash flows* are relevant.

How do you determine incremental cash flows? The answer is simple. Look at the cash flows to the firm without the project and then consider the cash flows to the firm with the project. The difference is the incremental cash flow. For example, without the diet drink project, the company in our example was generating a cash flow of $100 million per year from 10 million units of the regular drink sale. With the project, it will generate $90 million from the sale of nine million units of the regular drink and $50 million from the sale of five million units of DietQuoque. The total with the project is, therefore, $140 million per year. The incremental cash flow, therefore, is $140 − $100 = $40 million per year.

We will designate an incremental cash flow using the symbol Δ before a variable. Thus, ΔRevenue means the revenue the company expects to earn with the new project minus what it believes it would have earned without the new project. Thus, ΔRevenue considers all "other effects" on the revenue associated with the project. Then, our appropriate net cash flow equation will now be:

$$\Delta NCF = (\Delta Revenue - \Delta Costs) \times (1 - t_c) + (t_c \times \Delta Depreciation)$$

Although this equation may appear simple, in reality, estimating incremental cash flows is much more complicated than it appears. The capital budgeting analyst must actually construct pro forma income statements and balance sheets for the entire company for every year of the project assuming that the project is *not* undertaken, and then construct corresponding pro forma income statements and balance sheets for every year of the project assuming that the project *is* undertaken. Net cash flows from operating activities are then determined for each scenario and these are subtracted to find annual incremental cash flows.

4. Allocated Costs, Sunk Costs, and Opportunity Costs

Suppose that a firm is evaluating a project. This project will use the firm's mainframe computer. The firm's current operations use approximately 40% of this computer's capacity and even with the project, will use only 50% of the capacity. The firm's accounting department has allocated $30,000 per year as computer usage costs for this project. Is this $30,000 a relevant cash flow for the project? If you think within the framework of the cash flows of the firm with and without the project, you will notice that the firm's computer costs with the project are the same as what they are without the project. Therefore, this $30,000 is not an incremental cash flow.

There are many instances of such allocated costs that might not be incremental, and hence would be irrelevant from the point of view of the project's cash flows. These allocated costs could include several types of expenses such as rent, supervisory salaries, administrative costs, and many other overhead expenses that you can think of. Remember that these costs are not always incremental. The best litmus test for determining whether a cost is incremental is the comparison of the cost category to the firm with and without the project.

Suppose that your firm has paid $100,000 to a consulting firm for conducting some market research. On the basis of the consultant's recommendations, your firm has decided to undertake a project. Should the $100,000 paid to the consultant be considered as a cost of the project? The normal temptation is to say yes. But think about it a little more. Suppose you do not take on the project. Will you get this $100,000 back? Certainly not! Thus, the $100,000 is gone whether you do or do not undertake the project. Hence, this amount should not be considered as a part of the cost of the project. Such costs are called *sunk costs* and should not be included in the cost of the project. Examples of this include R&D expenses, consultant fees, and others. Sunk costs are by definition irrecoverable and, therefore, should not be considered relevant to the project.

A common situation where the above logic becomes important is when someone makes the following type of statement: "Unless we spend an additional million dollars, we will have wasted the $10 million that we have already spent." By now you can see the fallacy of this type of an argument. The only reason that you would spend the additional million dollars would be if the additional cash inflow that it generated had a present value of greater than a million dollars. The fact that $10 million are already invested is no reason to spend another million dollars. You might not be immediately convinced of the logic of this argument. Think about it for a while and hopefully you will realize that it does indeed make sense. You will also then begin to notice how often and how much money firms (or individuals) and, even more often governments, spend based on such arguments. It's scary.

Suppose that your firm is deciding whether it should build a new factory. The factory will be built on a piece of land that the firm already owns. The market value of this piece of land is $500,000. Should the value of the land be included in the cost of the project? The answer is yes. The argument for its inclusion is a subtle variation of the incremental argument and is called the *opportunity cost* argument. If the firm did not take on the project, it could sell the land for a half a million dollars. By taking on the project, the firm is forgoing the opportunity of selling the land. Therefore, the value of the land, and other such opportunity costs *should* be included in the cost of the project.

Including opportunity costs as relevant costs is akin to the notion that there is no such thing as a "free" asset. Everything has some cost, whether implicit or explicit. Buying a new machine for $1,000,000 has an explicit cost that can easily be identified. Using a piece of land that the company already owns has no explicit cost, because the company does not have to actually put out money to buy the land—the company already owns it! The land, however, has an implicit cost. As noted above, if the company uses the land for a given project, the land cannot be sold. The land is not "free" to this project, and therefore its cost must be estimated. The most accurate estimated, or implicit, cost, is what the land would return if it were sold.

5. Net Working Capital

As noted before, annual changes in forecasted net working capital (that is, changes in accounts receivable, inventory, accounts payable, and accruals) must be considered when computing annual net cash flows. This requires generating annual pro forma balance sheets for every year of the project. Although realistic, such detail is again beyond the scope of any introductory finance course. It can easily be avoided by merely assuming that annual net working capital changes will be zero (i.e., the balance sheets are "frozen" throughout the life of the project). For simplicity, we will make this assumption for all problems in this chapter. Thus, it will not be necessary to construct annual pro forma balance sheets. To determine annual net cash flow, all that will be required will be to add incremental depreciation to incremental net income.

We will, however, assume that most projects will require an initial increase in net working capital. For example, suppose that by taking on the project, the inventory of the firm will rise by $2 million and all other components of working capital will remain the same. Thus, there is a net increase of $2 million in the net working capital of the firm because of the project. Is this relevant? Absolutely! If you take on the project, you will have to maintain the higher level of inventory. This additional $2 million, the increase in the net working capital, should, therefore, be added to the cost of the project. What happens to this inventory at the end of the life of the project? As a matter of convention (mostly convenience), it is assumed that this additional working capital is liquidated at the end of the project's life. Therefore, the increase in working capital is added to the project's initial cost and also is considered a cash inflow in the last period. By the same logic, if the taking on of a project reduces the net working capital, then the magnitude of this decrease in working capital should be subtracted from the project's initial cost and also for the last period cash inflow.

Example Problem: After reading the last section of this chapter, Imo Sherman, owner/manager of Imo's Immediate Delivery (IID), realizes that he has forgotten to include the initial net working capital change in his cash flow estimates. Recall that Imo estimated that the bicycles, land, and building would cost $200,000. He now figures that the project will also require an $8,000 increase in inventory, the firm's minimum cash balance will need to increase by $3,500, higher sales will cause accounts receivable to increase by $18,000, accounts payable will increase by $2,500, and accruals are estimated to increase by $500. This change in net working capital will need to be funded immediately. The total amount will be recovered at the end of the life of the project. Compute the initial change in net working capital.

Solution: Change in Net Working Capital = $8,000 + $3,500 + $18,000 − $2,500 − $500 = $26,500.

An increase in net working capital must be funded; therefore, this amount represents a required cash outflow. If instead, the change in net working capital would have been negative, the amount would represent a cash inflow at year 0. Thus,

| Increase in net working capital | Cash outflow in Year 0 | Cash inflow at end of project |
| Decrease in net working capital | Cash inflow in Year 0 | Cash outflow at end of project |

Including this figure in the project cash flows will cause the initial cash outflow (that is, the total cost of the project) to increase to $226,500. Because we will assume that this expenditure will be recovered at the end of the life of the project, we will have a non-operating cash inflow of $26,500 in year 5. This will make the total cash inflow in year 5 equal to $90,000 + $26,500 = 116,500. In summary, the cash flows from the bicycle project are expected to be:

Year	Estimated Net Cash Flow
0	($226,500)
1	$ 50,000
2	$ 60,000
3	$ 75,000
4	$ 80,000
5	$116,500

Problem 10.3: Given the new cash flow estimates in the chart above, compute the NPV, IRR, and PI of the bicycle project assuming an appropriate discount rate of 18%.

Problem 10.4: Should IID accept or reject this project?

Obviously, inclusion of the initial net working capital effect is important. By ignoring this relevant cost, IDD would have accepted a project that in fact should have been rejected. This in turn would have reduced the value of the company, and therefore would have reduced the shareholder's (that is, Imo Sherman's) wealth.

6. *Treatment of Inflation*

When we began the study of the time value of money, we considered the effect of inflation on interest rates (that is, on investors' required rates of return). We noted that the relation between the nominal and real returns with inflation at i was given by

$$(1 + r_{nominal}) = (1 + r_{real}) \times (1 + i).$$

Let us consider a single-period project that costs C_0 and generates a cash flow of C_1 at the end of the first year. Consider first the case when we use the real values for all variables. Then the real NPV of this project will be given by

$$NPV_{real} = \frac{C_1}{(1+r_{real})} - C_0.$$

Now consider the case when there is inflation and we want to use the nominal values for all variables. We know the relation between the nominal and real interest rates. Thus, the denominator of the NPV expression is easy to adjust. Because inflation implies a general rise in prices, suppose that we assume that the cash inflow also increases by i percent. Then the NPV with nominal values becomes

$$NPV_{nominal} = \frac{C_1 \times (1+i)}{(1+r_{nominal})} - C_0.$$

Substituting for $r_{nominal}$, we obtain

$$= \frac{C_1 \times (1+i)}{(1+r_{real}) \times (1+i)} - C_0.$$

You will notice that the $(1 + i)$ terms in the numerator and the denominator cancel each other and we are left with the expression for the real NPV. Does this mean that inflation has no effect on project valuation or selection? What is your gut feel? We are sure that you are not convinced of the validity of this result. And you shouldn't be. There is no mathematical error in the above analysis.

There is, however, a conceptual error. When we multiply C_1 by $(1 + i)$ to determine the nominal cash inflow, we are implicitly assuming that all components of the firm's operations that result in this cash inflow are affected by the same amount of inflation. This is clearly not the case. The sales will increase at a different rate than will costs. In particular, labor costs move at different rates than the rate of inflation. Also, because the depreciation expense is not affected by inflation, the tax expenses are affected by an amount that is not proportionate to the inflation rate of i. In summary, it is not correct to adjust the cash flows by simply multiplying them by $(1 + i)$. In an inflationary environment, each component of the income statement has to be individually adjusted to account for inflation.

For simplicity, we will assume that there is NO inflation in the world for all problems we use in this chapter. Thus, we do not have to worry about these many important adjustment effects. Recall that we warned you that good capital budgeting is difficult and companies often spend days, weeks, even months doing project analysis. Most companies find that they continually improve in their abilities to identify and estimate all relevant cash flows (and to exclude all not relevant cash flows) as they do more and more project evaluations. Capital budgeting is most certainly a "learn by doing" process, but now that you understand the basics of what to include and what to exclude, you at least can appreciate what the process is all about. And, as long as we keep them simple, you can even work a few problems to apply some of these techniques in practice.

10.3 A Capital Budgeting Example

We have discussed quite a few concepts in this chapter so far. Let us illustrate these with the help of the following (extremely) comprehensive problem.

Example Problem: You are given the responsibility of conducting the project selection analysis in your firm. You have to calculate the NPV of a given project. The appropriate cost of capital is 12% and the firm is in the 30% tax bracket. You are provided the following pieces of information regarding the project:

a. The project will be built on a piece of land that the firm already owns. The market value of the land is $1 million.

b. If the project is undertaken, prior to construction, an amount of $100,000 would have to be spent to make the land usable for construction purposes.

c. To come up with the project concept, the company had hired a marketing research firm for $200,000.

d. The firm has spent another $250,000 on R&D for this project.

e. The project will require an initial outlay of $20 million for plant and machinery.

f. The sales from this project will be $15 million per year, of which 20% will be from lost sales of existing products.

g. The variable costs of manufacturing for this level of sales will be $9 million per year.

h. The company uses straight-line depreciation. The project has an economic life of 10 years and will have a salvage value of $3 million at the end.

i. Because of the project, the company will need additional working capital of $1 million, which can be liquidated at the end of 10 years.

j. The project will require additional supervisory and managerial manpower that will cost $200,000 per year.

k. The accounting department has allocated $350,000 as allocated overhead cost for supervisory and managerial salaries.

In solving the above problem, the first thing to note is that the computations are not going to be particularly difficult but we have to figure out which information is relevant and which is not.

a. $1,000,000 for the land should be included in the cost of the project (opportunity cost).

b. $100,000 for land improvement should be included in the cost of the project (incremental cost).

c. $200,000 to the marketing research firm are sunk costs and should be ignored.

d. $250,000 on R&D are sunk costs and should be ignored.

e. $20 million for plant and machinery should be included in the cost of the project.

f. The *incremental* sales from the project are only $15,000,000 × 0.8 = $12,000,000.

g. The variable costs of $9 million are relevant for the project.

h. Straight-line depreciation, along with 10-year economic life and $3 million salvage value, implies that the depreciation expense will be

$$\frac{20,000,000 - 3,000,000}{10} = \$1,700,000 \text{ per year.}$$

The $3 million in salvage value will be added to the cash flow at t = 10. Unless we are specifically given a price for which fixed assets will be sold at the end of the life of the project, we will ALWAYS assume these will be sold for their salvage value.

i. The additional working capital of $1 million implies that the initial outlay will be higher by $1 million and $1 million will be added to the cash flow at t = 10.

j. The $200,000 for *additional* managerial manpower is an incremental cash outflow and is relevant to the project.

k. The allocated expense should be ignored.

Having analyzed each piece of information, we suggest that you approach the solution of this problem in four steps as follows:

Step One: Compute the Initial Cash Flow (i.e., CF0)

The initial cash flow involves the following items:

ITEM	ASSOCIATED CASH FLOW
Buy land	($1,000,000)
Improve land	($100,000)
Buy plant and machinery	($20,000,000)
Change in net working capital	($1,000,000)
CF0	($22,100,000)

Step Two: Estimate ΔNCF for Each Year of the Life of the Project Using the Equation:

$$\Delta NCF = (\Delta Revenue - \Delta Costs) \times (1 - t_c) + (t_c \times \Delta Depreciation).$$

Note from the list above, that:

- Incremental revenue = $12,000,000.
- Incremental costs = incremental variable costs + incremental managerial salaries = $9,000,000 + $200,000 = $9,200,000
- Incremental depreciation = $1,700,000
- $t_c = 30\% = .30$

So, we have:

$$\Delta NCF = (\Delta Revenue - \Delta Costs) \times (1 - t_c) + (t_c \times \Delta Depreciation)$$
$$= (\$12,000,000 - \$9,200,000)(1 - .30) + (.30)(\$1,700,000)$$
$$= \$2,470,000 \text{ per year for years } 1, 2, \ldots, 10$$

Note that ΔNCF is called the annual "operating" cash flow for the project. It is the cash flow that results from "operating" the new project.

Step Three: Compute Final Year Non-Operating Cash Flow

At the end of the life of the project, a few items will usually occur that will produce a possible cash flow. These are non-operating items such as selling plant and equipment, land, or other assets and recovering (or replacing) new working capital. This non-operating cash flow is in addition to the operating cash flow for the final year of the project. Thus, the total final year cash flow for the project will be ΔNCF in final year + final year non-operating cash flow.

For this project, the additional cash flows at the end of the project are:

ITEM	ASSOCIATED CASH FLOW
Sell plant and equipment for salvage value	$3,000,000
Recover net working capital	$1,000,000
Final Year Non-operating cash flow	**$4,000,000**

Thus, the total final year expected cash flow for this project is $2,470,000 + $4,000,000 = $6,470,000.

Step Four: Construct Cash Flow Summary Table and Compute Desired Value

Summarizing the cash flows for this project, we have the following:

Year	Net Cash Flow
0	($22,100,000)
1	$2,470,000
2	$2,470,000

| | 9 | $2,470,000 |
| | 10 | $6,470,000 |

We can now calculate any of the capital budgeting valuation metrics we learned in the previous chapter. At a discount rate of 12%, we derive the following values and decisions:

Technique	Value	Decision
NPV	−$6,856,056.17	Reject
IRR	4.52%	Reject
PI	.069	Reject

Note two things here. First, if we had not recognized that 20% of the sales were from lost sales of existing products, the annual cash flow would have been $4,570,000, the NPV would have been positive and the project would have been accepted. Thus, a single mistake would have ended up causing the firm to invest $22.1 million in a bad project.

Now, using the same four-step process, see if you can derive the correct answers to the following problems. As usual, the answers are shown in Appendix A.

Problem 10.5: Spacely Sprockets is considering increasing its production of sprockets at its Orbit City plant. You have been provided the following pieces of information on this 10-year project.

- The expansion will require the immediate purchase of machinery costing $50,000,000.
- The firm has spent $750,000 to train workers to use the new machinery. If the project is accepted, the firm expects to spend an additional $350,000 in training costs payable today (t = 0).
- Sales from this project are expected to be $20,000,000 per year. Annual operating expenses (excluding depreciation) are expected to equal $11,000,000 per year.
- The company uses straight-line depreciation. The project has an economic life of 10 years and the machinery has a salvage value of $8,000,000. Spacely will sell the machine for salvage value at the end of the project (i.e., 10 years from today).
- Because of the project, the company will need additional net working capital of $300,000, which can be liquidated at the end of 10 years.
- Spacely's marginal tax rate is 40%.
- Spacely's cost of capital (WACC) is 10%.

  a. The initial cash flow (i.e., CF0 = final value for Step 1) for this project is $ _____.

b. The project's cash flow in year 9 (i.e., C09 = ΔNCF for this project) is $ _____.

c. The project's final year non-operating cash flow in year 10 (i.e., final value for Step 3) is $ _____.

d. The NPV of this project is $ _____.

Problem 10.6:   Woodard Boats, Inc. is considering beginning production of a new model of ski boat at its Owingsville, KY plant. You have been provided the following pieces of information on this 15-year project.

- The expansion will require the immediate purchase of machinery costing $32,000,000.
- The firm will house the new machinery in a building it already owns. The building is currently not being used. If Woodard does not use the building for this project, it will sell the building today for its current market value, which is estimated to be $14,000,000. If Woodard does use the building for this project, it will sell the building at the end of the life of this project (i.e., 15 years from today) for $14,000,000.
- Last year, Woodard spent $500,000 testing the product for consumer satisfaction. Results from that test indicate that the new model will most likely be very successful.
- Sales from this project are expected to be $24,000,000 per year. The operating expenses (excluding depreciation) are expected to equal $12,500,000 per year.
- Unfortunately, Woodard believes that sales of the new model will reduce expected sales of existing models. The company estimates that revenue from existing models will be reduced by $4,000,000, and the operating costs associated with these existing models will be reduced by $2,500,000. Because all equipment used for other models is fully depreciated, the incremental depreciation from this project will only be the annual depreciation associated with the new machinery.
- The company uses straight-line depreciation. The project has an economic life of 15 years, the machinery has a salvage value of $2,000,000 and will sold for that amount at the conclusion of the project.

- Because of the project, the company will need to invest in additional net working capital of $2,500,000 in Year 0. This investment will be recovered at the end of the life of the project.
- Woodard's marginal tax rate is 40%.
- Woodard's stock price is $34.25. The company just paid a dividend of $3 (i.e., $D_0 = 3.00$) and the market consensus is for constant 3% dividend growth forever.
- Woodard's bonds sell for $920. The bonds pay coupon interest semi-annually, have 7 years to maturity, a coupon rate of 4% and par value of $1,000.
- Woodard's marginal tax rate is 30%.
- The company's target capital structure is 60% equity and 40% debt.

a. What is Woodard's weighted average cost of capital?

b. What is this project's NPV, assuming that Woodard's WACC is the appropriate discount rate for the project?

10.4 Equivalent Annual Series

Suppose you have to choose between the following two mutually exclusive projects. The discount rate is 10%. Because we know that NPV is the better method for ranking projects than the IRR, we will consider only the NPV.

Project	C_0	C_1	C_2	C_3	C_4	NPV
L	−1,000	500	500	500	500	584.93
S	−600	500	500			267.77

Even though the NPV of L is higher, we should not rush to rank it higher than S. The reason is that the two projects have different lives, and comparing their NPVs would be equivalent to the proverbial comparison of apples and oranges. If we take on project L, we are locked in for four years. However, if we choose S, we can do something after two years. Therefore, to compare the two projects, we must consider what we can do in years 3 and 4 if we choose project S. The easiest assumption is that a firm's investment opportunities will remain the same in the future. Then, we can assume that at the end of the second year, the firm invests again in project S. In other words, it spends $600 at t = 2 and generates $500 in each of the next two years, three and four. This is called a *replacement chain*. For notational simplicity, we will call the replacement chain for S as the project S_{RC}. We will consider the two projects again.

Project	C_0	C_1	C_2	C_3	C_4	NPV
L	−1,000	500	500	500	500	584.93
S	−600	500	500			267.77
Second S			−600	500	500	220.66
S_{RC}	−600	500	−100	500	500	488.43

We now compare L with S_{RC} and determine that L is in fact the better project; its NPV is higher than that of the replacement chain of S, denoted by S_{RC}.

Attempt the following problems in the space provided and see if you obtain the answer shown in Appendix A.

Problem 10.7: Assume a discount rate of 12%. Which of the two mutually exclusive projects will you choose? Project A costs $12,000 and generates cash flows of $4,000 per year for eight years. Project B costs $8,000 and generates cash flows of $4,000 for four years.

Problem 10.8: The two projects G and H are mutually exclusive. The appropriate discount rate for both the projects is 14%. Project G costs $100,000 and generates cash flows of $50,000 per year for three years. Project H costs $53,000 and generates cash flows of $40,000 per year for two years.

In the above problem, the lives of the two projects were three and two years, respectively, so you will have to form replacement chains for both the projects. The common number of years for the two is six and therefore, you will invest in G once more and in H twice more to form the replacement chains.

The aspect of the replacement chain method that is depicted in the above problem makes its use extremely tedious. When the lives of the two projects were three and two years, the process was tedious enough. Imagine how boring it would be if the lives of the two projects were 11 and nine years, respectively. You would have to form replacement chains of the two projects for 99 years.

Fortunately, there is a better way. The whole idea behind forming replacement chains was to ensure that we compared two projects with equal lives. Another way to do the same thing would be to figure out a way to express NPV on a "per year" basis for any project and compare these values for projects. The project that has a higher per year NPV is the better project. This is achieved by constructing *equivalent annual series (EAS)*.

Suppose that we are trying to rank two mutually exclusive projects. Project J costs $12,000 and generates cash flows of $6,000 per year for three years. Project K costs $18,000 and generates cash flows of $7,000 for four years. The first step in constructing the EAS is to compute the NPV of each project. Assuming a discount rate of 10%, we find that

$$NPV(J) = \$2{,}921.11, \ NPV(K) = \$4{,}189.06.$$

The next step is to compute the EAS for each project. The EAS of a project is the payment on an annuity whose life is the same as that of the project and whose present value, using the discount rate of the project, is equal to the NPV of the project. The EAC for project J, denoted by EAS_J, then is the payment on the three-year (life of project J) annuity whose PV, using 10% as the discount rate, is equal to $2,921.11. In other words, we enter the following values in the calculator: $N = 3, I/Y = 10, PV = -2921.11, FV = 0, PMT = ?$. This yields $EAS_J = \$1{,}174.62$. To compute EAS_K, we enter the following values in the calculator: $N = 4, I/Y = 10, PV = -4{,}189.06, FV = 0, PMT = ?$. This yields $EAS_K = \$1{,}321.53$. Because $EAS_K > EAS_J$, K is the better project.

A very useful application of the EAS concept is in choosing between two machines that do the same job but have different costs and different lives.

Example Problem: Suppose that your firm is trying to decide between two machines, say lathes, that will do the same job. Lathe A costs $90,000, will last for 10 years, and will require operating costs of $5,000 per year. At the end of 10 years it will be scrapped for $10,000. Lathe B costs $60,000, will last for seven years, and will require operating costs of $6,000 per year. At the end of seven years it will be scrapped for $5,000. Which is a better machine? (The discount rate is 10%.)

Solution: Note that here there is no question of computing the NPV. Because both machines do the same job, we must choose the one with the least cost. Note, however, that their lives are different and therefore, we will need to use an adjustment similar to the EAS. The first step is to compute the present value of the costs for each of the two lathes.

$$
\begin{aligned}
\text{PV of costs (A)} &= \$90{,}000 + \text{PV of \$5{,}000 annuity for ten years} \\
&\quad - \text{PV of the scrap (at } t = 10\text{) value of \$10{,}000} \\
&= \$90{,}000 + \$30{,}722.84 - 3{,}855.43 \\
&= \$116{,}867.41
\end{aligned}
$$

PV of costs (B) = $60,000 + PV of $6,000 annuity for seven years

– PV of the scrap (at t = 7) value of $5,000

= $60,000 + $29,210.51 – $2,565.79

= $86,644.72

The next step is to compute the *equivalent annual cost series (EAC)* for each of the two projects. This involves finding the annuity that has the same present value as the PV of the costs of each of the machines. To compute EAC_A, we enter the following values in the calculator: N = 10, I/Y = 10, PV = –116,867.41, FV = 0, PMT = ?. This yields EAC_A = $19,019.63. To compute EAC_B, we enter the following values in the calculator: N = 7, I/Y = 10, PV = –86,644.72, FV = 0, PMT = ?. This yields EAC_B = $17,797.30. Therefore, lathe B is better. Remember, we are dealing with costs here and we want to choose the machine with the lower cost. In this case, it is Lathe B.

Example Problem: Assume the same decision as in the problem above. However, now assume that the firm pays tax at a rate of 30% and uses straight-line depreciation for tax purposes.

Solution: The problem is now somewhat more complicated because we have to consider everything on an after-tax basis. The depreciation expenses for the two machines are:

$$\text{Depreciation Expense (A)} = \frac{90,000 - 10,000}{10} = \$8,000 \text{ per year}$$

$$\text{Depreciation Expense (B)} = \frac{60,000 - 5,000}{7} = \$7,857.14 \text{ per year.}$$

Next, note that the operating expense of the machines is a tax-deductible expense and we will have to take the after-tax value of the cost. Then,

PV of cost (A) = $90,000 + PV of $3,500 ($5,000 × (1 – 0.30)) annuity for 10 years

– PV of the scrap (at t = 10) value of $10,000

– PV of $2,400 ($8,000 × 0.30) annuity for 10 years

= $90,000 + $21,505.98 – $3,855.43 – $14,746.96

= $92,903.59

EAC_A = $15,119.63

PV of cost (B) = $60,000 + PV of $4,200 ($6,000 × (1 – 0.30)) annuity for seven years

– PV of the scrap (at t = 7) value of $5,000

– PV of $2,357.14 ($7,857.14 × 0.30) annuity for seven years

= $60,000 + $20,447.36.97 – $2,565.79 – $11,475.54

= $66,406.03

EAC_B = $13,640.16

Since the EAC of B is lower, Lathe B is better.

10.5 Concluding Thoughts and Remarks

You have now completed the final chapter in the book. It is our sincere desire that you have enjoyed your experience and have learned a great deal about the world of finance. As professionals in the field, we appreciate the fact that finance is a central function of any successful business. Hopefully we have conveyed this fact throughout the book.

If you choose to continue your studies in finance, the material and lessons contained in this book will provide you with a solid foundation. If instead this is the only finance book that you ever read, we believe you will find that the knowledge about the field of finance you now possess will be useful in your career, regardless of your profession, and in your life. Because most of you will work for a company (or perhaps even own and operate your own company), you will undoubtedly interact with individuals from the finance department. Hopefully you will be able to understand what they are talking about and why they are concerned about certain issues.

Finally, finance major or not, most of you will someday own stocks and bonds, probably in a retirement account. The knowledge about valuation, financial reporting, efficient financial management, and risk that you have learned from this book will help you to make educated investment decisions. Although we cannot guarantee that this knowledge will lead to great riches, we *know* that educated decisions are much more likely to lead to favorable results than uneducated ones. Perhaps that is why we have chosen education as our career field—it most certainly is not because of great riches!

Good luck in whatever you do, and thank you for reading our book.

Assignment 10.1

1. FGH Corp. is considering investment in a project. The project involves an expenditure of $10 million in plant and equipment. These assets will generate $2 million per year for 10 years. The company uses straight-line depreciation to zero salvage value for tax purposes. The tax rate is 30% and the appropriate discount rate is 13%. Compute the NPV of the project.

2. A and B are mutually exclusive projects. Project A requires an initial outlay of $80,000 and generates cash flows of $18,000 per year for eight years. Project B requires an outlay of $40,000 and generates cash flows of $10,000 per year for eight years. Compute the NPV and IRR for each of the two projects. Assume that the discount rate is 10%. Which project would you select and why?

3. Two projects, A and B, are mutually exclusive and have the following cash flows. The appropriate discount rate is 13%.

Project	C_0	C_1	C_2	C_3	C_4
A	−28,000	6,000	10,000	12,000	18,000
B	−28,000	18,000	12,000	10,000	6,000

Compute the NPV and IRR of each project. Determine which is the better project.

4. P and Q are two mutually exclusive projects. Compute their NPVs for discount rates of 0, 5, 10, 15, 20, 25, 30, 35, 40, 45, and 50%. Plot the NPV profiles of the two projects on the same graph. From the graph, answer the following questions. At what cost of capital would you prefer P to Q? At what cost of capital would you choose project Q over P?

Project	C_0	C_1	C_2	C_3
P	−3,000	1,000	2,000	3,000
Q	−3,000	1,900	1,900	1,900

Assignment 10.2

1. RTY Co. is deciding between two machines to do a particular job. Machine X100 costs $45,000 to install, has operating costs of $5,000 per year, will last for five years, and has a salvage value of $6,000. Machine Y1300 costs $65,000 to install, has operating costs of $2,000 per year, will last for seven years, and has a salvage value of $10,000. If the firm's cost of capital is 12%, which machine will be better?

2. A company is deciding to introduce a new product to the market. In deciding on the product concept, the company spent $300,000 last year on a marketing research study. Once the product concept was decided upon, the company spent another $500,000 on the design of a new manufacturing process. The company is now ready to launch the product on a full scale. To do this, the company will have to invest $31 million in plant and machinery. This has an economic life of 20 years and will have a scrap value of $3 million at the end. The project is expected to generate sales of $5 million per year for the 20 years. Of these, 10% are due to lost sales of the existing products of the company. The variable cost of producing the product is 60% of sales. Other costs are $600,000 per year. Existing managerial manpower will be able to handle the project quite easily. The company's accountants have allocated $300,000 in supervisory salaries to this project. Investing in the project will result in a decrease of $2 million in the company's working capital. At the end of the project, working capital levels will go back to what they are without the project today. The company uses straight-line depreciation method for tax purposes and is in the 30% tax bracket. Assuming a discount rate of 11%, compute the NPV of the project.

Assignment 10.3

1. A firm is faced with the prospect of deciding between two manufacturing technologies. Technology Q36 will require machinery and equipment worth $3 million. This technology will result in operating cost savings of $600,000 per year for eight years. Technology Z96 will require an initial outlay of $4 million and will result in cost savings of $700,000 for 10 years. Assume straight-line depreciation, a 10% discount rate, and zero salvage values for both the technologies. The firm pays no taxes. Which technology would you recommend?

2. Assume the same number as in the previous problem. Assume, however, that the firm pays taxes at the 30% rate. Which technology would you now recommend?

Additional Questions and Problems

1. Rank the following mutually exclusive projects. Assume that the discount rate is 10%.

Project	C_0	C_1	C_2	C_3	C_4	C_5
A	−1,000	1,200				
B	−6,000	1,500	1,500	1,500	1,500	1,500
C	−29,000	14,100	22,340			
D	−17,000	0	0	34,200	8,200	

2. Determine which of the following is a relevant cash flow and which is not relevant for capital budgeting purposes. Also, where appropriate, determine whether the item is a sunk cost or an opportunity cost.

   a. The building will be built on land already owned by the company with a market value of $2 million. If the company does not accept the project, the land will be sold for $2 million.

   b. $100,000 in preliminary grading work has been done to prepare the site.

   c. The building will cost $10.5 million, and equipment will cost $4.5 million.

   d. The company paid a $1 million royalty to obtain rights to a production process.

   e. Additional royalty payments of 1% of gross revenues from the product will be required.

   f. Last year the company signed a non-cancelable 10-year lease on the building, requiring payments of $150,000 per year.

   g. The product is expected to generate sales of $2 million per year. Of these sales, 7% are expected to come from existing products, 30% are expected to come from a major competitor, and the rest will be entirely new sales to the industry.

   h. The plant and equipment will be depreciated for tax purposes on a straight-line basis to zero salvage value over a 10-year period. The tax rate is 36%.

   i. The variable costs of production will be $500,000 per year.

Advanced Topics in Capital Budgeting

j. Accounting plans to allocate supervisory and management costs of $25,000 per year to the project. No new supervisory or management personnel will be required.

k. Accounting plans to allocate electricity costs of $1,000 per month to the project due to the energy demands of the new equipment.

l. The inventor of the product left the company last year. She will receive non-compete payments of $50,000 per year for the next three years.

m. The project will require additional working capital of $2 million. The working capital can be recovered at the end of the life of the project.

n. The plant and equipment are expected to last for 15 years, at which time it is expected that they can be sold for $3.5 million.

3. An automobile company is deciding whether to manufacture the radiators that it uses in its cars or to buy them from a supplier. The annual requirement is for 100,000 radiators. The supplier is willing to sell these at a cost of $120 per radiator. If the company were to manufacture these radiators, it would need to invest in machinery worth $5 million. The manufacturing cost would be $80 per radiator. The economic life of the machinery is 10 years and the company uses straight-line depreciation for tax purposes. The tax rate is 30% and the discount rate is 9% for both projects. Assume that the life of both projects is 10 years. Should the company make or buy the radiators?

4. A and B are two mutually exclusive projects. Project A requires an initial outlay of $9,000 and generates a net cash flow of $4,000 per year for four years. Project B requires an initial outlay of $25,000, and will generate cash flows of $6,500 per year for eight years. Which project would you choose? Assume that the discount rate for both projects is 10%.

5. Hi Grade Tool Company is faced with the prospect of having to replace a large stamping machine. Two machines currently being marketed will do the job satisfactorily. The Superior Stamping machine costs $50,000 and will require cash operating expenses of $20,000 per year. The Peerless machine costs $75,000, and the operating expenses are $15,000 per year. Both machines have a 10-year useful life with no salvage value and would be depreciated on a straight-line basis. If the company pays a 30% tax rate and has a 12% after-tax required rate of return, which machine should be purchased?

6. Two mutually exclusive projects have projected cash flows as follows:

PERIOD	0	1	2	3	4
A	-$10,000	$5,000	$5,000	$5,000	$ 5,000
B	-$10,000	0	0	0	$30,000

a. Determine the internal rate of return for each project.

b. Assuming a required rate of return of 10%, determine the net present value for each project.

c. Which project would you select? Why?

7. The cash flows of two mutually exclusive projects X and Y are as follows:

YEAR	0	1	2	3	4
PROJ. X	(50,000)	25,000	20,000	15,000	5,000
PROJ. Y	(50,000)	5,000	15,000	20,000	30,000

   a. At what discount rate do the NPV profiles of the two projects cross?

   b. What is the NPV of the projects at this discount rate?

8. Which of the following items should be included in an incremental cash flow analysis when computing the NPV of an investment? For each item, why or why not?

   a. The reduction in the sales of the company's other products caused by the new product.

   b. The cost of R&D undertaken in the past year directly attributable to the product.

   c. Dividend payments that come from the cash flow to be generated from this product.

   d. The cost of additional consulting needed after the new project is launched.

   e. Variable costs associated with producing the product.

9. The president of White Star Line has asked you to evaluate the proposed construction of a new passenger ship, to be called the Titanic. White Star is expected to use the vessel for 10 years. The vessel's estimated construction cost is $4,000,000 and it is classified as an asset to be depreciated straight line over 10 years to a zero salvage value. The operation of the vessel would require an increase in net working capital of $120,000—this amount would be recovered at the end of the life of the project. The vessel would increase the firm's incremental net income by $300,000 per year. The firm's marginal tax rate is 30% and the project's cost of capital is 10%. Calculate the IRR of the proposed construction project.

10. After you discovered that a State University chemistry professor is planning to illegally produce liquor in his lab, you reported him to the police. He admitted to the police that he spent $12,500 to modify the lab's hot water boiler for this purpose, and that he expected to earn an annual net income of $6,000 on the black market for liquor. He did not plan to pay any taxes. Because he already had tenure, he estimated that he would be able to use the equipment until his retirement, that is, 20 years from now. Then he would sell the equipment for $2,500 to his son. Because of the enormous risk associated with this activity, he estimated a required rate of return of 37% p.a. What was the expected **NPV** of the project?

11. Albatros, Inc. is considering buying a piece of equipment (a cyclotron) from an unnamed Finance 3300 instructor for $47 million. By reducing Albatros's expenses for Proton-spectroscopy, the equipment will increase the company's **net income** by $4.3 million per year for the next 20 years. At the end of year 20, the company can sell the cyclotron's magnetic alloys for $2.0 million. The depreciable life of the cyclotron is 20 years and company can use straight-line depreciation to a $2 million salvage value. Albatros, Inc.'s corporate tax rate is 30%. The company estimates a discount rate of 15% p.a. for this project.

12. Williams Sisters, Inc. is contemplating the purchase of a clothing company to design new clothes for the Williams Sisters company employees. The cost of the clothing company is estimated to be $12,000,000. This entire amount can be depreciated over a 10-year life to a zero salvage value. A financial advisor to Williams Sisters, Inc. has told them that the appropriate cost of capital for such a purchase should be 16%, however, the Williams Sisters plan to pay for the clothing company with their own money. Williams Sisters estimates that the new clothing company will generate revenues less costs of $4,000,000 per year for the next 10 years. Williams Sisters plans to sell the company to the current owner's father at the end of 10 years for $0. Assuming that the tax rate is 40%, compute the NPV of this purchase.

13. BBB Electronics manufactures a variety of household appliances. The company is considering introducing a new product line. The company's CFO has collected the following information about the proposed product.

    - The project has an anticipated economic life of six years.
    - R&D costs for development of the new product line were $12 million.
    - The company will have to purchase a new machine to manufacture the new product line. The machine will cost the company $20 million to purchase and install, and will be depreciated on a straight-line basis to a $2 million salvage value over its six-year project life.
    - If the company goes ahead with the new product line, it will have an effect on the company's net working capital. At the outset (that is, at t = 0), inventory will increase by $1 million and accounts payable will increase by $800,000. At t = 6, the net working capital will be recovered after the project is completed.
    - The new product line is expected to generate sales revenue of $60 million per for each of the next six years. Operating costs, excluding management salaries, are expected to be $18 million per year. Allocated management salaries will be $2 million per year, although no new managers will be hired for this project.
    - Because the new product line is similar to another of BBB's existing products, sales in this other existing product will decrease by $5 million per year, net of cost, once the new product line is on the market. In addition, BBB expects that the product's introduction will cause its competitor's sales to also fall (by $1 million per year).
    - The company's interest expense each year will be $1.5 million.
    - The company's cost of capital (that is, the required rate of return on this project) is 10%.
    - The company's tax rate is 30%.

    Compute the NPV of this proposed new product line.

14. Atlanta Cookie (A Cookie) wishes to purchase a cookie making system that requires the purchase of a mixer costing $42,500 and an oven costing $35,000. This new cookie-making system project is expected to meet the firm's growing demand for fabulous, fat-free cookies for the foreseeable future. The firm plans to use a 12% cost of capital to evaluate the project. The before tax annual cookie sales revenues over the life the project are shown in the following table:

Year	Estimate Sales Revenue
1	$ 70,000
2	$112,000
3	$160,000
4	$163,000
5	$ 92,000

It is expected that the system will have a zero salvage value and be depreciated straight line over its five-year life. The equipment is not expected to have a market value in five years. The company will get bank financing at a rate of 8% effective annual interest rate for the initial investment. After purchasing the new cookie making system, A Cookie will hire Emanuel Jackson to maintain, operate, and train other employees on how to use the new equipment. Emanuel will require a salary and benefits totaling $70,000 per year. Emanuel previously worked for the consulting company that recommended this system to A Cookie. A Cookie paid Emanuel's firm $30,000 to determine which system was ideally suited for the company. Flour, sugar, a secret fat-free butter alternative, and other ingredients are estimated to cost 20% of sales annually. The system is so terrific that it is believed that A Cookie's baking process will become the industry standard and will open new distribution channels. However, the initial cost of setting up these new distribution channels is estimated to be $50,000. The increases in sales from the new customers are incorporated in the estimated sales revenue estimates above. The firm estimates that the project will require an increase in net working capital of $4,000, which will be recovered at the end of the life of the project. The company is in the combined 40% state and federal tax brackets.

Given the information above, compute:

a. The initial outlay (at T_0) for Atlanta Cookie to purchase the new cookie making system.

b. Atlanta Cookie's operating cash flow in year 3.

c. The non-operating cash flow in the fifth and final year of the project.

15. Seinfeld Creative Productions is evaluating the construction of a studio complex. The planned site is currently valued at $400,000, but this parcel would not need to be purchased because Seinfeld already owns it. (If the company does not use the parcel for this project, it will be sold today for its current value.) The studio construction would cost Seinfeld $1 million and would be depreciated for tax purposes using straight-line to a zero salvage value over 20 years. Costanza & Benis, LLP is retained as the creative consultant of this project. George Costanza is due $25,000 in fees next month for services already rendered in the design stage. Another $35,000 in advance fees is expected to be paid at the end of year 1 to Elaine Benis for additional services to be performed if the project is launched.

It is expected that the studio will increase Seinfeld's short-movie production by five new releases every year, with each of them bringing in $90,000 per year in royalty fees. The operation of the studio will necessitate additional marketing expenditures of $100,000 per year and other general expenses of $50,000 per year. Lost fees due to Seinfeld giving up stand-up comedy engagements would run at $50,000 per year. Seinfeld would be expected to increase its net working capital by $20,000 to accommodate increased investment in movies accounts receivable over the life of the studio ownership—this amount would be recovered at the end of the life of the project. Seinfeld Productions intends to sell the site parcel for $400,000 and to sell the studio for an additional $500,000 after 10 years.

The marginal tax rate of Seinfeld is 40%. For purposes of identifying the timing of cash flows, consider all project-related cash flows to occur at the end of the year. The construction will start immediately (i.e., in Year 0), the first year of operations will be Year 1, and the last year of operations is the Year 10. What is the project's NPV?

Appendix A

Appendix A Table of future value interest factors, $FVIF(i,n) = (1 + i)^n$: Future value of $1 invested today for n periods (i, per period interest rate)

To use this table, find the future value interest factor that corresponds to both a given time period n and an interest rate i. For example, if you want the future value interest factor for 5 years and 10%, move across from year 5 and down from 10% to the point at which the row and column intersect: 1.611.

n\i	1%	2%	3%	4%	5%	6%	7%	8%	9%	10%	11%	12%	13%	14%	15%	16%	17%	18%	19%	20%
1	1.010	1.020	1.030	1.040	1.050	1.060	1.070	1.080	1.090	1.100	1.110	1.120	1.130	1.140	1.150	1.160	1.170	1.180	1.190	1.200
2	1.020	1.040	1.061	1.082	1.103	1.124	1.145	1.166	1.188	1.210	1.232	1.254	1.277	1.300	1.323	1.346	1.369	1.392	1.416	1.440
3	1.030	1.061	1.093	1.125	1.158	1.191	1.225	1.260	1.295	1.331	1.368	1.405	1.443	1.482	1.521	1.561	1.602	1.643	1.685	1.728
4	1.041	1.082	1.126	1.170	1.216	1.262	1.311	1.360	1.412	1.464	1.518	1.574	1.630	1.689	1.749	1.811	1.874	1.939	2.005	2.074
5	1.051	1.104	1.159	1.217	1.276	1.338	1.403	1.469	1.539	1.611	1.685	1.762	1.842	1.925	2.011	2.100	2.192	2.288	2.386	2.488
6	1.062	1.126	1.194	1.265	1.340	1.419	1.501	1.587	1.677	1.772	1.870	1.974	2.082	2.195	2.313	2.436	2.565	2.700	2.840	2.986
7	1.072	1.149	1.230	1.316	1.407	1.504	1.606	1.714	1.828	1.949	2.076	2.211	2.353	2.502	2.660	2.826	3.001	3.185	3.379	3.583
8	1.083	1.172	1.267	1.369	1.477	1.594	1.718	1.851	1.993	2.144	2.305	2.476	2.658	2.853	3.059	3.278	3.511	3.759	4.021	4.300
9	1.094	1.195	1.305	1.423	1.551	1.689	1.838	1.999	2.172	2.358	2.558	2.773	3.004	3.252	3.518	3.803	4.108	4.435	4.785	5.160
10	1.105	1.219	1.344	1.480	1.629	1.791	1.967	2.159	2.367	2.594	2.839	3.106	3.395	3.707	4.046	4.411	4.807	5.234	5.695	6.192
11	1.116	1.243	1.384	1.539	1.710	1.898	2.105	2.332	2.580	2.853	3.152	3.479	3.836	4.226	4.652	5.117	5.624	6.176	6.777	7.430
12	1.127	1.268	1.426	1.601	1.796	2.012	2.252	2.518	2.813	3.138	3.498	3.896	4.335	4.818	5.350	5.936	6.580	7.288	8.064	8.916
13	1.138	1.294	1.469	1.665	1.886	2.133	2.410	2.720	3.066	3.452	3.883	4.363	4.898	5.492	6.153	6.886	7.699	8.599	9.596	10.699
14	1.149	1.319	1.513	1.732	1.980	2.261	2.579	2.937	3.342	3.797	4.310	4.887	5.535	6.261	7.076	7.988	9.007	10.147	11.420	12.839
15	1.161	1.346	1.558	1.801	2.079	2.397	2.759	3.172	3.642	4.177	4.785	5.474	6.254	7.138	8.137	9.266	10.539	11.974	13.590	15.407
16	1.173	1.373	1.605	1.873	2.183	2.540	2.952	3.426	3.970	4.595	5.311	6.130	7.067	8.137	9.358	10.748	12.330	14.129	16.172	18.488
17	1.184	1.400	1.653	1.948	2.292	2.693	3.159	3.700	4.328	5.054	5.895	6.866	7.986	9.276	10.761	12.468	14.426	16.672	19.244	22.186
18	1.196	1.428	1.702	2.026	2.407	2.854	3.380	3.996	4.717	5.560	6.544	7.690	9.024	10.575	12.375	14.463	16.879	19.673	22.901	26.623

n																				
19	1.208	1.457	1.754	2.107	2.527	3.026	3.617	4.316	5.142	6.116	7.263	8.613	10.197	12.056	14.232	16.777	19.748	23.214	27.252	31.948
20	1.220	1.486	1.806	2.191	2.653	3.207	3.870	4.661	5.604	6.727	8.062	9.646	11.523	13.743	16.367	19.461	23.106	27.393	32.429	38.338
21	1.232	1.516	1.860	2.279	2.786	3.400	4.141	5.034	6.109	7.400	8.949	10.804	13.021	15.668	18.822	22.574	27.034	32.324	38.591	46.005
22	1.245	1.546	1.916	2.370	2.925	3.604	4.430	5.437	6.659	8.140	9.934	12.100	14.714	17.861	21.645	26.186	31.629	38.142	45.923	55.206
23	1.257	1.577	1.974	2.465	3.072	3.820	4.741	5.871	7.258	8.954	11.026	13.552	16.627	20.362	24.891	30.376	37.006	45.008	54.649	66.247
24	1.270	1.608	2.033	2.563	3.225	4.049	5.072	6.341	7.911	9.850	12.239	15.179	18.788	23.212	28.625	35.236	43.297	53.109	65.032	79.497
25	1.282	1.641	2.094	2.666	3.386	4.292	5.427	6.848	8.623	10.835	13.585	17.000	21.231	26.462	32.919	40.874	50.658	62.669	77.388	95.396
26	1.295	1.673	2.157	2.772	3.556	4.549	5.807	7.396	9.399	11.918	15.080	19.040	23.991	30.167	37.857	47.414	59.270	73.949	92.092	114.475
27	1.308	1.707	2.221	2.883	3.733	4.822	6.214	7.988	10.245	13.110	16.739	21.325	27.109	34.390	43.535	55.000	69.345	87.260	109.589	137.371
28	1.321	1.741	2.288	2.999	3.920	5.112	6.649	8.627	11.167	14.421	18.580	23.884	30.633	39.204	50.066	63.800	81.134	102.967	130.411	164.845
29	1.335	1.776	2.357	3.119	4.116	5.418	7.114	9.317	12.172	15.863	20.624	26.750	34.616	44.693	57.575	74.009	94.927	121.501	155.189	197.814
30	1.348	1.811	2.427	3.243	4.322	5.743	7.612	10.063	13.268	17.449	22.892	29.960	39.116	50.950	66.212	85.850	111.065	143.371	184.675	237.376
31	1.361	1.848	2.500	3.373	4.538	6.088	8.145	10.868	14.462	19.194	25.410	33.555	44.201	58.083	76.144	99.586	129.946	169.177	219.764	284.852
32	1.375	1.885	2.575	3.508	4.765	6.453	8.715	11.737	15.763	21.114	28.206	37.582	49.947	66.215	87.565	115.520	152.036	199.629	261.519	341.822
33	1.389	1.922	2.652	3.648	5.003	6.841	9.325	12.676	17.182	23.225	31.308	42.092	56.440	75.485	100.700	134.003	177.883	235.563	311.207	410.186
34	1.403	1.961	2.732	3.794	5.253	7.251	9.978	13.690	18.728	25.548	34.752	47.143	63.777	86.053	115.805	155.443	208.123	277.964	370.337	492.224
35	1.417	2.000	2.814	3.946	5.516	7.686	10.677	14.785	20.414	28.102	38.575	52.800	72.069	98.100	133.176	180.314	243.503	327.997	440.701	590.668
36	1.431	2.040	2.898	4.104	5.792	8.147	11.424	15.968	22.251	30.913	42.818	59.136	81.437	111.834	153.152	209.164	284.899	387.037	524.434	708.802
37	1.445	2.081	2.985	4.268	6.081	8.636	12.224	17.246	24.254	34.004	47.528	66.232	92.024	127.491	176.125	242.631	333.332	456.703	624.076	850.562
38	1.460	2.122	3.075	4.439	6.385	9.154	13.079	18.625	26.437	37.404	52.756	74.180	103.987	145.340	202.543	281.452	389.998	538.910	742.651	1,020.675
39	1.474	2.165	3.167	4.616	6.705	9.704	13.995	20.115	28.816	41.145	58.559	83.081	117.506	165.687	232.925	326.484	456.298	635.914	883.754	1,224.810
40	1.489	2.208	3.262	4.801	7.040	10.286	14.974	21.725	31.409	45.259	65.001	93.051	132.782	188.884	267.864	378.721	533.869	750.378	1,051.668	1,469.772

Appendix B

Appendix B Table of present value interest factors, PVIF $(i,n) = 1/(1+i)^n$: Present value of $1 to be received at the end of n periods (i, per period interest rate)

To use this table, find the present value interest factor that corresponds to both a given time period n and an interest rate i. For example, if you want the present value interest factor for 11 years and 9%, move across from year 11 and down from 9% to the point at which the row and column intersect: 0.3875.

n \ i	1%	2%	3%	4%	5%	6%	7%	8%	9%	10%	11%	12%	13%	14%	15%	16%	17%	18%	19%	20%
1	0.9901	0.9804	0.9709	0.9615	0.9524	0.9434	0.9346	0.9259	0.9174	0.9091	0.9009	0.8929	0.8850	0.8772	0.8696	0.8621	0.8547	0.8475	0.8403	0.8333
2	0.9803	0.9612	0.9426	0.9246	0.9070	0.8900	0.8734	0.8573	0.8417	0.8264	0.8116	0.7972	0.7831	0.7695	0.7561	0.7432	0.7305	0.7182	0.7062	0.6944
3	0.9706	0.9423	0.9151	0.8890	0.8638	0.8396	0.8163	0.7938	0.7722	0.7513	0.7312	0.7118	0.6931	0.6750	0.6575	0.6407	0.6244	0.6086	0.5934	0.5787
4	0.9610	0.9238	0.8885	0.8548	0.8227	0.7921	0.7629	0.7350	0.7084	0.6830	0.6587	0.6355	0.6133	0.5921	0.5718	0.5523	0.5337	0.5158	0.4987	0.4823
5	0.9515	0.9057	0.8626	0.8219	0.7835	0.7473	0.7130	0.6806	0.6499	0.6209	0.5935	0.5674	0.5428	0.5194	0.4972	0.4761	0.4561	0.4371	0.4190	0.4019
6	0.9420	0.8880	0.8375	0.7903	0.7462	0.7050	0.6663	0.6302	0.5963	0.5645	0.5346	0.5066	0.4803	0.4556	0.4323	0.4104	0.3898	0.3704	0.3521	0.3349
7	0.9327	0.8706	0.8131	0.7599	0.7107	0.6651	0.6227	0.5835	0.5470	0.5132	0.4817	0.4523	0.4251	0.3996	0.3759	0.3538	0.3332	0.3139	0.2959	0.2791
8	0.9235	0.8535	0.7894	0.7307	0.6768	0.6274	0.5820	0.5403	0.5019	0.4665	0.4339	0.4039	0.3762	0.3506	0.3269	0.3050	0.2848	0.2660	0.2487	0.2326
9	0.9143	0.8368	0.7664	0.7026	0.6446	0.5919	0.5439	0.5002	0.4604	0.4241	0.3909	0.3606	0.3329	0.3075	0.2843	0.2630	0.2434	0.2255	0.2090	0.1938
10	0.9053	0.8203	0.7441	0.6756	0.6139	0.5584	0.5083	0.4632	0.4224	0.3855	0.3522	0.3220	0.2946	0.2697	0.2472	0.2267	0.2080	0.1911	0.1756	0.1615
11	0.8963	0.8043	0.7224	0.6496	0.5847	0.5268	0.4751	0.4289	0.3875	0.3505	0.3173	0.2875	0.2607	0.2366	0.2149	0.1954	0.1778	0.1619	0.1476	0.1346
12	0.8874	0.7885	0.7014	0.6246	0.5568	0.4970	0.4440	0.3971	0.3555	0.3186	0.2858	0.2567	0.2307	0.2076	0.1869	0.1685	0.1520	0.1372	0.1240	0.1122
13	0.8787	0.7730	0.6810	0.6006	0.5303	0.4688	0.4150	0.3677	0.3262	0.2897	0.2575	0.2292	0.2042	0.1821	0.1625	0.1452	0.1299	0.1163	0.1042	0.0935
14	0.8700	0.7579	0.6611	0.5775	0.5051	0.4423	0.3878	0.3405	0.2992	0.2633	0.2320	0.2046	0.1807	0.1597	0.1413	0.1252	0.1110	0.0985	0.0876	0.0779
15	0.8613	0.7430	0.6419	0.5553	0.4810	0.4173	0.3624	0.3152	0.2745	0.2394	0.2090	0.1827	0.1599	0.1401	0.1229	0.1079	0.0949	0.0835	0.0736	0.0649
16	0.8528	0.7284	0.6232	0.5339	0.4581	0.3936	0.3387	0.2919	0.2519	0.2176	0.1883	0.1631	0.1415	0.1229	0.1069	0.0930	0.0811	0.0708	0.0618	0.0541
17	0.8444	0.7142	0.6050	0.5134	0.4363	0.3714	0.3166	0.2703	0.2311	0.1978	0.1696	0.1456	0.1252	0.1078	0.0929	0.0802	0.0693	0.0600	0.0520	0.0451
18	0.8360	0.7002	0.5874	0.4936	0.4155	0.3503	0.2959	0.2502	0.2120	0.1799	0.1528	0.1300	0.1108	0.0946	0.0808	0.0691	0.0592	0.0508	0.0437	0.0376

19	0.8277	0.6864	0.5703	0.4746	0.3957	0.3305	0.2765	0.2317	0.1945	0.1635	0.1377	0.1161	0.0981	0.0829	0.0703	0.0596	0.0506	0.0431	0.0367	0.0313
20	0.8195	0.6730	0.5537	0.4564	0.3769	0.3118	0.2584	0.2145	0.1784	0.1486	0.1240	0.1037	0.0868	0.0728	0.0611	0.0514	0.0433	0.0365	0.0308	0.0261
21	0.8114	0.6598	0.5375	0.4388	0.3589	0.2942	0.2415	0.1987	0.1637	0.1351	0.1117	0.0926	0.0768	0.0638	0.0531	0.0443	0.0370	0.0309	0.0259	0.0217
22	0.8034	0.6468	0.5219	0.4220	0.3418	0.2775	0.2257	0.1839	0.1502	0.1228	0.1007	0.0826	0.0680	0.0560	0.0462	0.0382	0.0316	0.0262	0.0218	0.0181
23	0.7954	0.6342	0.5067	0.4057	0.3256	0.2618	0.2109	0.1703	0.1378	0.1117	0.0907	0.0738	0.0601	0.0491	0.0402	0.0329	0.0270	0.0222	0.0183	0.0151
24	0.7876	0.6217	0.4919	0.3901	0.3101	0.2470	0.1971	0.1577	0.1264	0.1015	0.0817	0.0659	0.0532	0.0431	0.0349	0.0284	0.0231	0.0188	0.0154	0.0126
25	0.7798	0.6095	0.4776	0.3751	0.2953	0.2330	0.1842	0.1460	0.1160	0.0923	0.0736	0.0588	0.0471	0.0378	0.0304	0.0245	0.0197	0.0160	0.0129	0.0105
26	0.7720	0.5976	0.4637	0.3607	0.2812	0.2198	0.1722	0.1352	0.1064	0.0839	0.0663	0.0525	0.0417	0.0331	0.0264	0.0211	0.0169	0.0135	0.0109	0.0087
27	0.7644	0.5859	0.4502	0.3468	0.2678	0.2074	0.1609	0.1252	0.0976	0.0763	0.0597	0.0469	0.0369	0.0291	0.0230	0.0182	0.0144	0.0115	0.0091	0.0073
28	0.7568	0.5744	0.4371	0.3335	0.2551	0.1956	0.1504	0.1159	0.0895	0.0693	0.0538	0.0419	0.0326	0.0255	0.0200	0.0157	0.0123	0.0097	0.0077	0.0061
29	0.7493	0.5631	0.4243	0.3207	0.2429	0.1846	0.1406	0.1073	0.0822	0.0630	0.0485	0.0374	0.0289	0.0224	0.0174	0.0135	0.0105	0.0082	0.0064	0.0051
30	0.7419	0.5521	0.4120	0.3083	0.2314	0.1741	0.1314	0.0994	0.0754	0.0573	0.0437	0.0334	0.0256	0.0196	0.0151	0.0116	0.0090	0.0070	0.0054	0.0042
31	0.7346	0.5412	0.4000	0.2965	0.2204	0.1643	0.1228	0.0920	0.0691	0.0521	0.0394	0.0298	0.0226	0.0172	0.0131	0.0100	0.0077	0.0059	0.0046	0.0035
32	0.7273	0.5306	0.3883	0.2851	0.2099	0.1550	0.1147	0.0852	0.0634	0.0474	0.0355	0.0266	0.0200	0.0151	0.0114	0.0087	0.0066	0.0050	0.0038	0.0029
33	0.7201	0.5202	0.3770	0.2741	0.1999	0.1462	0.1072	0.0789	0.0582	0.0431	0.0319	0.0238	0.0177	0.0132	0.0099	0.0075	0.0056	0.0042	0.0032	0.0024
34	0.7130	0.5100	0.3660	0.2636	0.1904	0.1379	0.1002	0.0730	0.0534	0.0391	0.0288	0.0212	0.0157	0.0116	0.0086	0.0064	0.0048	0.0036	0.0027	0.0020
35	0.7059	0.5000	0.3554	0.2534	0.1813	0.1301	0.0937	0.0676	0.0490	0.0356	0.0259	0.0189	0.0139	0.0102	0.0075	0.0055	0.0041	0.0030	0.0023	0.0017
36	0.6989	0.4902	0.3450	0.2437	0.1727	0.1227	0.0875	0.0626	0.0449	0.0323	0.0234	0.0169	0.0123	0.0089	0.0065	0.0048	0.0035	0.0026	0.0019	0.0014
37	0.6920	0.4806	0.3350	0.2343	0.1644	0.1158	0.0818	0.0580	0.0412	0.0294	0.0210	0.0151	0.0109	0.0078	0.0057	0.0041	0.0030	0.0022	0.0016	0.0012
38	0.6852	0.4712	0.3252	0.2253	0.1566	0.1092	0.0765	0.0537	0.0378	0.0267	0.0190	0.0135	0.0096	0.0069	0.0049	0.0036	0.0026	0.0019	0.0013	0.0010
39	0.6784	0.4619	0.3158	0.2166	0.1491	0.1031	0.0715	0.0497	0.0347	0.0243	0.0171	0.0120	0.0085	0.0060	0.0043	0.0031	0.0022	0.0016	0.0011	0.0008
40	0.6717	0.4529	0.3066	0.2083	0.1420	0.0972	0.0668	0.0460	0.0318	0.0221	0.0154	0.0107	0.0075	0.0053	0.0037	0.0026	0.0019	0.0013	0.0010	0.0007

Appendix G

Appendix C Future value interest factor of annuity, FVIFA $(i,n) = ((1+i)^n - 1)/i$: Future value of an (ordinary) annuity of $1 per period for n periods (i, per period interest rate)

To use this table, find the future value interest factor of annuity that corresponds to both a given time period n and an interest rate i. For example, if you want the future value interest factor of annuity for 10 years and 10%, move across from year 10 and down from 10% to the point at which the row and column intersect: 15.937.

n \ i	1%	2%	3%	4%	5%	6%	7%	8%	9%	10%	11%	12%	13%	14%	15%	16%	17%	18%	19%	20%
1	1.000	1.000	1.000	1.000	1.000	1.000	1.000	1.000	1.000	1.000	1.000	1.000	1.000	1.000	1.000	1.000	1.000	1.000	1.000	1.000
2	2.010	2.020	2.030	2.040	2.050	2.060	2.070	2.080	2.090	2.100	2.110	2.120	2.130	2.140	2.150	2.160	2.170	2.180	2.190	2.200
3	3.030	3.060	3.091	3.122	3.153	3.184	3.215	3.246	3.278	3.310	3.342	3.374	3.407	3.440	3.473	3.506	3.539	3.572	3.606	3.640
4	4.060	4.122	4.184	4.246	4.310	4.375	4.440	4.506	4.573	4.641	4.710	4.779	4.850	4.921	4.993	5.066	5.141	5.215	5.291	5.368
5	5.101	5.204	5.309	5.416	5.526	5.637	5.751	5.867	5.985	6.105	6.228	6.353	6.480	6.610	6.742	6.877	7.014	7.154	7.297	7.442
6	6.152	6.308	6.468	6.633	6.802	6.975	7.153	7.336	7.523	7.716	7.913	8.115	8.323	8.536	8.754	8.977	9.207	9.442	9.683	9.930
7	7.214	7.434	7.662	7.898	8.142	8.394	8.654	8.923	9.200	9.487	9.783	10.089	10.405	10.730	11.067	11.414	11.772	12.142	12.523	12.916
8	8.286	8.583	8.892	9.214	9.549	9.897	10.260	10.637	11.028	11.436	11.859	12.300	12.757	13.233	13.727	14.240	14.773	15.327	15.902	16.499
9	9.369	9.755	10.159	10.583	11.027	11.491	11.978	12.488	13.021	13.579	14.164	14.776	15.416	16.085	16.786	17.519	18.285	19.086	19.923	20.799
10	10.462	10.950	11.464	12.006	12.578	13.181	13.816	14.487	15.193	15.937	16.722	17.549	18.420	19.337	20.304	21.321	22.393	23.521	24.709	25.959
11	11.567	12.169	12.808	13.486	14.207	14.972	15.784	16.645	17.560	18.531	19.561	20.655	21.814	23.045	24.349	25.733	27.200	28.755	30.404	32.150
12	12.683	13.412	14.192	15.026	15.917	16.870	17.888	18.977	20.141	21.384	22.713	24.133	25.650	27.271	29.002	30.850	32.824	34.931	37.180	39.581
13	13.809	14.680	15.618	16.627	17.713	18.882	20.141	21.495	22.953	24.523	26.212	28.029	29.985	32.089	34.352	36.786	39.404	42.219	45.244	48.497
14	14.947	15.974	17.086	18.292	19.599	21.015	22.550	24.215	26.019	27.975	30.095	32.393	34.883	37.581	40.505	43.672	47.103	50.818	54.841	59.196
15	16.097	17.293	18.599	20.024	21.579	23.276	25.129	27.152	29.361	31.772	34.405	37.280	40.417	43.842	47.580	51.660	56.110	60.965	66.261	72.035
16	17.258	18.639	20.157	21.825	23.657	25.673	27.888	30.324	33.003	35.950	39.190	42.753	46.672	50.980	55.717	60.925	66.649	72.939	79.850	87.442
17	18.430	20.012	21.762	23.698	25.840	28.213	30.840	33.750	36.974	40.545	44.501	48.884	53.739	59.118	65.075	71.673	78.979	87.068	96.022	105.931
18	19.615	21.412	23.414	25.645	28.132	30.906	33.999	37.450	41.301	45.599	50.396	55.750	61.725	68.394	75.836	84.141	93.406	103.740	115.266	128.117

19	20.811	22.841	25.117	27.671	30.539	33.760	37.379	41.446	46.018	51.159	56.939	63.440	70.749	78.969	88.212	98.603	110.285	123.414	138.166	154.740
20	22.019	24.297	26.870	29.778	33.066	36.786	40.995	45.762	51.160	57.275	64.203	72.052	80.947	91.025	102.444	115.380	130.033	146.628	165.418	186.688
21	23.239	25.783	28.676	31.969	35.719	39.993	44.865	50.423	56.765	64.002	72.265	81.699	92.470	104.768	118.810	134.841	153.139	174.021	197.847	225.026
22	24.472	27.299	30.537	34.248	38.505	43.392	49.006	55.457	62.873	71.403	81.214	92.503	105.491	120.436	137.632	157.415	180.172	206.345	236.438	271.031
23	25.716	28.845	32.453	36.618	41.430	46.996	53.436	60.893	69.532	79.543	91.148	104.603	120.205	138.297	159.276	183.601	211.801	244.487	282.362	326.237
24	26.973	30.422	34.426	39.083	44.502	50.816	58.18	66.76	76.79	88.50	102.17	118.16	136.83	158.66	184.17	213.98	248.81	289.49	337.01	392.48
25	28.243	32.030	36.459	41.646	47.727	54.865	63.25	73.11	84.70	98.35	114.41	133.33	155.62	181.87	212.79	249.21	292.10	342.60	402.04	471.98
26	29.526	33.671	38.553	44.312	51.113	59.156	68.68	79.95	93.32	109.18	128.00	150.33	176.85	208.33	245.71	290.09	342.76	405.27	479.43	567.38
27	30.821	35.344	40.710	47.084	54.669	63.706	74.48	87.35	102.72	121.10	143.08	169.37	200.84	238.50	283.57	337.50	402.03	479.22	571.52	681.85
28	32.129	37.051	42.931	49.968	58.403	68.528	80.70	95.34	112.97	134.21	159.82	190.70	227.95	272.89	327.10	392.50	471.38	566.48	681.11	819.22
29	33.450	38.792	45.219	52.966	62.323	73.640	87.35	103.97	124.14	148.63	178.40	214.58	258.58	312.09	377.17	456.30	552.51	669.45	811.52	984.07
30	34.785	40.568	47.575	56.085	66.439	79.058	94.46	113.28	136.31	164.49	199.02	241.33	293.20	356.79	434.75	530.31	647.44	790.95	966.71	1,181.88
31	36.133	42.379	50.003	59.328	70.761	84.802	102.07	123.35	149.58	181.94	221.91	271.29	332.32	407.74	500.96	616.16	758.50	934.32	1,151.39	1,419.26
32	37.494	44.227	52.503	62.701	75.299	90.890	110.22	134.21	164.04	201.14	247.32	304.85	376.52	465.82	577.10	715.75	888.45	1,103.50	1,371.15	1,704.11
33	38.869	46.112	55.078	66.210	80.064	97.343	118.93	145.95	179.80	222.25	275.53	342.43	426.46	532.04	664.67	831.27	1,040.49	1,303.13	1,632.67	2,045.93
34	40.258	48.034	57.730	69.858	85.07	104.18	128.26	158.63	196.98	245.48	306.84	384.52	482.90	607.52	765.37	965.27	1,218.37	1,538.69	1,943.88	2,456.12
35	41.660	49.994	60.462	73.652	90.32	111.43	138.24	172.32	215.71	271.02	341.59	431.66	546.68	693.57	881.17	1,120.71	1,426.49	1,816.65	2,314.21	2,948.34
36	43.077	51.994	63.276	77.598	95.84	119.12	148.91	187.10	236.12	299.13	380.16	484.46	618.75	791.67	1,014.35	1,301.03	1,669.99	2,144.65	2,754.91	3,539.01
37	44.508	54.034	66.174	81.702	101.63	127.27	160.34	203.07	258.38	330.04	422.98	543.60	700.19	903.51	1,167.50	1,510.19	1,954.89	2,531.69	3,279.35	4,247.81
38	45.953	56.115	69.159	85.970	107.71	135.90	172.56	220.32	282.63	364.04	470.51	609.83	792.21	1,031.00	1,343.62	1,752.82	2,288.23	2,988.39	3,903.42	5,098.37
39	47.412	58.237	72.234	90.409	114.10	145.06	185.64	238.94	309.07	401.45	523.27	684.01	896.20	1,176.34	1,546.17	2,034.27	2,678.22	3,527.30	4,646.07	6,119.05
40	48.886	60.402	75.401	95.026	120.80	154.76	199.64	259.06	337.88	442.59	581.83	767.09	1,013.70	1,342.03	1,779.09	2,360.76	3,134.52	4,163.21	5,529.83	7,343.86

Appendix D

Appendix D Table of present value interest factor of annuity, PVIFA $(i,n) = (1 - 1/(1 + i)^n)/i$: Present value of an (ordinary) annuity of $1 per period for n periods (i, per period interest rate)

To use this table, find the present value interest factor of annuity that corresponds to both a given time period n and an interest rate i. For example, if you want the present value interest factor of annuity for 10 years and 10%, move across from year 10 and down from 10% to the point at which the row and column intersect: 6.145.

n \ i	1%	2%	3%	4%	5%	6%	7%	8%	9%	10%	11%	12%	13%	14%	15%	16%	17%	18%	19%	20%
1	0.990	0.980	0.971	0.962	0.952	0.943	0.935	0.926	0.917	0.909	0.901	0.893	0.885	0.877	0.870	0.862	0.855	0.847	0.840	0.833
2	1.970	1.942	1.913	1.886	1.859	1.833	1.808	1.783	1.759	1.736	1.713	1.690	1.668	1.647	1.626	1.605	1.585	1.566	1.547	1.528
3	2.941	2.884	2.829	2.775	2.723	2.673	2.624	2.577	2.531	2.487	2.444	2.402	2.361	2.322	2.283	2.246	2.210	2.174	2.140	2.106
4	3.902	3.808	3.717	3.630	3.546	3.465	3.387	3.312	3.240	3.170	3.102	3.037	2.974	2.914	2.855	2.798	2.743	2.690	2.639	2.589
5	4.853	4.713	4.580	4.452	4.329	4.212	4.100	3.993	3.890	3.791	3.696	3.605	3.517	3.433	3.352	3.274	3.199	3.127	3.058	2.991
6	5.795	5.601	5.417	5.242	5.076	4.917	4.767	4.623	4.486	4.355	4.231	4.111	3.998	3.889	3.784	3.685	3.589	3.498	3.410	3.326
7	6.728	6.472	6.230	6.002	5.786	5.582	5.389	5.206	5.033	4.868	4.712	4.564	4.423	4.288	4.160	4.039	3.922	3.812	3.706	3.605
8	7.652	7.325	7.020	6.733	6.463	6.210	5.971	5.747	5.535	5.335	5.146	4.968	4.799	4.639	4.487	4.344	4.207	4.078	3.954	3.837
9	8.566	8.162	7.786	7.435	7.108	6.802	6.515	6.247	5.995	5.759	5.537	5.328	5.132	4.946	4.772	4.607	4.451	4.303	4.163	4.031
10	9.471	8.983	8.530	8.111	7.722	7.360	7.024	6.710	6.418	6.145	5.889	5.650	5.426	5.216	5.019	4.833	4.659	4.494	4.339	4.192
11	10.368	9.787	9.253	8.760	8.306	7.887	7.499	7.139	6.805	6.495	6.207	5.938	5.687	5.453	5.234	5.029	4.836	4.656	4.486	4.327
12	11.255	10.575	9.954	9.385	8.863	8.384	7.943	7.536	7.161	6.814	6.492	6.194	5.918	5.660	5.421	5.197	4.988	4.793	4.611	4.439
13	12.134	11.348	10.635	9.986	9.394	8.853	8.358	7.904	7.487	7.103	6.750	6.424	6.122	5.842	5.583	5.342	5.118	4.910	4.715	4.533
14	13.004	12.106	11.296	10.563	9.899	9.295	8.745	8.244	7.786	7.367	6.982	6.628	6.302	6.002	5.724	5.468	5.229	5.008	4.802	4.611
15	13.865	12.849	11.938	11.118	10.380	9.712	9.108	8.559	8.061	7.606	7.191	6.811	6.462	6.142	5.847	5.575	5.324	5.092	4.876	4.675
16	14.718	13.578	12.561	11.652	10.838	10.106	9.447	8.851	8.313	7.824	7.379	6.974	6.604	6.265	5.954	5.668	5.405	5.162	4.938	4.730
17	15.562	14.292	13.166	12.166	11.274	10.477	9.763	9.122	8.544	8.022	7.549	7.120	6.729	6.373	6.047	5.749	5.475	5.222	4.990	4.775
18	16.398	14.992	13.754	12.659	11.690	10.828	10.059	9.372	8.756	8.201	7.702	7.250	6.840	6.467	6.128	5.818	5.534	5.273	5.033	4.812

19	17.226	15.678	14.324	13.134	12.085	11.158	10.336	9.604	8.950	8.365	7.839	7.366	6.938	6.550	6.198	5.877	5.584	5.316	5.070	4.843
20	18.046	16.351	14.877	13.590	12.462	11.470	10.594	9.818	9.129	8.514	7.963	7.469	7.025	6.623	6.259	5.929	5.628	5.353	5.101	4.870
21	18.857	17.011	15.415	14.029	12.821	11.764	10.836	10.017	9.292	8.649	8.075	7.562	7.102	6.687	6.312	5.973	5.665	5.384	5.127	4.891
22	19.660	17.658	15.937	14.451	13.163	12.042	11.061	10.201	9.442	8.772	8.176	7.645	7.170	6.743	6.359	6.011	5.696	5.410	5.149	4.909
23	20.456	18.292	16.444	14.857	13.489	12.303	11.272	10.371	9.580	8.883	8.266	7.718	7.230	6.792	6.399	6.044	5.723	5.432	5.167	4.925
24	21.243	18.914	16.936	15.247	13.799	12.550	11.469	10.529	9.707	8.985	8.348	7.784	7.283	6.835	6.434	6.073	5.746	5.451	5.182	4.937
25	22.023	19.523	17.413	15.622	14.094	12.783	11.654	10.675	9.823	9.077	8.422	7.843	7.330	6.873	6.464	6.097	5.766	5.467	5.195	4.948
26	22.795	20.121	17.877	15.983	14.375	13.003	11.826	10.810	9.929	9.161	8.488	7.896	7.372	6.906	6.491	6.118	5.783	5.480	5.206	4.956
27	23.560	20.707	18.327	16.330	14.643	13.211	11.987	10.935	10.027	9.237	8.548	7.943	7.409	6.935	6.514	6.136	5.798	5.492	5.215	4.964
28	24.316	21.281	18.764	16.663	14.898	13.406	12.137	11.051	10.116	9.307	8.602	7.984	7.441	6.961	6.534	6.152	5.810	5.502	5.223	4.970
29	25.066	21.844	19.188	16.984	15.141	13.591	12.278	11.158	10.198	9.370	8.650	8.022	7.470	6.983	6.551	6.166	5.820	5.510	5.229	4.975
30	25.808	22.396	19.600	17.292	15.372	13.765	12.409	11.258	10.274	9.427	8.694	8.055	7.496	7.003	6.566	6.177	5.829	5.517	5.235	4.979
31	26.542	22.938	20.000	17.588	15.593	13.929	12.532	11.350	10.343	9.479	8.733	8.085	7.518	7.020	6.579	6.187	5.837	5.523	5.239	4.982
32	27.270	23.468	20.389	17.874	15.803	14.084	12.647	11.435	10.406	9.526	8.769	8.112	7.538	7.035	6.591	6.196	5.844	5.528	5.243	4.985
33	27.990	23.989	20.766	18.148	16.003	14.230	12.754	11.514	10.464	9.569	8.801	8.135	7.556	7.048	6.600	6.203	5.849	5.532	5.246	4.988
34	28.703	24.499	21.132	18.411	16.193	14.368	12.854	11.587	10.518	9.609	8.829	8.157	7.572	7.060	6.609	6.210	5.854	5.536	5.249	4.990
35	29.409	24.999	21.487	18.665	16.374	14.498	12.948	11.655	10.567	9.644	8.855	8.176	7.586	7.070	6.617	6.215	5.858	5.539	5.251	4.992
36	30.108	25.489	21.832	18.908	16.547	14.621	13.035	11.717	10.612	9.677	8.879	8.192	7.598	7.079	6.623	6.220	5.862	5.541	5.253	4.993
37	30.800	25.969	22.167	19.143	16.711	14.737	13.117	11.775	10.653	9.706	8.900	8.208	7.609	7.087	6.629	6.224	5.865	5.543	5.255	4.994
38	31.485	26.441	22.492	19.368	16.868	14.846	13.193	11.829	10.691	9.733	8.919	8.221	7.618	7.094	6.634	6.228	5.867	5.545	5.256	4.995
39	32.163	26.903	22.808	19.584	17.017	14.949	13.265	11.879	10.726	9.757	8.936	8.233	7.627	7.100	6.638	6.231	5.869	5.547	5.257	4.996
40	32.835	27.355	23.115	19.793	17.159	15.046	13.332	11.925	10.757	9.779	8.951	8.244	7.634	7.105	6.642	6.233	5.871	5.548	5.258	4.997